# Communicational Anthropology

**By the Same Author**

— Anthrolopolgical Research Methodology
— Bio-Cultural Evolution
— Developmental Anthropology
— Neo Anthropological Theory
— Social-Cultural Anthropology
— Contemporary Anthropology
— भारतीय जनजातीय संस्कृति
— भारतीय मानवशास्त्र
— मानवशास्त्रीय अनुसंधानः विधि एवं तकनीक
— चिकित्सात्मक मानवशास्त्र
— जटिल समाज का मानवशास्त्र
— जैविक सांस्कृतिक उद्विकास
— मानवशास्त्रीय सिद्धांतः शास्त्रीय एवं आधुनिक
— संप्रेषणात्मक मानवशास्त्र
— भारतीय प्रागैतिहासिक पुरातात्विक मानवशास्त्र

---

**The Author**

**Gaya Pandey** (*b.* 1954) is a very Senior Faculty Member of the Department of Anthropology, Ranchi University, Ranchi, Jharkhand. Ever since his joining in the department as faculty in 1985, he has been sincerely and academically engaged in teaching and researches in Post-graduate Department of Anthropology. He has contributed a lot in organising a number of national seminar, symposium and workshop in the department. He has attended three dozens seminars and symposium of national and international level. He has to his credit three and half dozen articles in Journals of national and international repute. He has to his credit nine books under co-authorship and fourteen books under single authorship. Some of his recently published books are *Bio-cultural Evolution*, *Jaivik Sanskritik Udvikasa*, *Bharatiya Pragaitihasik-Puratattvik Manavashastra*, *Sampreshanatmak Manavashastra*, *Neo-Anthropological Theory*, *Chikitsatmak Manavashastra*, *Social-cultural Anthropology*, *Anthropological Research Methodology: Theory and Practice* and *Indian Prehestoric Archaeological Anthropology*.

# COMMUNICATIONAL ANTHROPOLOGY

Gaya Pandey

**CONCEPT PUBLISHING COMPANY PVT. LTD.**
**NEW DELHI-110059**

**ISBN-13: 978-93-86682-48-2 (HB)**

**ISBN-13: 978-93-86682-49-9 (PB)**

First Published 2018

*Published and Printed by*

Concept
Since 1974

**Concept Publishing Company Pvt. Ltd.**
A/15-16, Commercial Block, Mohan Garden,
New Delhi-110059 (India)
*T* : 91 11 25351460, 91 11 25351794
*E* : publishing@conceptpub.com, *W*: www.conceptpub.com

**Cataloging in Publication Data**--Courtesy: D.K. Agencies (P) Ltd. <docinfo@dkagencies.com>

**Pandey, Gaya,** 1954- **author.**
Communicational anthropology / Gaya Pandey.
pages cm
Includes bibliographical references and index.
ISBN 9789386682482 (HB)
ISBN 9789386682499 (PB)

1. Communication in ethnology. I. Title.

LCC GN307.5.P36 2018 DDC 305.80014 23

**Dedicated to**

Mother Smt. Anshuiya Devi, wife Smt. Indu Devi, Daughters—Sudha, Suman, Sarita and Anu, Son—Shekhar, Grandsons—Kushagra and Harshit with great gratitude and love who have always been behind me as a source of support in completion of this book.

# Preface

The book "Communicational Anthropology" has been written with the support of a number of persons at different levels such as teachers, students and researchers, who have contributed in such an anthropological academic area where there is no any systematic book covering all aspects of communication under single cover. The book is an excellent attempt to solve the problem of students, researchers and scholars interested in the study of communication. Now, it is my pious duty to extend gratitudes and thanks to all of them collectively and individually who became the source of help and encouragement in completion of the book.

I would like to extend my sincere gratitude to all teachers and students of Anthropology Department, Ranchi University, Ranchi, Jharkhand, and all M. Phil. and Ph.D. scholars of the department who encouraged me in completing the book in English medium for wider circulation.

I am thankful to librarian of Department of Anthropology and other Staff for their co-peration in completing the book with care.

My family members have always been a source of inspiration to all my academic ventures. I extent my sincere gratitude to all of them collectively and individually.

I am thankful to Sri Ashok Kumar Mittal, Managing Director, Concept Publishing Company (P) Ltd., New Delhi and his team who took every care in publishing my handwritten manuscript of the book with meticulous care.

**Gaya Pandey**
Department of Anthropology,
Ranchi University
Ranchi, Jharkhand

# Contents

# 1
# Introduction

Communicational Anthropology is a sub-branch of Anthropology, which deals with study of meaning, nature, characteristics, types, techniques, channels, agents and culture of human communication. Although communication is a special features of all creatures including man. But human communication is quite different from the communication of birds and animals. Every birds and animals pronounce some kind of sound to attract fellows and members of their community. But they utter some definite types of sound for the purpose of communication. It has been observed that dogs and cats utter 3 types of sound, cows utter 8 types of sound, Gorillas utter 24 types of sound and whales utter 36 types of sound for the purpose of communication. But human beings can utter indefinite types of sounds for the purposes of communication. Another feature of animals and birds communication is that they communicate only for the purpose of satisfaction of needs related to food or hunger, sex and fear. But human communication is related to various kinds of exchange of messages. They are not related to food, hunger, sex and fear only. Human beings fulfil all kinds of their needs through communication. We can say that human communication is life line of any kind of relationships and roles.

In animals and birds communication takes place with their own community members, but human communication is related to all ethnic groups of the world. Another feature is that human communication is related not only with human beings. But human beings also make communication with birds, animals, plants, trees, rivers, mountains, seas, Gods, Goddesses and ancestors.

For the purpose of communication, human beings have evolved languages. Language is a means of communication. It is language which acts as a medium of communication between two or more human individuals. For the purpose of communication human beings have evolved verbal and non-verbal languages. In verbal languages communication is made by uttering or pronounciating sounds. But sounds are uttered not only in haphazard manner. They are uttered as per the cultural lexicon and cultural grammar of the speech community concerned. Those who do not utter sounds as per culture lexicon and cultural grammar, their communication is taken as meaningless or irrelevant. Sometimes they are treated as mad, too.

Each linguistic community has its own cultural lexicon and cultural grammar. The members of speech community acquire them as a member of community. The cultural lexicon of a community is not static, rather, it is dynamic. Cultural lexicon accommodates changes. Lexicon is enriched by taking new terms from other communities or giving a specific meaning to a specific term in specific situation. A number of old terms lose its use and become extinct. In this way, substraction and addition take place in cultural lexicon of a community.

Each linguistic community has its own cultural grammar. The cultural grammar includes, noun, pronoun, verb, adverb, terms of reference, terms of address, terms of exclamation, idioms, phrases, riddles, proverbs, number, gender, person, case etc. The rules of cultural grammars are followed in verbal communication.

In human communication, message form occupies significant place. The message form may be of a word, a sentence, a paragraph, song, story, ballad, idioms, riddles, proverbs etc.

The human communication also uses codes like flag, Temple, Mosque, Church, Gurudwara, colour, drumbeat, and clapping sound. Each speech community has its own codes for the purpose of communication.

In human communication, topic occupied significant place because all rules of cultural lexicon and grammar revolve round the topic of communication.

Speech situation, speech act and speech event play valuable role in human communication. The speech situation reveals a situation in which communication takes place such as birth, marriage, death, worship, thiefly, dacoity, rape, fire, flood, femine and many others. Human communication differs from speech situation to speech situation.

The speech acts are those acts which initiate, continue and discontinue the human communication. For example Yes, No, good, very good, excellent, bad, very bad, worst, well done, bravo and so on. These speech acts play significant role in human communication.

Speech events also contribute very much in human communication.

Speech events are those events which occur at the time of communication such as laughing, weeping, serious faces, red eyes, keeping mum, speaking very loudly, shouting, keeping finger between lips, high pitch, low pitch and medium pitch sounds.

One of significant aspects of human communication is multilingualism. Multilingualism refers to a speech condition in which some members of a speech community acquire languages of other neighbouring communities. In this way, they possess expertise of communicating in more than one languages. Multilingualism is a feature of every speech community. It is because neighbouring speech communities have frequent mutual contacts through marriage, market and trade. Mutual or reciprocal exchange in marriage, markets and trade encourages multilingualism. Our Government is promoting multilingualism by providing modern education through national and regional languages such as Hindi, English, Sanskrit, Urdu and local regional languages. Multilingualism is not anti of local linguism. It is rather progressive and modern job oriented. Educated persons are, thus, equipped in communicating through local, regional, national and international languages.

Another significant feature of human communication is digglosia. Digglosia refers to a speech variety in which members of a speech community use different languages for different social groups speaking the same language. For examples in each speech community, different languages are used for children, adult, aged, male, female, castes and occupational groups. At the time of human communication, cultural lexican and cultural grammar of digglosia are followed.

Besides the above significant features of verbal human communication, non-verbal symbols are also used in human communication. Non-verbal language is known as body language. It includes gesture, facial expression, eye contact, handshake, touching feet, meeting shoulder-to-shoulder, movements of body parts, different poses and so on. Thus, in human communication body language also plays significant role. Non-verbal behaviour in communication tells many thing more than verbal behaviours. Generally, in human communication verbal and non-verbal behaviours go together.

In human communication, channels play significant role. The channels used for the purposes of communication are of two types: (i) Verbal channels and (ii) Non-verbal channels.

The verbal channels are divided in to four groups: oral, written, visual and audio-visual. The non-verbal channels are gesture, facial expression, eye contact, handshake, feet touch, putting hands on heads or shoulders, meeting shoulder-to-shoulder, holding in arms, different poses and movement of body parts.

The human communication is marked by communicators or agents. The communicators or agents can be divided in to three groups: Traditional, modern, and international agents. In modern communication the role of media cannot be ignored. The media of communication can also be divided in to two groups, folks media and mass media.

Now-a-days, we are living in communication revolution. Information technologies are playing vital role in our communication system. They have enriched our different areas of knowledge and have made us powerful. The communication revolution has been able to redefine the concept of time, space and distance with the help of knowledge revolution and information technologies.

Today, we are living in a world of development and business management. In both these areas communication plays significant role. Without proper communication, development and business cannot occur in proper way. Therefore, the role of communication in development and business is of great importance.

Although, communication plays significant role in human progress, but human communication has to face a number of impediments, such as physical, cultural, social, economic, political, religious, health, education and natural impediments.

Besides natural impediments, human communication is marked by taboo. There is a taboo to have a sexy and loose communication in presence of elders and youngers. But such types of communications are allowed between joking relative. Abusive words are generally avoided but their exchange is allowed in joking relatives.

Human communication has a feature of loss. Communication loss takes place when a message passes on from ears to ears among several individuals. Sometimes entire communication is partially conceived or sometimes entire message is wrongly perceived. This is because communicator tells something and receiver receives something.

Although every human individual acquires the attributes of communication as a member of speech community through mother tongue, but all individuals do not possess equal communication skill. Some individuals are well skilled in sending and receiving messages, while others are semi-skilled and some remains unskilled in communication.

Human communication may be divided in to two types : interpersonal communication and mass communication. Again human communication can be divided into intra-group communication and intergroup communication. Communication can also be divided in to self-communication and other communication.

The human communication employs two types of method for the purpose of communication. They are: informal method and formal method.

In human communications, besides language, some other means are employed. They are traditional means, modern means and international means.

The human communication can be understood in better way by anthropological, sociological and ecological approaches.

The ethnography of communication can be recorded on the basis of following facts:

- Speech Community
- Speech Situation
- Speech Acts
- Speech Events
- Message Sender
- Message Receiver
- Message Form
- Message Code
- Message Channel
- Message Topic
- Message Scene

From above discussion on introductory attributes of communicational anthropology, the scope of Communicational Anthropology becomes quite clear before us.

**Scope of Communicational Anthropology**

The scope or subject matter taught under communicational anthropology are as follows:

- Communication: Meaning, Definition, Role and Function
- Communication: Nature and Characteristics
- Communication: Types, Techniques and Means
- Impediments to Communication
- Communication Loss
- Communication Skill
- Communication Channel

- Communication Agents
- Communication Media
- Communication Revolution
- Development Communication
- Business Communication
- Approaches to Study of Communication
- Ethnography of Communication
- Structure of Human Communication.

## Initiation of Communicational Researches in Anthropology

The credit of initiating communicational researches in anthropology goes to E.B. Tylor. Tylor had visited deaf and dumb children's school in Mexico Province. His main purpose was to study communication among deaf and dumb. Among deaf and dumb communication takes place through sign languages and body languages. On the basis of his observation he had defined communication as mutual give and take of messages. He had described communication system in detail in his book, *Anthropology*: *An Introduction to Man and His Civilization* (1888).

After Tylor, Franz Boas, Edward Sapir and Bloomfied made significant contributions on language and communication system. Since then human communication is being studied following different approaches, methods and techniques in anthropological researches.

# 2

# Communication: Meaning, Definition, Role and Function

The meaning of communication in simple term is to give and take of messages through languages. In communication messages are sent and messages are received. Here language acts as a medium because for communication of messages a medium is required. This medium is language. Messages are sent or received through language. Without language communication cannot take place. Human language is of two types—verbal and non-verbal. Verbal language is known as sound language and non-verbal language is known as body language. Human beings use both kinds of languages in communication. The communication system has following parts :

- Message Sender
- Message Receiver
- Message Form
- Message Code
- Message Channel
- Message Topic
- Message Scene

Communication is a both way process. It is because messages are sent and received through communication. Thus, human individual is sender as well as receiver of communication. At one point he/she is sender of messages but at another point he/she is receiver of the message. Each individual of a speech community is both sender as well as receiver of messages. This can be understood in better way by the diagram given below:

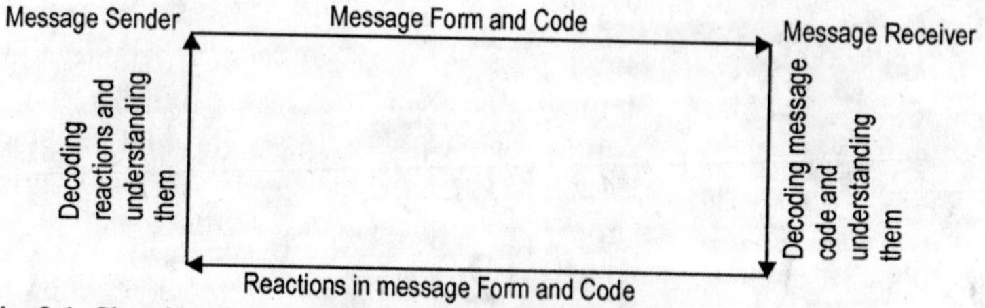


**Fig. 2.1:** Showing Communication as a both way process

## Acquisition of Communication

When an individual is born, he/she is only a mass of bones and flesh. But as he/she enters in to infancy and from infancy to childhood, he/she starts acquiring communication. As soon as he/she is delivered, he/she starts weeping. Weeping symbolises that the baby is not dumb. After few months if he/she starts paying attention through calls. Now, it is believed that the child is not deaf. Being deaf and dumb is taken as a physical barriers of communication. In order to participate in a speech community an individual should not be deaf and dumb.

The speech community has a common language. The members of a community acquires the language of a speech community through participation and use. The speech community makes an individual a communicating being. Since the language of community is acquired by an individual in the lap of mother, it is also known as mother tongue. The child acquires the cultural lexicon and cultural grammar of the speech community in family and neighbour.

The acquisition of communication takes place through following stages:

- Babbling Stage
- One word Stage
- Two word Stage
- Telegraphic Stage

***Babbling Stage*:** When an individual is in between 6 months to 12 months stage, he/she starts communicating with family members through laughing, weeping, babbling. This is known as babbling stage. In this stage, the child spends most of his/her time with mother. The communication takes place only between mother and the baby. Only mother understands and decodes the meaning of baby's weeping, laughing and babbling. The child also develops attention towards the call of mother.

***One word Stage***: When an individual attains an age of 12 months to 24 months, he/she enters in to one word stage of communication. In this stage, the child starts communicating with members of his/her speech community through one words, such as *mumma, papa,* grand pa, grand ma, uncle, aunty, brother, sister, cow, goat, dog, crow and so on. Hearing the utterance of one word from the mouth of a child, family members and neighbour try to understand what a child wants to communicate.

***Two word Stage***: When a child attains an age of 24 months to 36 months, he/she enters in the two-word stage of communication. In this stage, a child starts communicating with his/her family members and speech community members through two words. For example, *mumma-papa, bhaiya-didi,* cat-dog, mango-guava, glass-water, rice-bread, brinjal- pumpkin and so on.

***Telegraphic stage***: When a child acquires an age of 36 months to 60 months, he/she enters in the telegraphic stage of communication. He/she gradually becomes aware of cultural lexicons and cultural grammars of the speech community. By the time of achieving 5 years of age, a child attains the telegraphic stage. He/she becomes an active participants of the speech community.

**Theory of Communication Acquisition**

Two theories have been propounded regarding the acquisition of the communication. They are as follows:

- Imitation Theory and
- Enforcement Theory

***Imitation Theory***: According to this theory, a child acquires the communication through imitation theory. He/she hears the communication between father-mother, brother-sister, uncle-aunt and other members of the speech community. The child acquires the communication by observing the communication behaviour of speech community members. He/she remembers the cultural lexicon and cultural grammar and uses them as community members of old generation use them. This is related to heard and remembered tradition of communication behaviour. The children imitate not only the verbal utterances of speech community members, but they also follow the body language of their speech community members.

***Enforcement Theory***: According to this theory, the child is enforced to follow correct pronounciation of terms and correct rules of cultural lexicon and cultural grammar. The child is enforced to use such terms and cultural grammar which are socially accepted and which have positive social sanction for communication.

The child is enforced to avoid the use of those terms and grammar which have negative sanction for communication.

### Acquisition of Communication in Multilingual Situation

A child acquires more than one language when he/she participates in multilingual situation. In practice, a child has to face a multilingual situation. His/her father belongs to one speech community and mother belongs to another speech community. Again in the *Haat-bazaar*, a child faces an another lingual situation. Thus, the multilingual situation forces a child to acquire communication in multilanguages.

Now-a-days, all schools are promoting multilingualism. It is because multilingualism enhances the job opportunities. The children learn local or regional languages, Hindi, English, and Sanskrit in schools. Multilingual knowledge helps an individual to communicate in more than one languages.

### Definition of Communication

From the above presented discussion we can define communication in minimum terms as a method of exchange of messages between two individuals, an individual and a group or a group and an individual. In this method there are sender and receiver of messages. Messages are sent and received through language. In this way, it is language which acts as a medium of communication between sender and receiver.

### Role and Function of Communication

As referred to earlier that communication is a system of give and take of messages of various kinds between two individuals, an individual and a group or a group and an individual. With the help of this system mankind has been able to fulfil his various kinds of needs. As needs are varied, therefore, role and function of communication is also varied. The communication performs following roles and functions for the members of speech community:

- Cultural Role
- Social Role

- Educational Role
- Economic Role
- Political Role
- Religious Role
- Career Building Role
- Tour and Travelling Role
- Health and Hygiene Role
- Administrative Role
- Legal Role
- Entertainment Role
- Psychological Role
- Safety Role
- Welfare Role
- Accident Management Role
- Developmental Role
- Business Administration Role
- Migration Role
- Dissemination of Science and Knowledge Role
- Rumour Control Function
- Riot Control Function
- Transmission of Games, Play and Sports
- Transmission of Folklore

***Cultural Role***: The communication plays significant cultural roles. It helps in transmission of cultural traits from one generation to the next, from one ethnic group to another and from one place to another. It helps in making people aware of their cultural identity. It makes people known that each ethnic group has its own culture. But culture is neither superior nor inferior, neither rich nor poor, neither developed nor undeveloped. The culture is valuable for the members of the community concerned. We cannot judge the cultural value of a community from our own point of view. The communication helps in extending the ideas that we should respect not only our own culture, but also the culture of other communities. Communication makes members of the speech community known about the cultural lexicon and cultural grammars, cultural agents, cultural media communication and cultural performances.

***Social Role***: The communication performs significant social roles. It makes the members aware of Social organisation, Social structure, Social functions, Social groups and role status of individuals. It makes people known about social rights, duties, privilages, rewards, punishment, social sanction, social customs, morals and values. It also makes people known about the social manner, etiquette and social qualities, co-operation, competition and conflict. In this way, communication makes an individual a social being. Through communication individuals become participants of social behaviour. They become a potential member of the community. They lead healthy social life. It extends help in maintaining social relation and controlling social disorganisation.

***Educational Role*:** The communication performs educational roles for the members of speech community. Each speech community has its own traditions, customs, knowledge, value and usages. It is communication which provides education about the norms, values, customs, traditions, knowledge and usages.

No only in traditional education, but also in modern education communication contributes significantly. For providing modern education, there are teachers, students, reading materials and writing materials. Teachers communicate knowledge on a particular topic and subject to the students. Teachers also write reading materials like books, articles, essays for the purpose of knowledge communication among students, scholars and readers.

***Economic Role*:** Communication plays significant role in economy of a community. With the help of communication, the members of speech community acquire knowledge about economic institutions like production, consumption, distribution, exchange, trades market, capital, reciprocity, wages, loan, saving, small business and entrepreneurship. The members of speech community also make exchange of hospitality, gift and presentation through communication. The members also become aware of different types of economic organisations, jobs, professions and employment with the help of communication.

***Political Role*:** The communication also performs political roles. The members of the speech community know about customary laws, tradition of residence pattern, marriage rules, structure of family, inheritance rule, succession rule, village head, inter-village head, chieftainship, village officials, leaders, elites, caste Panchayats, modern political institutions, ward members, *mukhia*, *sarpanch*, Panchayat Samiti, Zilla Parishad, MLA, M.P., Ministers, Chief Minister, Prime Minister, President, Political parties, symbols of Political parties and so on. Thus, communication plays significant role related to political organisation, political institutions, political systems, elites, and leadership.

***Religious Roles*:** The communication plays significant role in transmission of religious traditions, sacred centres, Gods, Goddesses and their abodes, religious symbols, religious specialists, religious performance, worship, rituals, procession, religious tales, mythological stories, religious song, prayers and a number of beliefs and practices from one generation to another, from one place to another and from one group to another. In this way, communication performs transmission functions for the religions.

***Career Building Role*:** The communication plays valuable role in career building. It is helpful in building traditional career as well as modern career. In traditional career, an individual adopts family occupation. For example agriculture, artisan, share cropping, labour, priesthood, barber, gardener, shoe-making, *Jajmani* system-related work. But in modern career people are engaged in service, business and enterprenureship. But in transmitting the knowledge of traditional as well as modern career, the communication has to play significant roles. It is because both traditional and modern knowledge travels from one individual to another, one generation to another and one place to another place through communication channels. Modern education and skills are acquired through communication method and channels.

***Tour and Travelling Role*:** Communication plays significant role in tour and travelling. It makes people known about the tourist places and mode of travelling to go there. On the basis of communication with travel agencies people are able to manage ticket of buses, train, plain, taxi, cars and so on. People are also able to book advance ticket and rooms to stay at different places in hotels and lodges. With the help of modern communication system, tour and travelling has become very easy and comfortable.

***Health and Hygiene Role*** : The communication contributes significantly in maintenance of health and hygience. It transmits the concept of health, hygiene, traditional medicine man, folk medicine, *Jharphuk* method, different types of medical systems, such as Ayurveda, Yoga, Unani, Siddha, Homoeopathy, Naturopathy, Allopathy, health tourism, modern medicine and modern concept of general health, reproductive health, lactating health, health programmes and control of diseases like Diarrhoea, Maleria, AIDS, Cancer, infant mortality, mother mortality and so on. People are utilisting benefit of health and disease management with the help of communication.

***Administrative Role*** : The communication plays significant role in communication of administrative rules. There are concept of rural and urban administration. In rural areas administration is provided with the help of traditional and modern Gram Panchayats. But in urban areas administration is provided by municipality, municipal corporation, mega municipal corporation, cantonment board, notified area and other Governmental machinery such as civil servants and police. The communication makes the people aware of different types of agencies associated with administration in rural and urban areas.

***Leagal Role***: Communication makes valuable contribution in transmission of traditional laws, modern laws, functions of Government, new acts, statutes, modification and prohibition in previous acts. It also makes people aware of legal institutions and authority like thana, police, court, lawyer and judges. It also empowers people by creating legal awareness and human rights awareness among the people.

***Entertainment Role*** : The communication plays valuable roles in transmission of traditional and modern means of entertainment. For example, folkdance, music, drama, song, cockfight, bullfight, sheepfight, puppet show, bioscope, theatre, T.V., Cinema, Internet, radio, mobile and so on. In this way, communication contributes significantly about traditional and modern means of communication.

***Psychological Role***: The communication plays significant role in satisfaction of psychological needs. It performs great roles in controlling stress, tension, conflict, emotions, fear and so on. It also transmits social qualities like sympathy, pity, co-operation, competition and pardon. It helps in development of balanced personality and controlling disorganised and deviant behaviour.

***Safety Role***: The role of communication in transmission of safety mechanism is of great value. For healthy living and long life safety is essential. Our life is full of danger. We need safety from diseases, safety from enemies, safety from natural calamities like flood, famine, epidemic fire and so on. It is communication system which empowers us from different types of dangers by making us aware of different kinds of safety mechanism.

***Welfare Role***: Communication plays significant roles related to welfare activities. There are a number of Governmental, Non-Governmental Organisations and voluntary agencies which extend different types of welfare services related to disabled and needy persons. It is communication which makes us aware of welfare agencies and types of services they render. Thus, needy persons are benefited through communication.

***Accident Management Role***: The communication contributes significantly in accident management. Accident can take place anywhere and any time in our life. Our life is full of accident. Accident may occure due to own fault or fault of others. But there is always chance of loss of life and disability. It is communication system, which makes us alert form different kinds of accidents and where and whom to approach first in case an accident takes place.

***Developmental Role***: Communication plays significant role in development of human being. Man is a developmental being. Ever since his emergence on earth from his animal ancestry man is progressing continuously through contacts, communication, migration and mitual give and take of different kinds of technology. Now-a-days, attempts after attempts are being made by the Government to bring all ethnic groups and families in the mainstream of development. For this purpose, a number of developmental programmes have been launched for the people. There are a number of Governmental and Non-Governmental agencies who act as communicator of development programmes. They act as a medium between people and the Government. They communicate about the benefits of development programmes and make people aware to become more and more participants of development programme.

***Business Administration Role***: The communication system is contributing significantly in business, business management and business administration. It is because without proper communication, business administration and management are not possible. Each business company, takes help of communicators who make people aware of the benefits of business products. The communicators increase the sell of the company products.

***Migration Role***: People are migrating for better earning and livelihood. It is communication which makes people aware of benefits and demerits of migration. In search of better livelihood people are migrating. It is communication which tells them when and where to go for better earnings. It also tells them problems related to migration.

***Dissemination of Scientific Knowledge*** : The communication system plays significant role in disseminating scientific knowledges among the people. The benefits of scientific knowledges and achievements are communicated to the people of the globe. The people of the globe get benefit from the scientific knowledge and technology.

***Rumour Control Role***: The communication plays significant role in control of rumour. On the occasions of wars and riots, rumour mongers try to create panic in the society on the basis of wrong messages. The Government has to clarify the rumour and aleart the people from rumour mongers.

***Riot Control Role***: The communication plays valuable role in controlling riots. The Government takes every step to control different types of riots such as caste, regional, communal and lingual. The communication makes aware the people about riots which occured in particular places. It makes people to develop safety mechanism. It communicates the people about the steps taken by the Government to control the riot situation.

***Transmission Role of Play, Games and Sports***: The communication system plays significant role in transmission of traditional and modern plays, games, and sports from one generation to next generation and one place to another. Each ethinic group has its own traditional play, games and sports which are integral part of their culture. Besides traditional games, plays and sports, each community also practice modern games, and sports. This has become possible due to communication.

***Transmission Role of Folklore***: Folklore is literature of common man. It is spoken orally. It has different forms such as tales, ballads, songs, riddles, proverbs, idioms, phrases, knowledge, traditions, verbal jokes, action jokes, dance, music, drama, and so on. The folklore of a speech community is communicated from one generation to the next orally. Now-a-days, attempts have been made to record the oral traditions of a speech community. In this way communication plays significant role in transmission of folkloric traditions.

From the above presented description, it is quite clear that communication contributes significantly in the life of human beings and human societies. In fact, there is no aspect of human life left uninfluenced by the communication system. In fact, the life of human beings is fully dependent on communication. It is cradle to rebirth arrangement of human beings. One cannot even dream to survive in absence of communication. The communication system has made human beings as human. It has distinguished human beings from their animal ancestors. It is life line of all kinds of relationship, functions and roles.

# 3

# Communication: Nature and Characteristics

As referred to earlier, communication is a process dealing with mutual exchange of messages. It is a both way process or dual process. It is a method of sending and receiving messages. It requires a medium for performing its roles. The language acts as medium for exchange of messages between sender and receiver and *vice versa*. It forms many significant functions in the life of human beings. Human beings use communication for the fulfilment of their various kinds of needs. Human needs are countless. Therefore, the functions of communication are also countless. In fact, there is no area of human life where communication is not required. Considering such varied functions in the life of human beings, it will be the fitness of the thing to present here the nature and characteristics of human communication. The main nature and characteristics of communication are as follows:

### Communication is Human

Although all creatures of the world utter some kind of communication, but yet communication is human. It is because other creatures utter some fixed kinds of sound again and again for communicating something to their community fellows and opposite sex members. For example cat and dog utter 3 types of sounds for the purpose of communication. Cows utter 8 types of sound for communication. Chimpanzee uses 24 types of sound and whales create 34 types of sound for communication. But human beings can utter countless types of sound and provide social-cultural meaning to them. Another point is that in other animals communication is related only to satisfaction of hunger, sex and safety.

They are not related to past, present and future. In human beings communication is related to countless needs. It is also related to past, present and future. Thus, it is quite clear that human communication has its own characteristic. It makes human a human and distinguishes human beings from their animal ancestry.

## Language is Medium of Communication

For communication a medium is required. Without medium communication cannot take place between sender and receiver and *vice versa.* The language acts as a medium of communication. The language may be verbal or sound language, non-verbal or body language and sign language. But there is always a language behind communication. In speech community, members acquire communication channels and behave according to them. The verbal language may be local, regional, national and international. Mother tongue represents language of local speech community. Linguafranca represents language of regional speech community. English is taken as language of international community. Thus, we find that language has been a medium of communication between members belonging to local, regional, national and international speech community.

## Communication is a Both Way or Dual Process

Communication is not a one way process. Rather, it is dual or both way process. The same member is sender of messages at onetime, but he/she becomes receiver of messages on other time. In this way sender and receiver of messages have reciprocal exchange of messages. Communication is not only a system of sending messages, but is also a system of receiving feedback and reactions of the receiver.

## Communication is Universal as well as Local

Communication is universal phenomenon. It is found in every human society prevalent in the world. Everywhere human beings fulfil their various kinds of needs through communication. Human speech organs and movements of body parts are similar universally. Hence, body language and sound languages are universal phenomenon. But inspite of all these universal features, communication is local, too. It is because sound languages are different in different speech communities of the world. Each speech community has its own language which reveals local attributes of communication. In this way communication is universal as well as local.

**Communication is a Social Heritage**

It is true that communication takes place through speech organs and movement of body parts, i.e., sound and body languages but is not a biological heritage. Rather, it is a social heritage. We do not acquire communication from womb. We acquire communication as a member of speech community. The speech community provides us occasion to learn cultural lexicon and cultural grammars. By learning cultural lexicon and Grammar, a member is able to participate fully in the communication of the speech community.

**Communication is Stable as well as Changing**

The communication was existing in past, communication is existing today and it will continue to exist in future. Thus, communication is stable. But this cannot mean that communication is not changing. The cultural lexicon and grammars are changing. A good number of terms are included and adapted in local cultural lexicon and grammar with change in time, contact and technology. A good number of terms are also excluded from the cultural lexicon because they had lost their utility. Thus, communication is stable as well as changing.

**Communication is Learnt**

We are not born with language for communication. We are born with speech organs and hear organs. We gradually acquire communication with the help of our hear and speech organs as a member of the community. It is because each community has a language through which members acquire communication expertise with their fellow community members.

**Communication is Transferred**

Each society has its own words, lexicon and grammar for the purpose of communication. Words, lexicon and grammar of a society are transferred from one generation to the next generation, from one place to another place and from one group to another group. Each individual acquires communication from older generation and gives it to the younger generation. In this way each and every member of the community are participants of the communication and take part in its transfer.

**Communication is Related to Past, Present and Future**

Communication is such a method by which informations related to past, present and future are given and taken. Through communication we know about a number of pre- historic and historic events which had taken place in past. We become aware through communication about the things which are taking place in present. With the help of communication we are also able to predict the events which are supposed to take place in future. Thus, communication is related to all periods—Past, Present and Future.

**Communication is for an Individual and Mass both**

Communication can take place between two individuals or an individual with a mass. When communication takes place between two individuals, it is called interpersonal communication. But when it takes place between an individual and mass, it is known as mass communication.

**Communication may be with Self or Others**

Human beings are such beings who communicate not only with others but also with self. There are a number of situations in which human beings communicate with themselves for example right, wrong, good, bad, worst, sin, virtue, honesty, character etc. while taking decisions about these things human beings communicate not only with others but also with themselves.

**Communication is also with Non-human Beings**

Human beings communicate not only with human but they also make communication with non-human beings. For example human beings make communication with Gods, Goddesses, spirits, ancestors, domestic animals, birds and also with plants and trees. In this way human communication is not only with human beings, but also with deities, spirits, plants, animals and birds.

**Communication has to Follow some Rules**

Communication does not occur in haphazard manner. Rather, it has to follow some rules. That is why it is rule governed. In course of communication different terms of address and terms of reference are frequently used for children, young, adult and old, men, women, castes, for occupational groups. That is known as diglossia.

**Multilingualism is also a Feature**

Those individuals who know more than one languages can make communication in more than one language. Thus, multilingualism is also a feature of communication.

**Communication is Dependent on Channel**

For communication a number of channels are used. Channels are used to make communication effective. All communication channels may be divided in to two verbal and non-verbal channels. Verbal channels include oral, written, visual and Audio-visual channels. Non-verbal channel includes body language and body guesture.

**Communication has Traditional and Modern Institutions**

Since communication is being transferred from one generation to another since time immemorial, therefore, communication has traditional as well as modern institutions both. It reveals continuity as well as change. Priest, assistant of priest, barber, functional castes of *Jajmani* system, village head, village Panchayat, caste Panchayat, inter-village Panchayat, Prayer song party, Ram Leela party, Krishna Leela party, Nautanki party, dance party etc. are traditional institutions related to communication. But Post office, Telegraph, Radio, Television, Cinema, Newspapers, Information and Broadcasting Ministry are modern institutions of communication.

**There are Impediments to Communication**

Communication is everywhere and for all. But communication has to face a number of impediments. The communication has to face natural, physical, geographical, social, cultural, economic, political, religious, educational and psychological impediments.

**Communication has to Face Loss**

Communication has to face loss. There is a difference butween saying and hearing. The communicator is saying what and the receiver is receiving what. Both differs. The communicator tells in his own terms and in his own way. The receiver hears and understands in his own ways. This difference between communicator and receiver creates communication loss. On many occasion the original communication is lost or misunderstood. Thus, in course of travelling from one individual to another individual, communication has to suffer a loss.

# 4

# Communication: Type, Method, Technique and Tools

As referred earlier, communication is a method of sending and receiving different kinds of messages. The individual who sends messages is called as sender and the person who receives messages is known as receiver. Thus, communication is a system of sending and receiving messages between two or more persons. There may be more than one communicator and receivers in a system. Therefore, types of communication depends upon the individual and groups. The communication may take place between two individuals, an individual and a group, a group and an individual or an individual and public or public and an individual. Keeping these aspects in mind communication may be divided in to following types:

- Intra Personal Communication
- Inter Personal Communication
- Mass Communication
- Intra Group Communication
- Inter Group Communication
- Informal Communication
- Formal Communication

**Intra Personal Communication**

When a person communicates with himself or herself, it is known as intrapersonal communication. In this case the same person is sender of message and receiver of message. An individual faces a number of situation in his or her day to day life. In these situations he/she has to make communication with himself and herself. For example for right and wrong decisions, for punishment or excuse, for supporting or not supporting, favouring, not favouring, allowing or disallowing, accepting or rejecting and so on. In such situations an individual has to make communication with himself or herself.

**Inter Personal Communication**

When communication takes place between two persons, it is known as inter personal communication. The interpersonal communication takes place between husband-wife, brother-brother, sister-brother, sister-sister, father-son, father-daughter, mother-son, mother-daughter, master-servant, seller-buyer, teacher-student, leader-follower, leader-leader, Minister-Prime Minister and so on. Thus, when communication occurs between two persons having different relations, posts and even strangers, it is known as inter-personal communication. Here communicator and communicatee both are two different persons.

**Mass Communication**

When communication takes place between an individual and mass or people or public, it is known as mass communication. For example communication between village head and Village Panchayat, Mukhia and Gram Sabha, Ward member and ward assembly, teacher-student, leader-followers, religious leader-audience, Prime Minister-Public or people, News reader-public, officer-people and so on. The purpose of mass communication is to share news or messages with more and more people. Mass communication is dependent on modern information technology.

**Intra Group Communication**

When communication takes place between members of the same society, it is known as intra group communication. For example family members, lineage members, caste Panchayat members, village members, class student and so on. In this type of communication, the sender and receiver both belong to the same group and both are members of the same community. They understand easily language of each other.

**Inter Group Communication**

When communication takes place between two or more group it is known as inter-group communication. For example communication between two families, two lineages, two clans, two caste, two village heads, two states, two nations and so on. For intergroup communication, a common language must be known to both groups.

### Informal Communication

When the time, subject, speaker, audience and place of communication is not pre fixed, it is known as informal communication. Here the sender and receiver both do not follow any formality while communicating to each other. Such type of communication is found in family, lineage, clan, village, inter village, peer group, occupation group, and so on. The members of family make communication any time at any topic. Similar is the communication in members of lineage, clan, village and neighbouring villages. Such type of communication continues for few minutes or sometimes for hours. In this type of communication, there is no formality of time, place and topic.

### Formal Communication

When time, place, topic, speaker and audience of communication are prefixed, this is known as formal communication. Here, both communicator and communicatee have to follow formalities. This type of communication always takes place within the limit of formalities. Communication begins in time and is completed within time. Interactions also take place within time. Formal communication takes place in village assembly, caste assembly, tribe assembly, marriage, deathfeast, offices, schools, colleges, universities, state assembly, parliament, and different institutional and organisational meetings.

### Method of Communication

Although communication is itself a method of giving and taking messages, but communication has to follow a number of methods for give and take of messages. The chief methods used for the purpose of communication are as follows:

- Informal Method
- Formal Method
- Direct Method
- Indirect Method

- Positive Method
- Negative Method
- Open Method
- Closed Method
- Confidential Method
- Non-confidential
- Verbal Method
- Non-verbal Method
- Drama and Play Method
- Song and Dance Method
- Traditional Method
- Modern Method

Now, let us discuss about these methods one by one.

### *Informal Method*

In this method of communication, no formalities are required for communication. Communication can take place at any time at any place and at any matter. This method of communication is followed in informal group where relationship is face to face and where members reside together and know each other very well. For example couple, family, friend group, play group, occupation group, village, neighbourhood etc.

### *Formal Method*

In this method of communication, formalities are required for communication. Here communicator, communicatee, time, place and subject are prefixed. All participants of communication have to follow the rules and formalities of communication. Such type of communication is found at the time of marriage, death, festivals, plays, games, sports, institutes, colleges, universities, schools and a number of Governmental and Non-Governmental Institutions.

### *Direct Method*

In this method of communication, the communicator and communicatee participate directly. There is no other person between the communicator and communicatee. This types of communication is held in such group where persons are connected to each other directly. For example couple, family, friend group, occupation group, village, neighbourhood. In these groups, persons have direct relation to each other. That is why they have direct communication.

### *Indirect Method*

In this method of communication, communication between persons take place indirectly. Indirect communication takes place to follow social cultural taboos and where persons are related in hierarchical order. For example in family, the avoiding relatives have to follow in direct method of communication because they are not allowed to appear face to face before each other. Naturally, they have to take help of a third person who acts as a medium of communication between two avoiding relatives. For instance daughter-in-law takes help of his son or daughter for communication with father-in-law, mother-in-law, husband's elder brother. In a number of formal institutions a number of persons work on different posts. They are arranged in hierarchy. The order of top official is communicated to lower level officials indirectly.

### *Positive Method*

In this method, the communicator makes an attempt to know the positive impact of his/her communication. He or she as communicator puts such questions before audience as am I right, do you understand, do you agree and so on. By using these questions he/she tries to understand whether his/her communication is being followed or not.

### *Negative Method*

In this method, the communicator makes an attempt to know negative impact of his/her communication. He/she puts negative questions before the audience to know the negative impact of his/her communication. For example how many of you do not agree, how many do not understand, how many consider it right. By putting these questions, the communicator makes an attempt to know the negative impact of his/her communication.

### *Open Method*

In this method of communication, the response of audience or receivers is kept open. Here choices are not closed. It is left upon the receivers to answer according to their choices. The communicator asks to audience such questions whose answers are open for the receivers. For example in your opinion, what is the best method of communication, what is the best solution to check communication loss? How communication gap can be filled up. The answers of these questions are left to the receivers. Receivers are left to answer according to their choices.

### *Closed Method*

In this method of communication, the choice is closed by the communicator himself/herself. Here, the communicator provides only two, three or four choices. The receivers have to select any one choice. For example, Do you support communication through songs and dances? The choices of this answer has been closed by Yes, No, No response. Now, the receiver is bound to select any one choice among three choices given. This method of communication is very useful to know the responses of receivers where choices are limited and known to communicators.

### *Confidential Method*

In this method of communication, the communicator communicatees secretly to a receiver whom he/she wants to communicate a secret message. He/she tells something in the ear of the receiver isolating the message from other receivers or he/she puts some written symbols in a paper in the hand of receiver concerned. This method of communication is very much useful when some secret message is to be conveyed to a receiver in a group.

### *Non-confidential Method*

In this method of communication, the communicator makes the message common for all receivers. Here, he/she does not isolate any receiver for communicating a special message. Rather, he/she makes the message public for all receivers. For example he/she makes announcement for all receivers present there. Here, the communicator does not keep any thing confidential for any receiver.

### *Verbal Method*

In this method of communication, communication is made through verbal symbols which may be oral, written, pictorial and audio-visual. This method of communication is very much used by receivers and communicators both.

### Non-Verbal Method

In this method of communication, communication is made by body language such as facial expression, gesture, poses, eye contact, shaking hand, meeting chest to chest, and movements of different body parts.

### Drama and Play Method

In this method of communication, communication is made through staging drama and play. The communicator stages drama and play on theme which he/she has to communicate among the receivers. Communication by this method brings positive impact on the receivers.

### Song and Dance Method

In this method of communication, the communicator organises song and dance on the theme which he/she wants to communicate among the receivers. This is also an effective method of communication among the mass.

### Procession Method

In this method of communication, the communicator organises procession to communicate the receivers the matter which he/she wants to communicate. This is very effective method of communicating various types of demands and strength to Government and authorities.

### Traditional Method

In this method of communication, the speech organs, hear organs and body language are used for the purpose of communication. This method also utilises different types of traditional codes such as social, economic, political, religious, health, epidemic, drum, bird, animal, plants, trees, love, war, friendship etc. for the purpose of communication.

### Modern Method

In this method of communication, modern means are used for the purpose of communication. For example, post office, telegraph, press, cell phones, phones, internet, T.V., Cinema etc. for the purpose of communication.

### *Techniques of Communication*

The techniques are part of a method of communication. It is a means by which a communicator sends messages to receiver or receivers and *vice versa.* Techniques are related to linguistic symbols. The linguistic symbols may be verbal and non-verbal both. Therefore, the technique of communication may be divided in to following two parts:

- Verbal Technique of Communication
- Non-verbal Technique of Communication

Verbal Technique of Communication may be divided in to following groups:

- Oral Technique
- Written Technique
- Visual Technique
- Audio-Visual Technique

### *Oral Technique*

This technique is most important technique because it is followed by both illiterate and literate people in their day-to-day communication. Here, communication takes place through speech and hear organs. In our country, there has been a tradition of heard (*Shruti*) and remembered (*Smriti*) since time immemorial. In every communication, this technique is used besides other techniques.

### *Written Techniques*

In this technique, messages are communicated in written symbols. The written symbols may be pictorial, graphic, algebraic or alphabetic. Each symbol carries a social-cultural meaning. The communication is made in written form and the receiver decodes the social cultural meaning by observing and reading them. Literacy was a pre-condition for the emergence of this technique of communication. Prior to the emergence of written method, oral tradition was the only technique of communication. Even to day oral technique is most preferred technique of communication in a speech community. Written technique of communication is used where formality of writing is essential.

### *Visual Technique*

In this technique of communication, communicator makes communication by showing pictures, photographs, maps, charts, tables, diagrams and graphs of the thing which he/she wants to communicate to the receivers. Visual communication is made with the help of visual aids.

### *Audio-visual Technique*

In this technique of communication, communication of theme is made with the help of audio-visual aids. With the help of audio-visual aids, the communicator is able to communicate the receivers the theme which he/she wants to show the receivers with the help of photographs and sounds.

### *Non-verbal Techniques*

In communication, human beings use not only verbal techniques for communicating the messages to receives, but he/she also uses non-verbal techniques to communicate the message of various kinds. The non-verbal technique is also of various types. The chief types of non-verbal communication are as follows:

- Gesture
- Facial Expression
- Eye Contact
- Hand Shake
- Chest Shake
- Poses
- Nodding Head
- Movement of Body Parts
- Clapping
- Jumping
- Sitting
- Smiling
- Seeing Angrily
- Laughing

- Weeping
- Avoiding
- Not Keeping mum
- Emotional scene
- Keeping mum

Even today, non-verbal techniques have been able to establish their significant position in communication of various types of messages to receivers.

**Tools of Communication**

Closely related to the techniques of communication, there are tools by which techniques of communication are employed. The important tools related to various techniques of communication are as follows:

- Human speech organs
- Human hearing organs
- Different parts of Human body
- Writing materials
- Reading materials
- Printing press
- Photographs
- Graphs
- Tables
- Report
- Visual Aids
- Projector
- C.D.
- V.C.D.
- V.C.R.
- Phone
- Cell Phones
- Internet
- T.V.
- Cinema
- Radio
- Booklets
- Books
- Letters
- Pamphlets

- Wall writing
- Procession
- Flags
- Drums
- Loud speakers
- Slogan shouting
- Morning prayer

# 5
# Impediments to Communication

Communication is a human speciality. It is one of systems established by human beings for the fulfilment of their various kinds of need. With the help of communication system human beings were able to fulfil their needs in past, they are fulfilling their needs today and they will continue to fulfil their needs in future. So long as needfulfilment is attached to communication system, communication will maintain its existence. Although communication performs significant roles for human beings, but communication is not free from impediments. There are a number of factors which come in the way of communication. The chief factors creating impediments to communication are as follows:

- Physical Factor
- Natural Factor
- Ecological Factor
- Educational Factor
- Social Factor
- Cultural Factor
- Economic Factor
- Religious Factor
- Political Factor
- Health Factor
- Transportation Factor
- Transmission Factor
- Psychological Factor

**Physical Factor**

Human body has to pass through the stages of infancy, childhood, adolescence, younghood, adulthood and oldhood. During infancy the child is unable to communicate. Perhaps, the only way of communication in this stage is weaping and whispering. In childhood, the communication is acquired through imitation and enforcement method. In adolescene, an individual starts communicating with the members of his/her speech community. Now, he/she becomes a full participant of communication. In younghood and adulthood he/she remains full participants of communication in speech community. But in old hood he/she looses teeth and memory power. He/she is now not a full and active participant of the communication. Deaf and dumb are also unable to communicate properly as an active participant of communication in speech community. The physical conditions of an individual affects his/her participation in communication. Only persons with good health are the active participants of the communication. Unhealthy and diseased persons become non-participant of communication. In this way, physical factor creates impediments to communication.

**Natural Factor**

Natural factors like flood, storm, starvation, earthquakes and epidemic create impediments to communication. During natural calamity all communicational system gets paralysed and people are cut off from rest part of the country and globe. It takes time to get the communicational system revived.

**Ecological Factor**

The habitat of human being is not same every where in the world. It is located in hilly, plateau, forested, coastal, desert, plain and island areas. The communication system has to face hindrance in such areas. Mountain, river, sea, island and desert create impediment to communication.

**Educational Factor**

Education contributes a lot in communication. Illiteracy comes in the way of communication. It is true communication is above education. It is because uneducated people are also active participant of communication in their speech community. But there is no doubt that education develops communication skill. Skilled persons are able to communicate in better way than unskilled persons. Uneducated cannot communicate through writing and readings. Thus, illiteracy creates impediment to communication.

**Social Factor**

Society consists of persons belonging to different age, sex, caste and occupation groups. Each group has to follow social rules related to communication. Children do not communicate clearly. Youngers are not allowed to speak much before elders. Women are not allowed to talk with men of own caste as well as other castes. They are also not allowed to talk with avoidance relatives. The low caste people are not allowed to talk with high caste people. They have very limited communication occasions on limited issues. Thus, social taboos and law create impediment to communication.

**Cultural Factor**

Cultural taboos and rules of behaviours also play significant role in communication. Culture is way of life and it is acquired as a member of society. It is a social heritage. Different kin groups behave with each other following rules of kinship behaviour. It is also known as kinship usage. In this rule, some relatives are treated as avoiding relatives. They do not have direct communication. They have communication through an another non-avoiding relative. In our society *Sasur-damad*, *Sas-damad*, *Sasur-putravadhu*, *Sas-putravadhu*, *Bhawoh-Bhaisur*, *Jyestha Sali*—younger sister's husband are treated as avoiding relatives and they do not have direct communication.

At the time of marriage, bride and bridegroom are not allowed to talk to any stranger. In *Sasuralaya* bride and grooms are not allowed to have communication during day time. Even women of a family are not allowed to talk with any stranger. Young and adult males and females are not allowed to have free discussion on sex-related matters. They are not allowed to share sex problems with elders and youngers, but they are allowed to have communication with friends and joking relatives.

When quarrel takes place between husband and wife, communication is suspended temporarily. With enemies communication is broken permanently. One is not allowed to have communication through abusive words. When a person or a family is out casted, all members break communication. Communicationally, he is ousted member of the society.

In this way, we can say that a number of cultural customs, rules and taboos create impediment to communication.

**Economic Factor**

Economic factor is also responsible for impediment to communication. On the basis of property and wealth possession people are divided in to rich and poor. The poor are those who do not have house and are unable to feed themselves and their family members both ends. Poverty is taken as curse. The poor have their own world and world view. They struggle hard to maintain their existence. They do not have communication with other people. They do not want to know what is happening in nation and the world. They do not have proper communication of poverty alleviation programme. They remain cut off from the mainstream of nation. The rich, on the other hand, take benefit of proper communication of every types of events occurring in country and the world. They take all benefits related to communication development. In this way, economic factor creates hindrance in the way of communication system.

**Religious Factor**

Religious factor also creates impediments to communication. Each religion has its own holy book, festivals, symbols, pilgrim centres, and fairs. Religious authorities incalcate the belief that only their religion is superior. But this is not true. All religions have equal value for their followers. They should not isolate one religious followers from other religious followers. But they should play role to integrate people of all religious faith through secularism. Wrong communication and fanatics create riots causing harm to life and property. Riots create hatered towards other religious faith. People start fearing from the communication with people of other religious faiths. Due to lack of communication, people do not know the goodness of other religions. Thus, religious factor comes in the way of proper communication.

**Political Factor**

Political factor is also responsible for impediment to communication. In traditional political system, women do not play political role. They do not enjoy their say even in decision-making in family. They do not participate in traditional Village Panchayat. They are represented by their father, brother and husband. Now-a-days, women are participating in elections. They are also wining elections as ward member, Mukhia, Panchayat Samiti chair person. Zilla Samiti chair person, M.L.A., M.P. and so on. But the concept of Ward Pati, Ward Putra, Mukhia Pati, Mukhia Putra, Pramukh Pati, Pramukh Putra, Adhyaksha Pati, Adhyaksha Putra, Vidhayak Pati, Vidhayak Putra etc. have also come in to existence. This shows that women are still being deprived in decision-making. This also indicates that women are not empowered politically and communicationally as yet. Thus, political factor create hindrance in proper communication.

### Health Factor

Health factor also creates impediment to communication. It has been observed that healthy persons are the best, efficient and active participant of communication. Unhealthy persons remain cut off from the participation in communication. Persons having different types of physical disability and suffering from communicable serious diseases remain cut off from participation of communication.

### Transportation Factor

Transportation takes place through road ways, railways, waterways and airways. In order to carry goods and messages, these transportation systems have been established. Truck, bus, car, rail, ship and aeroplanes are used for the purpose of transportation. Transportation finally helps in communication. But when some troubles arise either in ways or means of transportation system, communication is badly effected. Flood, storms and earthquakes disturb transportation system. Disturbance in transportation system creates impediments to communication.

### Transmission Factor

Transmission factor is also responsible for impediment to communication. Transmission of news and views takes place through radio, T.V., Cinema and Internet. But these means of transmission are dependent on electricity supply. Electricity supply is adversely affected when production is not up to demand. Flood, storms and earthquakes also disturb electric supply. The disturbance in electricity supply creates hindrance in transmission of news and views. The hindrance in transmission ultimately creates impediments to communication.

**Psychological Factor**

Psychological factor also creates an impediment to communication. Without knowing the psychology of communicator and receiver it is very difficult to understand communication. What communicator has communicated and what receiver has understood is very difficult to know without knowing the psychology of sender and receiver. For example if a communicator says what a beautiful nose ?, its psychology is not clear. It is because beautiful nose is used to praise the beauty of nose of a person, but it is also used to make a fun of ugly nose of person. Thus, what a beautiful nose carries dual meaning. The dual meaning cannot be understood without knowing the psychology of the communicator. In the same way, the receiver says yes even without understanding the message sent by the communicator. Saying yes by receiver also indicates his confusion in mind.

A number of messages related to love, hatered, jealousy, enemity, goodness and badness carry dual meaning. The real meaning cannot be understood without knowing the psychology of communicator and receiver. In this way, psychological factor creates hindrance in communication.

After going through a good deal of discussion over various factors related to impediments to communication, it is quite clear that communication is not free from impediments. Communication has to face a number of impediments. The impediments come in the way of proper communication.

# 6
# Communication Loss

As discussed earlier in nature and characteristic of communication, communication is a system of giving and taking messages. But proper give and take of messages takes place only when sender and receiver know the meaning of messages. If give and take of messages do not take place properly, communication has to suffer a loss. The incidence of loss suffered by communication is termed as communication loss. The communication loss can be understood in a better way by the examples given below.

**Example 1:** In a class the teacher asked all students to stand in a queue. All students obeyed his/her class teacher and stood in a line. He called the monitor of the class and communicated a news in his ear. The message was like this; "Tomorrow each student will sing a song in the last class." The teacher asked the monitor to convey this message in the ear of 1st student. The 1st student will convey to the 2nd one, the 2nd one to the 3rd one…….to the last 50th one. In this way, the news was communicated to all students of the class through ear to ear. When the teacher asked the last 50th student what he had received, it was found that he received only a message of singing song tomorrow. The message like "each student in the last class" was lost completely. This example reveals clearly that when news passes from ear to ear, some parts of news are lost or news are received completely changed. This reveals communication loss.

**Example 2:** In an another class, a teacher asked his student to take a sheet of paper, fold it and tear it in to equal half. Some student folded the sheet once and tore it in two equal half. While some students folded the Sheet twice and tore it in equal haves. While still some other students folded the sheet again twice and tore it in to equal haves. Thus, the same message was received differently by different students of the class. This example also shows us incidence of communication loss.

**Example 3:** In an another class, a teacher asked his students to answer write or wrong about one k.g. of sugar is heavier than one k.g. of cotton. Majority of students replied that sugar is heavier than cotton.

Like above three examples, a number of examples can be cited dealing with communication loss. But it is also true that communication loss occurs every where. Some people receive message properly, while others receive them partly. In these situation, partly lost messages are example of communication loss.

## Causes of Communication Loss

Communication loss occurs due to following causes:

- Not listening properly to message conveyed by sender
- Not understanding the meaning of message
- To give own meaning to the message heard
- Not proper communication by sender
- Unclear language of sender
- Unreadable writing of sender
- Unimpressive personality of sender
- Dual meaning of the message
- Failure of loud speaker
- Failure of Electricity
- Disturbance in transmission system
- Failure of transport system
- Not proper communication of heard message

### *Not Listening Properly to Message Conveyed by Sender*

Communication loss takes place when a receiver does not pay proper attention towards the message conveyed by the sender. As a receiver does not pay proper attention, he/she looses some traits of messages sent. This behaviour of receiver results in communication loss.

### *Not Understanding the Meaning of the Message Received*

The communication loss occurs when a receiver does not understand the meaning of the messages sent. In a number of instances, the receiver does not understand the real meaning of the messages received. He/she is able to understand partly the meaning of messages conveyed. This brings ultimately communication loss.

### *To Give Own Meaning to Message Received*

Sometimes it so happens that the receiver provides his/her own meaning to the message received. The own meaning of receiver becomes quite different from the original meaning of the message. In this way communication loss occurs.

### *Not Proper Communication by Sender*

Communication loss also occurs when there is no proper communication of message by the sender. In some instances the sender himself or herself remains confused. As a result he/she does not communicate the message in proper way. This results in communication loss.

### *Unclear Language of the Sender*

Sometimes, the sender uses such a language which does not make the message clear. The receiver tries to know the meaning of the message. But he/she becomes unable to know. As a result communication loss takes place.

### *Unreadable Writing of Sender*

Sometimes the handwriting of the sender is not clear and even unreadable. In this circumstances, the receiver does not understand the meaning of the messages received. This ultimately brings communication loss.

### *Unimpressive Personality of Sender*

The personality of sender or communicator also attracts the hearing efficiency of receiver. Persons with handsome personality and good oration attract the receiver more and more. As a result there is no chance of communication loss. But unimpressive personality of a communicator, on the other hand, brings boring impact on receiver. The receiver does not pay proper attention towards the message conveyed by such a person. Thus, unimpressive personality brings communication loss.

### *Dual Meaning of Message*

Dual meaning of the message is also responsible for communication loss.

There are a number of words and sentences which have dual meaning. The words and sentences having dual meaning creates confusion in the mind of receiver. The confusion regarding meaning brings communication loss. For example, the Hindi word *Pani* has two meanings–one water and the other hand. When a sender sends a message that bring *Pani*, the receiver gets confused wheather the sender is asking for water or hand. Similarly, if a communicator sends message like what a beautiful face, the receiver gets confused whether the communicator is praising the face, or making a fun on ugly face of a person.

### *Failure of Loud Speaker*

In mass gathering and meetings, arrangement of loud speaker is made to make the voice of communicator audible to all audience. But sometimes loud speaker gets failed suddenly due to some reasons. The failure of loud speaker does not make oration of communication audible to all people. The people sitting infront of the communicator receive messages properly, but the people sitting in last line do not receive messages properly. Thus, the failure of loud speaker brings communication loss.

### *Failure of Electricity*

Communication tools such as loud speaker, T.V., Cinema, internet etc. are dependent on electricity. Failure of power brings communication loss among mass.

### *Disturbance in Transmission System*

Radio, T.V., cinema and internet are dependent on satellite transmission system. The failure of transmission system brings communication loss.

### *Failure of Transportation System*

Communication is also made through roadways, waterways, railways and airways. But earthquakes, cloudy weather, and flood brings hindrance in communication system. As a result, communication loss takes place.

### *Not Proper Communication of Heard Message*

Communication loss occurs when a receiver does not communicate the heard messages properly to another receiver. Generally, the receiver adds his/her oral tradition in the messages heard.. Each receiver goes on adding his/her own tradition. As a result, communication loss comes in to existence.

From the above presented causes, it is clear that there is always a chance of communication loss. Inspite of taking a number of steps to check communication loss, communication loss is still a reality.

# 7
# Communication Skill

Communication is a system of give and take of messages. Through this system messages are given and taken. It is not a one way process. Rather, it is a two way process. A person who is a communicator at one hand becomes receivers at the other hand. In communication, there is always a chance of communication loss. In order to avoid communication loss, special emphasis is made on communication skill. All individuals do not possess equal communication skill, although they all are participant of communication in a speech community. The communication skill varies from individual to individual. To be a good communicator demands upon ones skill to communication. Thus, it is a skill which makes a person good communicator or a bad communicator. We can say that communication skill is an ability of an individual by which he/she makes communication efficiently and effectively.

While discussioning the nature of communication, it has been stated that communication is a social heritage. We acquire it as a member of our speech community. We are not born with communication from our mother's womb. Rather, we learn it in our speech community. But we acquire good communication skill, only when our speech organs and hearing organs are functioning properly. Deaf and dumb persons are not able to hear and speak. So, they are not in a position to communicate properly. However, they attempt to communicate through body languages and symbols. Now-a-days, deaf and dumb acquire education in schools through sign languages. With the help of sign languages, they are able to communicate among themselves. Blind can speak but cannot read. But they are also acquiring education through sign languages. They communicate very efficiently with people who are not blind. We also get education in schools and colleges and acquire communication. These indicate clearly that communication is acquired and learnt. Blind, dumb and deaf also acquire communication skill through education like common man.

It is also true that each members of the speech community participate in communication in day to day talk, but all individuals do not possess communication skill equally. People having communication on the same topic, differ in their communication skill. As an audience we are so attracted towards the communication of some communicators in such a way that we do not wan to miss even a word. But, on the other hand, we are so frustrated to hear the communication of some communicator that we leave the seat for not listening to them. The good communication skill develops interest in receivers through his/her each words and sentences. Receivers become pleased to hear them. But bad communicators create dispair in the mind of receivers. They do not create interest in receivers. The receivers do not clap for them, leave seat, or start sleeping to hear their speeches. Thus, all persons do not have equal communication skill.

Communicating again and again increases the communication efficiency of a communicator. It has been observed that persons having social, cultural, political and administrative posts, get more and more chances to communicate than common man. That is why their communication is more perfect and effective than common people.

In speech community, children and adolescents do not have freedom to communicate freely. Therefore, the communication skill of children and adolescents is not as affective and efficient as an adult.

It has also been observed that the aged lose their communication skill due to physical disability. Woman are not allowed to communicate with strangers and also at public place. This taboo deprives women from proper communication skill.

In caste system high castes have more opportunity of communication. As a result they have better communication skill than low castes.

More and more chances of communication increases communication skill. It makes a communicator more impressive.

Education provides occasion for communication in modern languages through which education is acquired. Education develops multilingual communication skill, where as speech community develops unilingual communication. More and more education enhances more and more communication skill of a person. It also increases multilingual communication. The educated persons possess communication skill in local, regional, national and international languages.

Three things are essential for communication skill. They are:

- Understandable messages
- Reliability of communicator
- Impact of message on receiver

On the basis of above parameters, communication skill of a sender is measured. If the message of a communicator is not understandable, his/her communication skill is measured negatively. If the communicator is not reliable, his/her communication skill is also taken as negative. If the message conveyed by a sender does not bring positive impact on the receiver, his/her communication skill is not taken positive. All these above mentioned matters are considered while measuring the impact of communication skill.

**Bases for Effective Communication Skill**

The effective communication skill depends on following bases:

- Clarity of Expression
- Completeness of Information
- Conciseness of Message
- Concreteness in Presentation
- Courtesy towards Recipient
- Correctness of Facts
- Consideration for Receiver

***Clarity of Expression***

Clarity of expression is closely related to communication skill. A communicator is treated as an expert of communication, only when he/she possess clarity of expression. Without clarity of expression, he/she is never recognised as skillful communicator. Thus, it is clarity of expression which makes a communicator skillful or skil!less.

***Completeness of Information***

The completeness of information is also closely associated with communication skill. If a communicator is not able to send complete message to receiver, his/her communication skill comes under criticism. Receivers start criticizing his/her communication skill. Without providing complete information, a communication is not recognized as a skillful communication.

### *Conciseness of Message*

Conciseness of message is one of bases of communication skill. It is closely related to communication skill of a communicator. A skillful communicator is one who sends message to receivers in concise form. If he/she fails in sending message in complete form his/her communication skill comes under question. Receivers start talking openly that the communication skill of communicator is not good. He/she always confuse us by sending message in unconscise form. Such remarks by receivers put a question marks on skill and expertise of a communicator.

### *Concreteness in Presentation*

A skillful communicator is one who always places concreteness at the time of presenting message. A skillful communicator always presents message in concrete form before the receiver. Those communicators, who present message before the receiver in abstract form, are not counted as skillful communicator. Communication skill of such communicator comes under criticism and question.

### *Courtesy Towards Recipient*

A skillful communicator is one who shows courtesy towards recipients or receivers. The courtesy towards recipient brings skillful influence on recipients. Recipients become pleased to see courtesy of communicators. This brings communication more and more successful.

### *Correctness of Facts*

A skillful communicator is one who presents correctness of facts before the recipient. If he/she is not able to present correctness of facts before the recipients, he/she is not counted as a skillful communicator. Rather, he/she is counted and criticized as skillless communicator.

### *Consideration for Receiver*

A skillful communicator is one who provides time for consideration to receiver. In a successful communication, it is necessary for a communicator to know the idea of receiver. Those communicators who do not provide time to receiver for consideration, their communication skill is criticised. Their communication skill comes under question.

**Essential Condition for a Successful Communication**

The essential conditions for a successful communication are as follows:

- Own your Message
- Offer Complete and Relevant Information
- Thinks of Recipient
- Obtain Feed back from Receiver
- Verbal and Non-verbal congruence
- Repeat, if necessary
- Do not judge values
- Rely on facts

***Own Your Message***

A successful communicator is one who always owns his/her messages communicated to receivers. Owning of ones own messages conveyed to receiver increases the respect and faith in the mind of receivers towards communicator. The receivers develop full faith in the messages communicated. This reciprocate with communicator in good manner. Owning of messages removes all types of doubt which receivers have towards the message of communicator. This enhances the successfulness of a communicator. Thus, owning ones messages is an essential condition for a successful communicator.

***Offer Complete and Relevant Information***

Offering complete and relevant information is an essential condition for a successful communication. A successful communicator always pays attention towards this essential condition. He/she always offers complete and relevant messages to receivers. This enhances faith of receiver towards communicator. The receiver provides true answer to the messages received. The communicator becomes a reliable person for the receiver. The reliability ultimately increases the success rate of communication.

***Think of Recipient***

Thinking for recipient is also one of essential conditions for success of communication. A successful communicator always pays special attention towards the recipient. He/she always think of recipient. He/she takes in to account the age, sex, educational, occupational, marital, religious and residential background at the time of communicating messages to receivers. The communicator tries to use language of messages understandable clearly to receivers. The receivers begin to consider communicator as one of members of own community. They develop full faith in communicator and provide positive result. Thus, thinking about the background of recipient is closely related to the success of communication.

***Obtain Feedback from the Receiver***

Obtaining feedback from the receiver is one of essential conditions for success of communication. A successful communicator is one who tries his/her best to get feedback from the receiver on messages communicated to them. The communicator maintains contact with receivers and attempts to know their feedback. The obtaining feedback from the receiver provides satisfaction to communicator regarding the messages which he/she had communicated.

***Verbal and Non-verbal Congruence***

For a successful communication, congruence between verbal and non-verbal communication is a must. For example, if a communicator conveys welcome message, then there must be a smile on his/her face. If he/she sends sorrowful message, then there should be a sorrowful sign on his/her face. Similarly, message of anger should follow angry face. Thus, for a successful communication, there should be a balance between verbal and non-verbal behaviour of a communicator.

***Repeat, if Necessary***

Repeating the messages on the request of receivers is an essential condition for the successful communication. Sometimes, the recipients are not in a situation to receive messages in one time. They request the communicator to repeat the messages. A successful communicator does not hesitate in repeating the messages. Rather, he/she feels pleasure and extends thanks to receivers. The receivers develop full faith in communicator. This increases the success of communicator.

### *Do not Judge the Value*

Not judging the value is an essential condition for successful communication. A successful communicator never attempts to judge the value of messages communicated or received. He/she never attempts to judge the value of receivers. Rather, he/she tries to see value from the point of view of receivers.

### *Rely on Facts*

Relying on fact is a key for a successful communication. A successful communicator always relies on facts. Because facts are truth or realities. The main purpose of a successful communication is to find out truth. He/she pays attention on evidences not only on saying.

### *Importance of Communication Skill*

The importance of communication skill has been every where, every fields and in every ages. But to-day, we are living in age of communication revolution. In this age, the importance of communication skill has increased more and more. To-day only those are powerful who have better communication skill. In every kinds of roles, in every professions and every occupations, the role of communication skill has become of prime importance. If your communication is skillful, you get success. If not, you are rejected. Thus, success and unsuccessful have been attached to communication skill. The persons with communication skill attains success after success. But persons without communication skill become failure after failure. Thus, the importance of communication skill has increased in our every spheres of life. We are powerful if we have sound communication skill, but we are powerless if we have weak communication skill.

# 8
# Channels of Communication

Channels of communication are those medium through which communication takes place in human society. As referred to earlier that for the purpose of communication a medium is required. Without a medium communication cannot take place. As air is required to act as medium of diffusion of smell good or bad, in the same way a medium is required to convey messages in communication. In communication language acts as a medium to convey messages from communicator to receivers. As human language has been classified in to two categories: Verbal and Non-verbal. Therefore, on the basis of language the channels of communication have also been classified in to two categories. They are as follows:

- Verbal Channels of Communication
- Non-verbal channels of Communication

These two categories of communication channels have also been divided in to a number of types. About them a detail description is being furnished below.

**Verbal Channel of Communication**

In Verbal Channel of Communication, a communicator attempts to communicate messages to receivers through speaking, writing, showing and showing-telling. In this way in verbal communication, four types of human actions are involved. They are speaking, writing, showing and showing telling. On the basis of these four actions, verbal channel of communication is further divided in to following types:

- Oral Communication Channel
- Written Communication Channel
- Visual Communication Channel
- Audio-visual Communication Channel

***Oral Communication Channels***

This is the most easy channel of communication. This channel of communication came in to existence much earlier than written channel of communication. But, it is still most easy and effective channel of communication prevalent in all types of human society–folk, peasant, urban, city metropolises and global. In this channel of communication, a communicator conveys messages to receivers through speech or oration of sounds. This channel of communication functions on the following occasions:

- Serving oral invitation
- Serving oral messages of different kinds
- Serving oral decision of village head and Panchayat
- Serving oral decision of Inter-village head and inter-village Panchayat.
- Oral sale and purchase of commodities
- Serving oral acceptance
- Serving oral complements
- Serving oral sorrowful message
- Oral Conversation between Individuals
- Oral proceedings of different kinds of meeting
- Speech Lecture
- Meeting Session
- Oral lease out and lease in of land
- Debate Competition
- Singing of folksongs and prayers
- Story telling
- Recitation of poetry
- Play of Riddles
- Play of Proverbs
- Folk plays and drama
- Interview conducting
- Dictation writing
- Teleconferencing
- Seminar-conferences

- News broadcasting
- Public messages transmission
- Telephone talks and cellular phone talks
- Discussions on different issues

### *Serving Oral Invitation*

In folk and peasant society, there is a tradition to serve invitation to relatives and friends orally. For this purpose one kin or relative of boy or girl visit in the house of each relatives and communicates the invitation to come and participate in social-ceremonial function. He/she brings sunfried rice coloured in turmeric power along with dub grass. If rice and dub grasses are accepted the invitation is supposed to be accepted by the relative. But when *dub* grass and sunfried rice are returned, it means, the invitation has not been accepted. Now, attempts are made to make the relative pleased so that he and his family members could participate in the function. Oral communication of invitation is served on the occasion of birth, mundan, marriage and death rituals. The tradition of serving oral invitation is still followed in rural and even urban societies.

### *Serving Oral Messages of Different Kinds*

In village societies, messages related to fire, flood, epidemic, starvation, thefty, dacoity, rape, gangrape, murder, madness, snake bite, dog bite, witchcraft, fair, festivals, haat-bazar, and a number of messages related to daily social life are communicated orally. These kinds of messages are communicated orally from mouth to mouth and ear to ear.

### *Serving Oral Decision of Village Head and Village Panchayat*

In tribal village, there are institutions of village head and village Panchayat. The village head is a social head of the village. He is chairman of the village Panchayat. All heads of families are members of the village Panchayat. The religious head is also an official of the Village Panchayat. The village head and the village priest have an assistant each. It is duty of the village assistant to communicate orally the date, time and place of village Panchayat meeting and its agenda. The village head officiates the meeting orally. All types of cases are heard orally. Decision, compensation and punishment are communicated orally. The institution of village head and village Panchayat functions orally.

### *Serving Oral Decision of Inter-village Head and Inter-Village Panchayat*

Indian tribals have an institution of inter village head and inter village panchayat. In Jharkhand State these institutions are known as Munda-Manki system, Pir Panchayat system, Paraha Panchayat system and Manjhi parganait system. These institutions also function orally. The assistant of inter-village head communicates orally the time, place and date of Panchayat meeting. In meeting inter-Village cases are heard and problems are solved. The entire procedure of the meeting is followed orally. Agrieved parties, witnesses, decision, compromise, compensation and punishment are heard and communicated orally.

### *Oral Sale and Purchase of Commodities*

In village and tribal areas, weekly *haat-bazaar* takes place. In local *haat-bazaar* sale and purchase of commodities take place orally Haggling and credit all go through oral tradition.

### *Oral Acceptance*

In villages and tribal areas people provide oral acceptance related to a number of works. People agree or disagree orally.

### *Serving Oral Complements*

In villages and tribal areas people extend good wishes on the occasion of birth, new year, marriage and festival orally. Now-a-days, good wishes and congratulation are communicated orally through telephones and cell phones.

### *Serving Oral Sorrowful Message*

The members of folk and urban societies serve sorrowful message like death, illness and accident orally to their friends and relatives. Now-a-days, communication of sorrowful messages take place through phones and cell phones.

### **Oral Conversation between Individuals**

In folk and peasant societies, oral conversation between individuals occupying different status and performing different roles takes place. In Village Panchayat, Caste Panchayat and religious meeting conversation takes place between individuals. The conversation may be between father-son, father-daughter, brother-brother, brother-sister, sister-sister, mother-son, mother-daughter, *malik-majdoor*, Priest-*jajman*, teacher-student, friend-friend, *mukhia*-villager and so on.

***Oral Proceeding of Meetings***

In villages village level and caste level meetings are organised time to time to raise funds for celebration of festivals and construction of road, school, Panchayat etc. The meeting is held orally. The proceeding of meeting is recorded orally. Different kinds of meetings also take place in urban areas. In meeting different officials and members express their opinions orally.

***Singing of Folk Songs and Prayers***

Oral communication of folk songs and prayers takes place in villages and in urban areas on the occasion of worship, festivals and rituals like birth and marriage. Songs and prayers are also sung in temples dedicated to different Gods and Goddesses. The communication of folk songs and prayer goes on from one generation to another orally.

***Recitation of Poetry***

In folk and peasant society, there are a number of folk poets who compose poetry related to Gods, Goddesses, social problems, social events and other cultural heroes and heroin. Sometimes, a programme of poetry recitation takes place. The prize distribution takes place, too, on this occasion. Poetry recitation is also organised in urban areas, too. Poetry recitation takes place orally.

**Story Telling**

In folk and peasant societies story telling is an important means of entertainment. Grand father and grand mother tell varieties of storis to their grandson and granddaughter. Tales are related to kings, animals, trees, Gods, Goddesses, queen, Prince, Princes, master, servant, demon, witch, spirit, ferry and son on. Communication of story telling takes place orally from one generation to the next generation.

### *Play of Riddles*

In folk and peasant society, play of riddles is organised among children. Each children is given time to tell a riddle for answer. All children make an attempt to answer the riddle. In this way play of riddle goes on orally.

### *Play of Proverbs*

In folk and peasant societies, a play of proverbs is organised. The proverb specialists take part in this play. The villagers are present to hear different kinds of proverbs. The proverbs are related to man, woman, children, teacher, students, middleman, agriculturist, wise, fool, king, queen, festival, dress, food and so on. Play of proverbs take place through oral tradition.

### *Folk Plays and Drama*

In folk and peasant society, play and drama are staged on festive and ceremonial occasions. The villagers play the roles of different actors in the play and drama. In break dances are organised. Plays and drama are related to social problems. The play like to-day's son, to-day's daughter, to-day's aged, honesty, political leader, dowry system, witchcraft, family planning, voting right and so on are staged orally.

### *Interview Conducting*

Interview is one of techniques to know something in detail from the interviewee. In interview there is interviewer and interviewee and conversation on a topic or topics goes on. This is also one of techniques of selecting candidates on different posts. The interview may be individual interview or group interview. But the entire process of interview takes place orally.

### *Dictation Writing*

This is a technique of communication of knowledge in schools. The teacher asks students to write dictation. The teacher communicates orally and students have to write the dictation. On the occasion of meeting, seminar, workshop, symposium, technical session, a number of media persons are present. They hear the speech given by different scholars. They prepare news on the basis of hearing speeches.

### *Teleconferencing*

Now-a-days, teleconferencing is organised by media person to make the people aware of views of different scholars, readers, politicians, academicians, economist and so on. Tele- conferencing is organised orally.

### Seminar and Conferences

Now-a-days, seminar, conference, workshop and symposium are organised to get opinions and views of different experts on a specific topic. These are held also for the dissemination of different kinds of messages among scholars and experts. The different scholars and expert present their views orally before the learned audience.

### *News Broadcasting*

National and international news are broadcasted on radios and televisions time to time by different news agencies. News are broadcasted orally in Hindi, English and local languages for the purpose of communication among the people who are interested in local, regional, national and international news of different kinds.

### *Public Message Transmission*

Different Ministers of State and National Governments make transmission of public interest messages to the people for their interest. The transmission of public interest messages is done orally.

### *Telephonic Talks*

Telephonic talks between different individuals take place orally with the help of phones or mobile cellular phones.

### *Discussion on Different Issues*

The State and National Assemblies have discussion hours in which a discussion is held on acts, statutes and problems of the people. The discussion in Assembly and Parliament takes place orally in which different members participate in presence of chairman or chair person.

### *Speech/Lecture*

In higher educational institutions and universities, special speech, talk or lecture of eminent national and international scholars is organised time to time. In these lectures, students and teachers are audience and participants. The lecture takes place orally. Question answer session also takes place.

### *Meeting Session*

A number of caste, religious, political, academic, play and games related meetings are organised in rural and urban areas on different occasion. The meetings are organised in different sessions. In different sessions, the different issues are discussed orally before reaching at a common conclusion.

### *Oral Leaseout and Lease in of Land*

In folks and peasant society, lease in and leaseout of land take place orally. This is still in practice. But now-a-days, lease in and lease out of land take place through written court document.

### *Debate Competition*

In schools and colleges, debates competition is held on a topic selected. In the debate competition, a number of students take part. They try their best to get prize. One who comes first is declared as winner and one who comes second is declared as runner. Some prizes and certificate are given to both winner and runner.

## Importance of Oral Communication Channels

Oral communication has occupied significant position even from those dark periods which are known as prehistoric periods. In historical period man acquired writing skill. Thus, development of literacy is taken as demarcating line between prehistory and history. Although man remained only a communicating animal in entire period of prehistory, but from historical period he became a writing animal. Now, man has developed full writing skill. But even after reaching the stage of writing, the importance of oral communication has not become less. Even today, oral communication is followed by each and every individuals residing in different parts of the globe. It is because man is a communicating animal and the most easy way of communication is oral communication. It needs only speech and hearing organs which every individual possesses. It also needs body language which every individual has. Thus, oral communication is still most preferred form of communication.

Our sacred texts *Ramayana*, *Mahabharata*, *Vedas*, *Puranas*, *Upanishads* all are orally communicated and staged. In *Ramayana* three communicators appear. They are Lord Shiva, Kagbhusundi and Tulsidas. The receivers are mother Parvati, Garuda and people.

Folk songs, stories, ballades, proverbs, idioms, riddles, phrases, jokes are still being communicated orally in folk and peasant society.

In schools, colleges, universities, institutes oral method of teaching by lectures is still preferred and favoured.

In Assembly and Parliament, oral discussions on various issues and problems take place.

In seminar, symposium, workshop, conference oral presentation of papers, views, comments, observations take place.

Exchange of invitation, news and views are also taking place orally even today. Oral transmission of news takes place through different news channels of T.V. and Radio.

Thus, the form of society may be folk, peasant, rural, urban, metropolitan or global, but the importance of oral communication is still maintained.

The oral communication channel occupies significant place in democracy to press public demand on Government. Rallies, *dharana*, *bandh* and slogan shouting take place through oral communication channel.

### *Advantages of Oral Communication Channels*

There are a number of advantages of oral communication channel. The chief advantages of oral communication channel are as follows:

- Saving of time
- Less expensive
- Occasion of getting feed back
- Occasion to provide clarification
- Message according to background of receiver
- Useful channel for announcement
- Useful for intra-group communication
- Useful for illiterate society

- Occasion to get back message

Now, let us discuss about these advantages of oral communication channel.

***Saving of Time***

The greatest advantage of oral communication channel is that it saves time of communicator and receiver both. There is no need of writing materials, reading materials and of being literate. Hence, it saves time of both communicator and receiver.

***Less Expensive***

In comparison to other verbal channels like written, visual and audio-visual, oral communication channel is less expensive. It is because it saves money of communicator and receiver in writing, reading, visual and audio-visual means.

***Occasion of Getting Feedback***

Oral communication channel provides an occasion to a communicator to get feedback of messages from the receivers. The oral communicator can know the feedback about the messages communicated to the receivers.

***Occasion to Provide Clarification***

The oral communication channels provides occasion to a communicator to clarify the messages communicated to receivers. The communicator has face to face relation with receivers. Therefore, he/she is available for receivers to clarify doubts related to messages communicated to receivers.

***Messages According to Background of Receiver***

In oral communication channel, messages are communicated according to the background of receivers. The communicator is in a position to communicate messages in useful tone, sound and terms which suit to the receiver. That is why, the receivers are attracted towards the messages communicated by communicators.

### *Useful Channel for Announcement*

The oral communication channel is very much useful for announcement. Ministers, administrators, Social-cultural officials use this channel very much for making announcement for the people and public.

### Useful for Intra Group Communication

The oral communication channel is very much useful for intra group communication. It is because in intra group communication the communicator and receivers know the language of each other. Generally, they belong to same speech community or are aware of languages through which communication takes place.

### *Useful for Illiterate Society*

Oral communication channel is very much useful for the members of illiterate society. It is because there is no need of writing and reading in this communication channel.

### *Occasion to Get Back Message*

Oral communication channel provides occasion to get the message back by the communicator from the receiver. If there appears some confusion or mistake, in the message communicated to receivers, the communicator is in a position to seek apology from the receiver and get the message back in few seconds. The receivers do not take it ill because they are aware of the possibility of human err in communication.

### *Disadvantages of Oral Communication Channels*

There is no doubt that oral communication channel has a number of advantages over other verbal channels. But this cannot be concluded that this channel does not have any disadvantages. This channel also has disadvantages. The main disadvantages of oral communication channel are as follows:

- Not always time saving
- Not always less expensive
- Not always effective
- Dependency on useful tone, sound and word

- Dependency on reaction and counter reaction
- Dependency on right communicator and receiver
- Dependency on how to say not what to say
- Totally dependency on hearing process
- No dependency on legal burden
- Not suitable for multilingual receivers

### *Not Always Time Saving*

The oral communication channel is not always time saving. Rather, it is more time consuming in certain situation. It takes more time in selection of right communicator and right receivers. Therefore, oral communication is not always time saving.

### *Not Always Less Expensive*

The oral communication channel is not always less expensive. In many situations it appears more expensive. The oral communication channel depends upon right selection of communicator and receivers. In selection of right communicator and receivers more and more money are spent. It includes expenses over journey, holtage and phone calls. Therefore in some situations, oral communication channels appear more and more expensive.

### *Not Always Effective*

The oral communication channel is not always effective. Unimpressive personality of communicator does not bring effective impact of communication on receivers. If a communicator is not a good orator, the communication does not bring effective result. In this way oral communication channel is not always effective.

### *Dependency on Useful Sound, Tone and Terms*

The success of oral communication channel depends upon useful sound, tone and terms of the communicator. If sounds, tones and terms of communicator are useful, only then oral communication channel brings positive result from the receivers. But if the sound, pitch and terms of the communicator are not useful, the oral communication channel does not bring positive result. In such cases, oral communication channel brings negative result. Thus, oral communication channel is totally dependent on useful sound, tone and oral terms.

### *Dependency on Reaction and Counter Reaction*

The oral communication channel is dependent on reaction and counter reaction of the communicator and receivers. If the reaction and counter reaction of the communicator and receivers are positive, only then oral communication channel gets success. But in some situations, the reaction and counter reaction of communicator and receiver are contrary. In these situations oral communication channel does not receive success.

### *Dependency on Right Communicator and Receiver*

The success of oral communication channels depends upon right communicator and right receiver. If communicator and receiver are right and proper persons, the oral communication gets success. But to get right communicator is really a difficult task. On many occasions communicator is right but some receivers are not right. In some other situations, receivers are right but communicator is not good. In both such cases, the success of oral communication goes towards negativity.

### *Dependency on How to say not on What to say?*

The success of oral communication channel depends upon how to say, not on what to say. How to say occupies significant place in oral communication channel? Receivers are attracted not towards what is being said, but they are attracted towards how are being said? A good communicator always makes emphasis on how to say to attract the receiver? If a communicator is not expert in how to say, the oral communication channel does not receive success?

### *Totally Dependent on Hearing Process*

The oral communication channel is totally dependent on hearing process. If a communicator or a receiver is suffering from hearing defects, the success of oral communication channel is not possible. Again for the purpose of oral communication channel, audible communication between communicator and receiver or receivers is a must. Only then oral communication channel can receive success.

### *No Dependency on Legal Burden*

The oral communication channel is free from legal burden. It is because the communicator relates confession and mistake to oral fault. The communicator does not share legal burden. Legal action is not possible because the communicator deny about wrong communication. One cannot depend legally on oral channel of communication.

### *Not Suitable for Multilingual Receivers*

The oral communication channel is not suitable in multilingual situation. For example the audience belongs to different linguistic groups and the communicator knows only one language. In this case, oral communication channel does not receive success.

### *Written Communication Channels*

Written communication channel is one of verbal channels of communication. In this channel, the communicator sends message to receivers in written form. Here, sounds are not uttered or pronounced by the communicator to make the receiver to hear messages. Rather, he/she provides written form to the sounds which he/she wants to communicate as messages. The messages are written in Hindi, English, or other local and regional scripts. In this communication channel, both communicator and receiver(s) must be educated. This channel depends upon writing and reading process, not on hearing process completely like oral communication channel. The written channel of communication functions through following means:

- Letter
- Diary
- Journal
- Periodicals
- Books
- Research Paper or Articles
- Answer books
- Newspaper
- Written order
- Written judgement
- Address
- Money order
- Report
- Thesis
- Graphs

- Chart
- Tables
- Bulletin
- Proceeding of meeting
- Poetry collection
- Story collection
- Riddle collection
- Proverbs collection
- Idioms and phrases collection
- Novel writing
- Life history
- Case study
- Autobiography
- Sacred Texts
- Collection of Folk traditions
- Questionnaire
- Application
- E-mail
- Fax
- SMS
- Advertisement
- Press release
- Document
- Land and House registration
- Sale and Mortgage of Land
- Business News and Price List
- Horoscope
- Marriage Invitation Card
- Certificate
- Telegram
- Cinema script
- Play or Drama script
- Proceeding of seminars

Now, let us discuss about these means of written communication channel one by one.

***Letter***

Letter is one of means of written communication channels. A communicator communicates his/her message to receiver by writing his/her personal letter. The letter conveys messages in written form. The receiver reads the messages communicated by the communicator and understands what kind of message has been communicated to him or her. He/she also knows the purpose for which communicator has written a letter. The letter may be personal, departmental, official, public. The letter may also be a reply letter if a receiver gives reply to the messages communicated by the communicator by writing a letter in reply. Previously letters were communicated through post office, though it is still a valid and legal source of communication. But letter is now also communicated and replied through e-mail.

### *Diary*

Diary is also taken as source of communication. The diary may be personal or official. But they provide very useful messages to the receiver. In diary writing, the communicator writes about a number of incidences which he/she faces in day to day life to communicate to interested receiver(s). The researcher or investigating agencies treat Dairy written by a person or an official as a valid source of messages. The diary writers write down a number of confidential messages which he/she does not want to make public without his/her permission. Some authors of diary express their desire to make messages of diary public after his/her death.

### *Journal*

Different university departments, technical and management institutes, ministries publish journals which contain a number of knowledgeable messages for interested scholars. The records of respective institutions are maintained in the office for interested readers, scholars and other persons who want to know something on some special issues.

In journal knowledge is preserved not only for present day scholars, but also for scholars of generations to come. The Journal are published quarterly, half yearly, and annually. Journals play significant role in dissemination of knowledge.

### *Periodical*

Periodicals are also a significant means of written channel. A number of Governmental and Non-Governmental institutions publish their periodicals regularly highlighting their achievements. They contain important development related news. They are circulated in different institutions for diffusion of achievement and knowledge.

### Books

Books are most import means of written communication channels. Students have to read books right from primary level schools to universities and technical institution. Through books different kinds of knowledge is communicated to the readers. The scholars and academicians work day and night to contribute books on different themes, subjects and discipline. Scientists, artists, novelists, literatrurists, academicians, technical institutions experts, higher education experts, planners, administrator, officials, politicians are contributing books to be read by present generation and the generations to come in future. There are Governmental, Non-Governmental and private libraries where books are preserved for generations to come.

Books may also be edited besides authored by a scholar. There may be single author or more authors of a book. The edited books consist of collection of papers written by different scholars on a particular theme arranged systematically by the author(s).

### Research Paper or Article

Different experts of their respective fields write their valuable articles or papers. They publish their research articles in journals of national and international repute. These articles contain messages related knowledge in different academic disciplines. The journal containing such articles are circulated in different libraries for record and to be read by different scholars time to time.

### Answer Books

Right form primary schools to universities, higher education and technical institutes, students have to appear at examination and answer the questions on answer books. The examiner evaluates answer books and provides marks to each students. In result, students are declared pass, promoted or fail. Thus, answer books contain valid written messages provided by students on questions set by the examiner. Answer books are written channel of communication.

***News Papers***

News papers are also an important channel of written communication. A number of news papers are published daily and weekly. These news papers are published in Hindi, English, and local languages. These news papers play valuable role in communicating various kinds of news to public readers. The readers of news paper remain waiting for reading news paper from early morning. Taking morning tea and reading news papers is a common hobby of a number of readers. It is one of the best and preferred written communication channel.

**Written Order**

The different Governmental and Non-Governmental Officials, businessman, institution heads, organisation heads, private companies, Government companies, multinational companies and other write official order or notice to their employees and their counter parts. Written order is a valid means of written communication channels.

***Written Judgement***

Written judgement is a valid means of written communication. In the judgement of Lower Court, High Court, Supreme Court, Special Court, C.B.I. Court, written judgement is provided to the parties. Through written judgement decision of court is communicated to the parties and institutions concerned. The judgement is read thoroughly for the purpose of appeal from lower to High and from High to Supreme Court. It is also read thoroughly by the lawyer of the parties for appeal in double or full bench. Judgements of different cases in different courts are preserved in the law Journal, periodicals, books etc. for future use by lawyers to get justice.

***Address***

The nation keeps record of addresses of their citizens through Aadhar card, voter card, ration card, passport, job card, MNREGA card, BPL card, APL card, different kinds of certificates and bank accounts. Different Governmental and Non-Governmental employers also keep record of address of their employees. Addresses are taken as valuable document for personal identification of an individual. It is one of written channels of communication.

### Money Order, Money Transfer, a Cheque and Bank Draft

Money order, money transfer, cheque and bank draft are valid documents and written channel of economic communication.

#### *Report*

Report is also one of written channels of communication. The report may be an annual report of Ministries, annual report of institutions—Social, cultural, economic, political, religious and health. It may be of an investigating agency or committee. It may be a research report. The reports consist of valuable messages for communication in written form. Therefore, reports are taken as one of valid and valuable written channels of communication.

#### *Thesis*

The students of undergraduate, postgraduate and doctoral researches have to write a thesis or dissertation on a topic of research selected for this purpose. Theses are evaluated by the examiners to provide degree to the students concerned. It is regarded as very valuable written channel of communication related to examination.

#### *Graphs*

In thesis and reports graphs are presented to illustrate, explain, analysize, and describe the informations. Graphs also have some written messages not only lines. Therefore, graphs are also taken as a valuable means of written communication channels.

#### *Chart*

In reports, books, theses, and dissertations charts containing messages are furnished here and there to illustrate description in meaningful way. Therefore, charts are taken as one of means of written channels of communication.

#### *Tables*

In papers, reports, theses, and dissertation tables are presented to describe, explain and analyse the data. Tables make presentation attractive and beautiful. Thus, tables are written communication channels.

### *Bulletin*

Different institutions publish their bulletin to make readers aware of their achievements and benefits. Thus, bulletins are written channels.

### *Proceeding of Meetings*

When official meetings are held, its proceeding is recorded as a witness and for the purpose of preservation and communication. The proceeding includes every steps of a meeting right from welcome and welcome address to vote of thanks. Proceedings are recorded in written form. Now-a-days, proceedings are also recorded through camera and videography.

### *Poetry Collections*

A number of poets publish their collection of poetries in book. The poetry collection books contain a number of messages related to social, cultural, political, religious, administrative and health issues, besides literature. Poetry collection books are written source of communication. Hence, they come under written communication channel.

### *Story Collection*

Some story tellers publish stories written by themselves in book form. The readers like story collection books because such books contain a number of messages which have social, cultural, religious, political, health, ferry, witch, spirits and humerous issues. These books have entertainment value, too.

### *Riddle Collection*

Some scholars interested in study of riddles, collect a good number of riddles and publish them in book form to preserve them for future generation. The riddles are based on knowledge of folk and peasant societies. Such books act as written communication channels.

### *Proverbs Collection*

Some scholars have interest in collection of folk proverbs. They collect oral traditions and publish them in book form for record and preservation for future generation. Proverbs collection books act as written communication channel.

### *Idioms and Phrases Collection*

A number of scholars interested in the study of folk idioms and phrase make a collection of them and get them published. They become a book containing all idioms and phrases of a folk and peasant society. Thus, idioms and phrases collection books become written communication channel.

### *Novel Writing*

A number of literaturists write novels and publish them. Novels are not only literature, but they are literature produced by author based on social, economic, political, religious national and global events. Novels act as written communication channel.

### *Life History*

Some scholars collect life histories of eminent scholars, academicians, politicians, leaders and others. They get them published. Thus, books on life histories become written channel of communication.

### *Case Study*

Some scholars collect cases of social pathology and get them published as book. Now, they become written channel of communication on social pathological behaviours.

### *Autobiography*

Some scholars write their own biography and get them published for public. Thus, they become written channel of communication.

### *Scared Texts*

Each religion has its own sacred texts. For example *Vedas*, *Ramayana*, *Mahabharata*, *Gita*, *Upanishads* and *Puranas* are sacred texts of Hindu. *Bible* is scared text of Christian, *Quran* is sacred text of Islam, *Gurugrantha Sahib* is sacred text of Sikh. In sacred texts principles of religion is communicated for the followers. Sacred texts are written communication channels.

### *Folk Traditions*

A number of scholars are interested in study of folk traditions. They make a research on folk and peasant traditions. They publish their researches in book form. Such books act as written channel of communication for the readers.

### *Questionnaire and Schedule*

For the purpose of research, the researcher prepares a questionnaire or schedule containing a list of questions to be answered by the sample informants. The written questions are printed and a cover page is provided to each set. Thus, questionnaire or schedule becomes a written communication channel for the researchers.

### *Application*

The students write application to their heads of institution for fees, scholarship, book grant and so on. The employee writes application to his/her head for leave. Similarly, people write application to officials for a number of causes. Applications are granted or rejected. In this way applications are written channels of communication.

### *e-mail*

e-mail is an important written communication channel prevalent all over the world. With the help of internet messages are communicated to an individual on his/her e-mail address.

### *Fax*

Fax is also a written channel of communication. With the help of fax machine and fax number written messages are communicated to individual and institution concerned.

### *SMS*

SMS is also a written channel of communication. Written messages are communicated with the help of cell phones through SMS.

### *Advertisement*

Advertisement is a written communication. Posts for appointment are advertised in news papers. Interested candidates apply for the post. They are sent admit cards and interview letters. When candidates become successful in written test and interview test, they get appointment letter. In this way, advertisement, admitcard, interview letter and appointment letter are written channel of communication.

### *Press Release*

Press release is also a written communication channel. The organisers of different meetings, seminars, conferences, workshops and symposium prepare written press release regarding the purpose, time, venue, date and outcome of the seminar. The press release is circulated to different news papers for circulation of news.

### *Documents*

Different notifications by Ministries and Governmental and Non-Governmental Institutions are known as documents. They are preserved for future use. Each institution keeps record of its documents. They are written communication channels.

### *Land and House Registration*

People purchase land and house. They get registry paper from the Government for ownership. The ownership is written document. It works as written communication channel regarding the ownership.

### *Mortgage of Land*

The mortgage of land is also taken through registry. It is treated as a written documents for both parties involved in the mortgage of land.

### *Business News and Price List*

Business news and price list are written documents for sell and purchase of commodities. Each trader has his/her own business news and price list on the basis of which sell and purchase of commodities produced take place.

### *Horoscope*

Horoscope is a written personal documents related to impact of different planets in different periods of life. Each individual keeps his/her horoscope and makes some useful attempts to please the planets for favourable and successful events in life.

### *Marriage Invitation Card*

Marriage card is taken as a useful document for marriage registration and also valid witness of marriage. It is a written communication channel which communicates the name of marriage partners, their relatives, date, place and time of marriage.

Like marriage invitation cards, there are death ritual card, participation in function card and so on. They are also written communication channel.

### *Certificate*

Certificate is treated as written communication channel. The certificate is regarded as valid document. The certificates may be related to examinations, competitive examinations, debate competition, play, games, sports championship, residence, caste, income, SC, ST, OBC, and others. For the purpose of admission and service these certificates are required. Birth and death certificates are also treated as valid document related to an individual and his dependents.

### *Telegram*

Telegram is also a written communication channel to communicate messages to receivers. But now-a-days, e-mail services are used for communicating messages to receivers.

### *Cinema Script*

Cinema script is also regarded as a written communication channel. Cinema script writers write script of cinema according to which cinema actors and actress have to perform roles.

### *Play or Drama script*

Play or drama script is also regarded as a written channel of communication. The play or drama script writers write the script of the play or drama according to which actors and actress have to perform roles.

### *Proceedings of Seminars*

A number of seminar, symposium, worshop, conferences are organised by the different higher academic institutions. The purpose of seminar is to gather knowledge on a subject concerned. The proceedings of the seminar are recorded in writing. Hence, proceeding of the seminar is regarded as a written channel of communication. The proceeding keeps the entire recording of the seminar from welcome to vote of thanks by the organisers of the seminars or symposium.

### *Advantages of Written Communication*

Written communication channel has a number of advantages over the other channels of communication. The main advantages of written communication channel are as follows:

- Legally valid
- Cannot be taken back
- Plenty of time for planning
- Review work possible
- Showing message possible
- Pointwise presentation possible

- Giving title and conclusion possible
- Letter communication for long time possible
- Preservation as document possible

***Legally Valid***

Written communication channel is regarded as legally valid. The court consider it as legally valid document for witness.

***Cannot be taken back***

The messages communicated by written communication channel cannot be taken back. It remains always as it was written at the time of communication.

***Plenty of Time for Planning***

The written communication channel provides plenty of time for planning messages. The messages communicated by written communication channel are well planned because it provides sufficient time to communicator to think and plan the messages to be sent to receivers.

***Review Work Possible***

In written communication channel, messages are communicated in written form. Therefore, review works of messages to be sent are possible.

***Showing Messages Possible***

As messages are communicated in written form in written communication channel, therefore, it is possible to show messages to others for the purpose of suggestions. The receivers can show it to others to get their suggestions before giving reply message.

***Pointwise Presentation Possible***

In written communication channel, pointwise presentation of messages is possible. The communicator is in a position to present messages pointwise. Similarly, receiver is also in a position to present reply messages pointwise.

***Giving Title and Conclusion Possible***

In written communication, it is possible to provide title and conclusion to messages to be communicated by the communicator. Similarly, it is also possible to provide title and conclusion to reply messages by a receiver.

***Long Time Letter Communication Possible***

In written communication channel, it is possible to have long time communication between communicator and receivers through letter, SMS or e-mail messages.

***Preservation as Document Possible***

Message communicated through written channel can be preserved as documents to be used in future. Thus, documentation of messages is possible.

***Disadvantages of Written Communication***

Although written communication channel has a number of advantages about which a description has been presented just above, but it cannot be concluded that written communication channel has no disadvantages. It has a number of disadvantages, too. The chief disadvantages of written communication channel are as follows:

- More time taking
- More expensive
- Dependency on literacy
- Dependency on technology
- Legal burden possible
- Influenced by psychology
- Influenced by limit of communicator
- Delay in getting feed back
- Delay in getting reply
- Not getting reply
- Lack of clarification
- Lack of congruence between verbal and non-verbal behaviour.

***More Time Taking***

The written communication channel takes more time in communicating news to receivers. It is because it takes time in writing and posting messages to receivers. It also takes more time in getting feed back and reply messages.

***More Expensive***

Written communication channel is not only more time taking but it is also more expensive. It includes writing materials, printing cost and sending costs. All these items increase the expenses over written communication channel.

***Dependency over Literacy***

Written communication channel is totally dependent on literacy. For this communication channel, the communicator and the receiver both should be literate upto such level so that they could read, write and understand the messages communicated and reply received.

***Dependency on Technology***

Written communication channel is dependent on technology such as writing materials, reading materials, printer, fax, post office, internet and so on. Therefore, dependency on technology creates disadvantage to written communication channel.

***Legal Burden Possible***

Written communication channel sometimes creates legal problem and expenditure on legal matters. Written documents are produced as witness in court. The sender or communicator can use it in their own favour for legal purpose.

***Influenced by Psychology***

The written communication seems to be influenced by the psychology of communicator. The written messages are not only messages but they also reveal the psychology of the communicators. The receiver has to reply in written the psychology of the communicator.

***Influenced by Limit of Communicator***

The written communication channel is not only influenced by the psychology of the communicator, but it is also influenced by the limit of communicator. Each, communicator has own limit of language, its grammar and script. Therefore, the written communication channel has to work within the limit of communicator.

### *Delay in Getting Feed Back*

In written communication channel, the communicator has to face the situation of delay in getting feed back from the receiver. Sometimes, receiver takes more time and sometimes he/she does not send feed back to communicator.

### *Delay in Getting Reply*

The written communication channel has to face the situation of delay in getting reply messages. The communicator communicates messages and keeps on waiting for reply messages. The receivers makes delay in sending reply messages to communicator knowingly or unknowingly.

### *Not Getting Reply*

In written communication channel, the communicator has to face sometimes the situation of not getting reply message. The communicator goes on writing for reply from the receiver, but the receiver does not send reply. He/she avoids the communication message sent to him/her by the communicator.

### *Lack of Clarification*

In written communication, the communicator and the receiver do not have face to face relation. Therefore, communicator is not before the receiver to clarify the message. Therefore, written communication lacks scope of clarification.

### *Lack of Congruence between Verbal and Non-verbal Behaviour*

In oral communication channel there is congruence between verbal and non-verbal behaviour of communicator and receiver. But in written communication channel, there is no chance of congruence between verbal and non-verbal behaviour.

***Essential Conditions for Effective Written Communication Channels***

For effective written communication channel, some essential conditions need to be followed by communicator and receiver. The related essential conditions are as follows:

- Selection of right terms
- Quite clear view
- No use of fanatic terms
- No use of ambiguous and confusing terms
- No use of sentimental terms
- No use of prestige hurting terms
- Well thought style
- Small sentence
- Simple presentation

Now, let us discuss about these essential conditions for effective written communication channel one by one.

***Selection of Right Terms***

The success of written communication depends upon the selection of right terms by both communicators and receivers. Unless a communicator communicates a receiver in right term, the receiver is unable to understand the meaning of messages received. Again if a receiver does not use right term in his reply message, the communicator will not be able to get clear feed back and reply message. Therefore, for achieving success in written communication channel, both communicator and receiver should use right terms in their messages and counter messages.

***Quite Clear View***

The success of written communication channel depends also upon clear view of communicator and the receiver. If communicator and receiver do not have clear cut view about messages to be communicated to receivers and to be counter communicated to communicator, the success of written communication channel cannot be expected.

***No Use of Fanatic Terms***

For the success of written communication channel, the use of fanatic terms should be avoided by both communicator and the receiver. The fanatic terms bring the situation of conflict between communicator and receiver. This creates hindrance in the success of written communication channel.

### *No Use of Ambiguous and Confusing Terms*

For a successful written communication channel, the communicator and receiver should avoid ambiguous and confusing terms. The use of ambiguous and confusing terms creates impediments to the success of written communication channel.

### *No Use of Sentiment Hurting Terms*

For a successful written communication channel, the sentiment hurting or sarcasting terms should be avoided by communicators and receivers. Sentiment hurting and sarcasting terms lead towards unsuccess of a written communication.

### *No Use of Prestige Hurting Terms*

In written communication channel prestige hurting terms should be avoided. Because such terms create trouble in success of written communication channel.

### *Well Thought Style*

The success of written communication channel also depends upon well thought style. The communicator and receiver should follow well thought style in communication and counter communication of messages, other wise, no success can be achieved.

### *Simple Sentence*

For the success of written communication channel, the communicator and receiver should follow communication and counter communication in simple sentence. The simple sentences are easy to read and understand. They increase the success of the written communication channel.

### *Simple Presentation*

The success of written communication channel also depends upon simple presentation of facts. Therefore, the communicator and receiver should follow simple presentation in their communication and counter communication of messages.

### *Visual Communication Channel*

Visual communication channel is one of verbal channels of communication. In this channel of communication, communication between communicator and receiver takes place through visual or visible messages. The visible messages can be shown to receiver through photographs, scenes, scenery, diagrams, graphs, tables and pictorial symbols. Along with these visible messages some written words are also shown which describes in brief what visual messages are communicating to the receivers. The receiver sees the visual messages and expresses his/her counter messages either orally or through written communication channels. The visual communication channels are as follows:

- Signature
- Photographs
- Sketch
- Scene and scenery
- Drawing
- Painting
- Images
- Diagram
- Graph
- Map
- Chart
- Table
- Design
- Exhibition
- Poster
- Cover page
- Party symbols
- Railway crossing signal
- Family planning signal
- Hospital signal
- Traffic signal
- Petrol Pump signal
- Slide
- Flip card

- Hording
- Without multimedia Internet
- Presentation through projector

***Signature***

Signature is visual communication channel. The signature of each individual differs from other individuals. Signature of individual is visible on application, admit card, passport and different types of certificates. On many occasions the people launch a signature campaign to make pressure on the Government. The signature of signatories can be shown through photographs and scanner machines. The real and false signature of a signatory is recognised by signature expert. The signature as a visual channel of communication plays significant role in communicating messages in support or against a decision of Government. It also communicates messages related to true or false communication of signature.

***Photographs***

Photographs are visual channel of communication. They reveal the typical observations of a communicator. Each individual, house, and institutions have their own photo. Photographs are taken as valid document. In each admit card, admission card, passport, voter card, ration card, BPL card, MNREGA card, certificates and Aadhar card, a photograph of individual concerned is attached dully attested by the official concerned. The photographs of each candidates communicate their individual identity.

Photographs may also be of plants, animals, birds, insects, river, ocean, mountain, religious places, Gods, Goddesses and all things which are visible to us. All visible things can be captured in photographs through camera or cell phones. The photographs can be shown to those persons who have not seen photos of those things and events.

Photographs are also presented in books, thesis, reports, bulletin, souvenir, periodicals to communicate visual message along with written description.

***Sketch***

Sketches are also visible means of communication. The police release sketches of criminals, naxalites, terrorists and a number of lost persons.

With the help of sketches released, they are caught and punished. The lost persons are found out.

### *Scene and Scenery*

Photographs of natural scene and scenery of forest, hills, waterfalls, riverbank, clouds, ice deposit, sea beach, and garden are also visual channel of communication. They present a living visual messages of the things seen by the communicator.

### *Drawing*

Drawing is a visual channel of communication. It communicates the art of an artist who makes messages to be communicate through the art of his/her drawing. Besides art it also communicates motif, sentiment, nature and feature of the figure drawn. Now-a-days, drawing competitions are organised in which different artist take part. They own prizes, too, in competition. We have a number of evidences of cave drawing left for us as an evidence of art by our prehistoric ancestors.

### *Painting*

Painting is also an art in which artists make paintings of different things observed. They consist of visual messages regarding the nature and characteristic of things observed and painted. It also indicates ssentiment of the artist. Prehistoric and historic paintings found in caves and rock-shelter communicates messages related to social, cultural, economics, political and religious life of our prehistoric and historic ancestors.

Under modern art and paintings artists and painters communicate messages related to modern art and paintings. They also exhibit regional, local, national and international level arts and painting.

### *Images*

Images are also visual communication channel. Images sculptured or carved on rocks, stones, marbles, metals and ceramic communicate messages related to non-human and human form of Gods and Goddess, their family members, their animals and bird *vahan* (vehicle). They also reveal messages of fight between *Deva* and *Asura* and the victory of *Devas* over *Asuras* or *Rakshasas* (Demons).

### *Diagrams*

Diagrams are visual communication channel. Diagrams may be of various types. For example linear, circular, histogram, bar diagram, pie diagram and so on. Through diagrams data of researches are presented in attractive and beautiful manner. Diagrams make data attractive and beautiful. With the help of diagram data are made communicable at a very first glance. Diagram can be shown through visual aids.

### *Graphs*

Graphs are visual channel of communication. They can be presented through visual aid before the learned audience. The graphs show correlation between two or more different variables. The correlation could be understood easily by observing the graphs.

### *Map*

Maps are also visual channel of communication. Through maps location of villages, towns, cities, metropolises, railway station, international and national aerodrum, temples bridges, rivers, mountains, forest, waterfalls, population, santuries and a number of sites are shown. Maps also indicate boundaries of different countries, continents, and states. Maps also reveal construction design of different bridges, overbridge and buildings. Maps can be shown through visual aids to the audience in seminar, symposium and conferences.

### *Chart*

Charts are also visual channel of communication. The chart related to varieties of data can be presented through visual aids in seminar, meeting and conferences. They present varieties of data of our place.

### *Tables*

Tables are visual channels of communication. They communicate data in short, attractive and beautiful manner. They are presented in report, thesis, papers and books.

### *Design*

Design are also visual channel of communication. The design may be of a building, temple, bridge, hospital, township, entertainment centres, park, hotel, college, universities and researches. The different designs are presented to officials, scholars and audience for seeing and seeking suggestions and permissions.

### *Exhibition*

Exhibitions are also visual channel of communication. On different occasions exhibitions of *khadi* clothes, silks clothes, woolen cloths, prehistoric excavations, historic, excavation, war weapons, flower gardens, drawing and paintings take place in which people are invited to see the exhibitions and to make some purchasing. The exhibitions reveal varieties of items prepared by different communities of different states and countries. People are attracted to see items in exhibitions and do not make a control over themselves to make purchasing of the things exhibited.

### *Posters*

Posters are also visual channel of communication. The posters may be of cinemas, heroes, heroins, villains, artists, scientists, hospitals, schools, colleges, universities institutes, social evils, family welfare programmes, development programme beneficiaries and on varieties of them. Poster communicates messages related to things and events.

### *Cover Page*

Cover pages are also visual channel of communications. Books, reports, bulletin, journals, theseses and dissertations have a cover page. The cover pages are attractive and communicate visual messages to the readers about the inside contents.

### *Party Flag and Symbol*

Each political party has its own flag and symbol. Flags and symbols communicate visual messages to the people. The followers regard flag and symbol of their political party very much.

### *Railway Crossing Signal*

Each railway crossing has a visible signal which sends visual message to people that be careful, the train will come any time. Before the time of crossing train railway crossing is closed.

### *Family Planning Signal*

In hospital, signals showing family planning methods are communicated visually. The people are attracted to see such visual signal.

### *Hospital Signal*

Hospital signals are also visual channel of communication. They are displayed on surface roads, stations, aerodrum, railway crossing and also on maps. Following the signals people reach hospital if and when required.

### *Traffic Signal*

At surface road crossings, there are traffic signals to help the vehicles crossing the road one by one. There are traffic police to extend punishment to traffic rule breaker. The traffic posts have red, yellow and green colour signals. Red signal says stops and green signal says go and yellow says in between.

### *Petrol Pump Signal*

Signals of petrol pump are displayed on road indicating the distance and direction from different places. These signals provide a visual message to car, bus, truck, two wheeler and auto drivers to go if they need petrol. It also communicates messages to check whether the vehicle has fuel to cover distance up to next petrol pump or to this destination.

### *Slide*

Slides are also visual communication channel. Slides are prepared to display facts on screen. A number of scholars, doctors and other professional use this channel to show the audience the facts preserved in slide.

### *Flip Card*

Flip cards are also visual channel of communication. It sends visual messages to the audience.

### *Hordings*

Hordings are also visual channel of communication. It shows messages to the people to follow or not to follow.

### *Without Multimedia Internet*

Without multimedia internets are also a visual channel of communication. It communicates visual messages to any part of the world.

### *Presentation through Projector*

In a number of seminars, symposium, conferences, presentation of facts is made through over head projector. The audience are able to see the facts presented by the scholar.

### *Advantages of Visual Communication Channels*

Visual communication channel has its own advantage over the other verbal channels. The main advantages of visual communication channel are as follows:

- Communication through showing
- To make communication authentic
- To make communication attractive
- To make communication interesting
- To show similarity and differences between designs
- To make communication reliable
- To describe facts with visual witness
- To attract crowed of receivers

### *Communication through Showing*

Visual communication channel has advantages over oral channel and written channels of communication. It is because messages are communicated by showing. People believe more on messages seeing through own eyes.

### *To Make Communication Authentic*

The visual communication channel makes communication of messages authentic. The messages communicated are authenticated by photographs, maps, chart, table, design and so on. They can be seen and understood by the receivers.

### *To Make Communication Attractive*

The visual communication channel is very much useful in making communication attractive with the help of photographs, graphs, diagrams, and paintings. The visual communication channel makes messages more and more attractive for the receivers.

### *To Make Communication More Interesting*

The visual channel of communication is helpful in creating interest in receiver. When receivers see photographs, drawing, painting and design, they are attracted towards the messages. In this way, visual channel of communication is useful in making communication more interesting.

### *To Show Similarity and Difference between Designs*

The visual channel of communication is helpful in showing similarity and difference between different items, quality, advantage and design. To see similarity and differences people are attracted towards the messages being communicated visually.

### *To Make Communication Reliable*

Visual channel of communication plays significant roles in making communication reliable. When a receiver not only hears, but sees a messages being communicated visually, he/she gets more reliable message. It is because nothing can be more reliable than seeing with own eyes.

### *To Describe Facts with Visual Witness*

The visual channel of communication is helpful in describing facts with visual witness. Receivers are attracted towards visual witnesses and develop faith in messages.

### *To Attract Crowd of Receivers*

The visual communication channel is helpful in attracting crowd of receivers more and more. The receivers are naturally attracted towards visual messages of communicators.

### *Disadvantages of Visual Channels of Communication*

The visual communication channel has following disadvantages:

- Time consuming
- Expensive
- Dependency on visual aids
- Dependency on satellite
- Dependency on electricity
- Hyper reality

### *Time Consuming*

Visual communication channel is more time consuming. It takes more and more time in photography, recording, slide making and presenting them through visual aids.

### *Expensive*

The visual communication channel is not only more time consuming, but it is also more expensive. It takes more money in taking photographs, making videograph, and making C.D. and slides. It needs visual aids and electricity. Thus, this channel is more expensive

### *Dependency on Visual Aids*

The visual communication channel is dependent on visual aid. The failure of visual aids creates hindrance in visual communication channel.

### *Dependency on Satellite*

The visual communication channel is dependent on satellite for world wide communication of visual messages. The trouble in satellite channels creates impediments to visual communication channel.

### *Dependency on Electricity*

Visual communication channel is dependent on electricity supply. All audio-visual aids work through electricity. Disruption in electricity supply creates hindrance in visual communication channel.

### *Hyper Reality*

Visual communication channel suffers from the problem of hyper reality. Messages which are communicated visually, sometimes remain far away from the truth. They bring negative impact on receivers.

### *Audio-Visual Channels of Communication*

Audio-visual communication channel is one of verbal channels of communication. Through this channel messages are communicated to receivers through audio-visual aids by the communicator. The audio-visual aids work as a medium between communicator and receivers. Here receivers are able to hear and see messages together. That is why it is known as audio-visual channel of communication.

Audio-visual communication of messages take place with the help of following aids:

- Television
- Cinema
- Videography
- Laptop
- Internet with multimedia
- Overhead projector
- Tablets

### *Television*

Television is an audio-visual channel of communication. The T.V. has a series of audio-visual channels, such as news, business, entertainment, market, discovery, sports, spiritual and so on. Through these channels T.V. communicates messages related to them.

### *Cinema*

Cinema is an audio-visual channel of communication. In cinema messages related to social, economic, cultural, political, economic, health, character, and social pathological nature are communicated to receivers with the help of audio-visual aids.

### *Videography*

Video-graphy is an audio-visual channel of communication. With the help of video-graphy marriage, meeting, seminar, conferences are recorded audio-visually. Video-graphs are communicated to receivers with the help of audio-visual aids.

### *Laptop*

It is also an audio-visual channel of communication. With the help of laptop, videography and C.D. are displayed on over head projector.

### *Internet with Multimedia*

This is also an audio-visual channel of communication. With the help of audio-visual aids messages are communicated to receivers located in different parts of the globe.

### *Overhead Projector*

It is an audio-visual channel through which audio-visual messages are communicated to receivers with the help of C.D. and internet.

### *Tablets*

Tablets are also audio-visual channel of communication. They are hand set computer and internet. With the help of it audio-visual communication is done to receivers.

### *Advantages of Audio-visual Channels of Communication*

Although audio-visual communication is one of verbal communication channels, but it has its own advantages over the other verbal channels of communication. The main advantages of audio-visual communication channel are as follows:

- More effective communication
- More attractive communication
- More impressive communication
- Anywhere Communication in the world
- More influence on memory of receivers

***More Effective Communication***

Audio visual communication channel makes communication more effective. It is because it involves the seeing and hearing processes together which make the communication more effective.

***More Attractive Communication***

Audio-visual communication channel makes communication more attractive. It is because sounds and pictures related to messages attract more and more receivers. It attracts a crowd of receives.

***More Impressive Communication***

Audio-visual channel of communication makes communication more impressive. By seeing and hearing messages, receivers are impressed more and more. That is why, it is regarded as more impressive channel of communication.

***Anywhere Communication in the World***

This audio visual-channel of communication can make communication of messages any where in the world. This is regarded as the most important channel of verbal communication.

***More Influence on Memory of Receivers***

The audio-visual communication channel brings more influence on memory of receivers because hearing and seeing of messages go together here.

***Disadvantages of Audio-visual Channels of Communication***

There is no doubt that audio-visual communication channel has a number of advantages, but this does not mean that this communication channel has no disadvantage. It also has some disadvantages. Main disadvantages of this channel are as follows:

- More time consuming
- More expensive
- Dependency on audio-visual aids
- Dependency on satellite
- Dependency on electric supply

Now, let us discuss about these disadvantages of audio-visual communication channel one by one.

### *More Time Consuming*

The audio-visual communication channel requires more time in taking photography, voice recording, making videography and presenting through audio-visual aids. That is why more time taking is a disadvantage of this communication channel.

### *More Expensive*

Audio-visual channel of communication is not only more time consuming, rather, it is also more expensive. It requires more money for photography, voice recording, videography and audio-visual communication aids. Thus, this channel is more expensive.

### *Dependency on Audio-visual Aids*

Audio-visual channel of communication is dependent on audio-visual aids. If audio-visual aids are functional, it brings positive result. But if audio-visual aids are non-functional, it brings negative result.

### *Dependency on Satellite*

This channel depends on satellite for world wide communication of messages. But if satellite medium is functional, it brings positive result, and if satellite medium becomes non-functional, it brings negative result.

### *Dependency on Electricity Supply*

This channel is also dependent on supply of electricity. The disruption in electricity brings negative result. Regular supply of electricity brings positive result.

### *Non-verbal Channels of Communication*

Non-verbal communication channel is such a channel which functions through body language. Body language is that language which is non-verbal. The communicator uses not only different types of verbal communication channels, which are based on verbal languages, but he/she also uses his/her body language which is known as non-verbal language. The oral communicator makes a congruence between verbal and non-verbal behaviours. The non-verbal channels of communication are as follows :

- Facial expression channel
- Gestural channel
- Pose channel
- Eye channel
- Handshake channel
- Head channel
- Mouth channel
- Nose channel
- Teeth channel
- Tongue channel
- Waist channel
- Palm channel
- Eye brow channel
- Forehead channel
- Legs and foot channel
- Finger channel
- Chest channel
- Shoulder channel
- Neck channel

Now, let us discuss about these non-verbal channels one by one.

### *Facial Expression Channel*

This is a kind of non-verbal or body language channel. Through this channel a number of messages are communicated to receivers. It is said that the face is index of mind. The expression of face reveals a number of messages related to pleasant mood, angry mood, supportive mood, unsupportive mood, accepting mood or non-accepting mood and so on. By observing the facial expression of communicator, the receiver understands his/her mood.

### *Gestural Channel*

Gestural channel of non-verbal behaviour deals with gestural messages which are sent through ear, nose, mouth, tongue, teeth, lips, nose, eyes, fingers, palm, and other body parts. The communicator communicates through gestures and receivers receive messages communicated by gestures.

### *Pose Channel*

The different poses of human body communicates messages to receivers. The poses may be related to *Aasan* (sitting), standing, bending, dancing, walking, running, exercising, eating, drinking, serving, singing, fighting, sleeping, riding, fishing, hunting, worshiping, seeking blessings, giving blessing and so on. Thus, human poses communicate a number of non-verbal messages.

### *Eye Channel*

The eye channel is also one of non-verbal communication channels. Human eyes communicate a number of messages to receivers. For example closing eye, opening eye, contacting eye, bowing eye, red eye, opening half eye, winking, closing one eye and so on. Each type of eye movement and poses send a message to the receiver from the communicator.

### *Hand Channel*

The hands of human body also communicate messages through non-verbal behaviour. For example shaking hand tightly, shaking hand loosely, withdrawing hands, showing hands, raising hands, extending hands, folding hands, clapping hands, exposing hands, helping hands and so on communicate some special message to receiver.

### *Head Channel*

Head channel is one of non-verbal channels of communication. With help of head channel, the communicator sends a number of non-verbal messages to the receivers. For example holding head with hand, rubbing head, combing head, holding head vertically, holding head horizontally and so on.

### Mouth Channel

It is also a non-verbal or body language channel. With the help of mouth channel a communicator sends messages to receiver. Full opening of mouth, half opening of mouth, closing mouth, smiling mouth, angry mouth, strait one finger on mouth, covering mouth with hands, and so on have non-verbal messages. The receivers decode those messages.

### Nose Channel

Nose channel is one of non-verbal or body language channels. With the help of nose communicator communicates non-verbal messages related sorrow, happiness, peace, angry and so on. For example widening nose, narrowing nose, rubbing nose, closing nose, cutting nose etc. have non-verbal messages which a receiver has to decode the meaning by observing nose behaviour.

### Teeth Channel

This is also one of non-verbal channels of communication. Through teeth, human being communicates a number of non-verbal messages. For example showing teeth, not showing teeth, broken teeth, white teeth, brown teeth, cutting teeth, chewing teeth, sivering teeth, and so on communicates non-verbal messages to a receiver. Such teeth behaviours have communicational value.

### Tongue Channel

Tongue channel is also a non-verbal channel of communication. With the help of it a communicator is able to send messages to the receivers. The tongue behaviours such as showing tongue, rubbing tongue on lips, creating sound by tongue, oscillating tongue and cutting tongue with teeth, etc. communicate message to receivers.

### Waist Channel

Waist channel is also a kind of non-verbal channel. With the help of waist behaviours news are communicated to receivers. Through waist behaviours such as thin waist, thick waist, flexible waist, strait waist, bend waist, both hands on waist, single hand on waist, holding waist etc. have communicative value for receivers.

### Palm Channel

Palm is also one of non-verbal channels of communication. With the help of palm, human being sends a number of messages to receivers. For example heavy palm, light palm, showing palm, lines of palm and folding palm. All such behaviours related to palm sends a number of messages. Those behaviours have communicative value. Palmistry has been developed as a science to study types of palm and lines in palm to know the impact of different planets on the life of individual. The palm construction reveals the personality and fortune of an individual.

### Eye brow Channel

Eyebrow channel is also a non-verbal channels of communication. The type of eye brows indicates the fortune and personality of the individual concerned. Thin eyebrow, thick eye-brow, connected eyebrow, no eye brow, shrinking eye brow communicate messages related to individual and his personality.

### Forehead Channel

Forehead channel is also one of non-verbal channels of communication. The construction and types of forehead communicates a number of messages related to personality of the individual concerned. The long forehead, thick forehead, flat forehead, lines on forehead communicate significant message regarding the personality of an individual. The forehead readers are able to decode those messages.

### Legs and Foot Channel

The leg and foot channel are also one of non-verbal channels of communication. The construction of leg and foot reveals messages related to personality and fortune of the individual concerned, Bent leg, strait leg, long leg, short leg, flat foot, long foot, curved foot, oscilating leg, sitting cross leg etc. send messages related to individual concerned.

### *Finger Channel*

The fingers are also non-verbal channel of communication. The construction of fingers sends messages about the personality and luck of individual concerned. Thick finger, thin finger, long finger, short finger, gap between fingers and lines in each finger send messages regarding the personality of person concerned. It also tells about he fortune of the person. Each finger and toe communicate some significant message. Showing toe, showing first, second, third and last fingers communicate different meaning. The first and second fingers together communicate some significant message. All fingers together communicate a different meaning. Folding fingers with palm communicates some different meaning.

### *Chest channel*

Chest channel is also a non-verbal channel of communication. Construction of chest and behaviour through chest communicate a number of messages regarding the person concerned. The length and width of chest, meeting chest to chest, hiding in chest, showing chest all such behaviours indicate the personality of the person and how he/she behaves with another person.

### *Shoulder Channel*

Shoulder channel is also a kind of non-verbal communication channel. The shoulder channel communicates a number of messages related to personality of the person concerned and also about social-cultural behaviour. Well built shoulder, meeting shoulder to shoulder, carrying shoulder load, not meeting shoulder to shoulder, communicate significant message related to social-cultural behaviour.

### *Neck Channel*

Neck channel is also a non-verbal channel of communication. The construction of neck and movements of neck communicate a number messages related to personality of a person and social-cultural behaviour. Small neck, long neck, no neck, movement of neck, forward backward, up-down convey significant messages regarding personality of the person and social-cultural behaviour.

Thus, from above discussion it is quite clear that each part of body is related to non-verbal communication channel. Rather, all parts of human body work as a non-verbal channel.

# 9
# Agencies of Communication

The form of society may by simple, or complex, folk or peasant, town or city, metropolitan or global, but there are always some institutions or associations involved in communication of messages at societal level. Those institutions or associations contributing in the communication of messages are known as agencies of communication. Some agencies involved in communications have changed, some have appeared in new form, while some others have lost their existence in new social situations.

For the purpose of study, we can devide agencies of communication in to following three types:

- Traditional agencies of communication,
- Modern agencies of communication, and
- International agencies of communication.

## Traditional Agencies of Communication

There are some agencies which are involved in communication of messages traditionally. They are existing since time immemorial. They are playing significant roles in communication since past. They are termed as traditional agencies of communication. For the purpose of study traditional agencies of communication may be divided in to following types:

- Traditional social agency of communication,
- Traditional cultural agency of communication,
- Traditional economic agency of communication,
- Traditional political agency of communication,
- Traditional religious agency of communication,

- Traditional health agency of communication,
- Traditional sport and entertainment agency of communication, and
- Traditional educational agency of communication.

Now, let us discussed about each these traditional agencies of communication one by one.

**Traditional Social Agency of Communication**

The traditional social agencies of communication can be discussed under following sub-headings:

***Family***

Family is a traditional social agency of communication. Each family has a head. All members are represented by family head. The family head communicates significant messages to family members. He/she also collects opinion messages from each adult members before reaching at final message to be communicated to receivers. All family members participate in decision-making messages. But if it is to be communicated to other families or individual, it is always communicated by the head of the family.

***Lineage***

Lineage is a collection of all present descendants of a known four or five generation previous ancestor. All families related through a common ancestor are taken as blood relative. Each lineage also has a lineage head who plays significant role in communication of lineage level decision messages. The lineage head plays significant role in intra-lineage and inter-lineage decision-making communication.

***Clan***

A clan is descendants of a mythical ancestor. Each clan has a head. The clan head plays significant role in intra clan and inter clan level decision-making communication.

***The Village Priest***

The village priest is religious head of the village. But he also plays significant roles in social communication. He plays significant role in marriage settlement communication. He reads the horoscope of boy and girl and makes communication whether the marriage will be suitable or unsuitable horoscopically.

The social communication regarding the settlement of marriage is communicated through his mouth.

### *The Barber*

The barber is traditional communication bearer for his *Jajman* under *Jajmani* system. It is he who makes formal communication to relatives, friends and castes functioning under *jajmani* system regarding birth, *mundan*, sacred thread (*Janeu*), marriage and death in the family of his *Jajman*. The barber serves oral or written communication on behalf of his *Jajman*. For this he is paid by the *Jajman*.

### *Gorait*

The Gorait is traditional communication bearer to *Zamindars* and *Rajas* or *Maharajas*. Each *Zamindar* family had a Gorait who worked as communication bearers on behalf of his Malik (master). The Gorait belonged it to *Dusadh* caste. As *Zamindari* system has been abolished, therefore, this agency of communication bearer has become vanished or it has become the thing of past. But Gorait (*Dusadh*) still consider themselves as superior to other Scheduled Castes because they were directly related to *Zamindars* and their family. They were also muscle man of *Zamindars*.

### *Village Head*

In each village, there is a traditional institution of village head. The village head is a secular head of the village. He is official head of the village and represents his village in intra village meeting. He plays significant role in intra village and inter village social communication. This agency is still prevalent in tribal villages.

### *Assistant to Village Head*

In each village, there is an assistant to village head who works as message bearer of village head. He uses to communicate messages of village head to villagers. This institution is still prevalent in tribal villages.

### Village Panchayat

The village Panchayat, as an assembly of all heads of family, is an important social communication agency where messages related to social pathology and social problems are communicated and discussed. It is headed by village head. The date, time, venue and issues to be discussed are declared and communicated by the village head with the help of his assistant who acts as message bearers of the village head. This communication agency is functioning in tribal areas.

### Inter Village Panchayat Head

In tribal areas, one finds the existence of traditional inter village Panchayat. It is an important social communication agency through which inter village social problems and social pathologies are discussed and on the basis of consensual decision a common message related to all villages forming an inter village Panchayat is communicated to all inhabitants. The inter village head is also a traditional social communication agency who officiates the inter village Panchayat. He has an assistant. All village heads are member of inter village Panchayat. In this Panchyat inter village social problems and social pathology are discussed. The time, venue, day, date and issue of inter village Panchayat is communicated with the help of inter village head assistant. The inter village Panchayat head communicates messages related to consensual decision regarding various issues to the heads of different villages. Such social communication agencies are found in tribal villages.

### Inter Village Head Assistant

Inter village Panchayat head assistant is functioning as social agency of communication. In fact, he is message bearer of inter village head. He communicates messages of inter village head to people and heads of different villages.

### Council of Elders

In some tribal villages, there is a social communication agency known as council of elders. This agency consists of elder members of the village community who provide social control in the society. The members of the council are selected in village Panchayat to assist the head. The number of members may be three, five, seven, nine, eleven depending upon the number of families in the village. The council of elders communicates message related to social norms, value, traditions and social control to the adolescent and young members of the community. They are incharge of social control. They share the responsibility of social control by communicating norms, values and traditions among the adolescent and young.

### Caste Panchyat

The caste panchayat is a social communication agency which communicates significant messages among members of a caste belonging to different neighbouring villages of a region related to social problems and social pathology. They have healthy discussion on these issues. They communicate consensual social messages among members of a caste concerned.

### Gram Pancha

Those villages which do not have village head and village Panchayat, have the concept of Gram Pancha. The Gram Pancha are selected informally by the villagers. They included the biggest ryot of the village, village Priest, village teacher and the most educated person of the village. The village Pancha acts as social agency of control. They communicate social control messages among villagers and help solving social problems.

### Kin Group

The kingroups work as traditional social agency of communication. They communicate a number of messages related to social value when they meet with each other. The members of the same kin group rely on messages communicated by their own kins. They also communicate messages related to extending help and conflict resolution.

### Friend Group

The friend group also works as traditional social agency of communication. The friend group communicates messages to each other which are of great social importance. They also exchange messages related to careers.

## Traditional Cultural Agency of Communication

The traditional cultural agency of communication can be discussed under the following sub-headings:

- Youth dormitory
- Sarana
- Sasandiri
- Akhra
- Cultural organisation
- Folk song singing party
- Folk story telling party
- Folk Dance party
- Musical instrument play party
- Drama party
- Nautanki party
- Rama Leela party
- Krishna Leela party
- Rash Leela party
- Mahabharata Party
- Traditional dress sewing party
- Traditional ornaments making party
- Food cooking party
- Food serving party
- Folk art party
- Bhajan kirtan party
- Domkach party
- Kajari geet or Jhula geet party
- Sohar Geet party
- Vivah geet party
- Family
- Lineage Group
- Clan Group
- Tribe/caste
- Kins groups
- Friend group

### *Youth Dormitory*

Youth Dormitory is a traditional cultural agency found in tribal village. Although for a number of villages, it is becoming the thing of past. But in traditional tribal villages, it is still performing a significant role as cultural agency. This cultural agency is known by different names in different tribes. For example Dumkhuria in oraon, Gitiora in Munda and Gothul in Gond. This cultural agency has membership of adolescent boys and girls under the supervision of a senior man in case of boys and a senior woman in case of girls or both in case of a bisexual youth organisation.

Practically, youth dormitory is a hut made house where adolescent boys and girls spent night and receive messages related to their culture such as belief, ritual, custom, song, stories, ballads, riddles, proverbs, jokes, knowledge, archery, playing *lathi* (stick) spear, and musical instruments. In this way cultural messages are communicated to tribal adolescents by the care takers of the youth dormitory. This agency communicates significant cultural messages even related to family and married life, offering *pranam* to elders and receiving *Ashirvad* from them, offering hospitality to guests at the time of coming and *Vidai* at the time of going. In this way, youth dormitory is very significant traditional cultural agency of communication.

### *Sarana*

Sarana is such a cultural agency which receives regards from all tribals residing in the same village. It is a patch of forest situated nearby a tribal village where all Gods and Goddess are suppose to reside. In this way, it is an abode of all village deities. It is maintained by both village head and the village priest with the assistance of all villagers. The Sarana communicates messages related to tribal deities and their functions in the life of tribal villagers. It communicates messages of unity, tension releasing and tradition enhancing with the help of village priest, his assistants and the village head.

### *Sasandiri*

This is also a traditional cultural agency of communication which communicates the messages related to grave yard culture of tribals. This culture occupies significant place in communication in tribals. It sends messages of death and death rituals of an individual. It sends message of unity among clan members to dig grave, put remains of dead body, fill up the grave with mud and cultural goods and place a stone slab in the memory of the dead. On this occasion all kins and villagers are present there.

### *Akhra*

Akhra is a traditional cultural agency which communicates significant cultural messages related to group dance, singing and playing traditional music. Akhra is a common dancing floor of a tribal village where tribals of the village perform the group dance along with singing and playing musical instruments. The adolescent, young and adult members belonging to both sexes perform group dance. Group members sing songs and some members play musical instruments. This cultural agency plays important roles in communicating messages related to song, dance, musical instrument, clapping and whistling from one generation to the next generation, one individual to another individual and one village to another village.

### *Cultural Organisation*

The tribal villages have cultural organisations such as Sarana samiti, Akhra samiti and youth organisation. These cultural organisations make significant contribution in the communication of cultural messages like cultural processions, festivals, dances, folk plays and so on.

### *Folk Song Singing Party*

In tribal and peasant villages there are folksong singers party. This party or group consists of adolescent and young members of the village community. There are separate party for boys and girls. Each party receive training on singing songs, playing musical instruments and performing dances under the supervision of adult males or females of the village. The boys sing song and the female sing geet. They communicate cultural messages through performing songs, or geet, dance and paying musical instruments. Thus, folk song singing party is a traditional cultural agency of communication.

### *Folk Story Telling Party*

In folk and peasant villages, there are folk story telling party. They use to communicate stories related to king, queen, ferry, farmer, wood cutter, lion, snake, birds, animals, wise man, foolman, and stories of a person related to several generation. Stories related to lame, deaf, dumb, one eyed, evil spirit, witch craft, gods, goddesses, cultural heroes and heroins are also communicated to adolescent and young generation people. Story telling party is a traditional cultural agency of communication which communicates cultural significance of story telling communication.

### *Folk Dance Party*

In order to perform folk dances, there are dance parties which communicate cultural significance of dances among members of folk and peasant villages. They are hired on the occasion of marriage, birth and celebration of festivals. The dance party has male or female dancers, a *dholak* or *tabala* player, a harmonium player, a flute player, *Jhal* player and some persons to assist them. The dance party works as traditional cultural agency of communication. It communicates the significance of cultural dances performed by professional dance party.

### *Musical Instrument Play Party*

In folk and peasant villages there are musical instrument playing party. They play *Dol, Nagara, Thali, Jhal, Kartal,* earthen pots and perform dances. They are hired on birth, death and festive occasions.

### *Drama Party*

There are some traditional professional drama parties which organise different types of drama and plays on stages on the request of cultural youth organisations of folk and peasant villages. They stage plays and drama of different ancient kings, queens, social problems, cultural and historical heroes, heroins, wiseman, foolman, victory of truth, *dharma* and honesty after hard examination. In this way traditional drama parties communicate messages in society related to different cultural characters and cultural values.

### *Nautanki Party*

*Nautanki* party is a traditional cultural agency of communication which communicates messages related cultural characters and values of a number of heroes, heroins, cultural problems, cultural conflicts, cultural assimilation and acculturation. The *nautanki* party stages plays in poetry form. That is why it is termed as *Nautanki* party, whereas party which organises plays in prose form is known as drama party.

### *Ramaleela Party*

It is a traditional cultural agency of communication which communicates messages related to ideal characters of Lord Rama of *Ramayana.* This party stages the entire episode of *Ramayana* in a month in simple manner. They remain moving from village to village performing *Ramayana* characters and war between Rama and Ravana, the demon king of Lanka. This party plays significant roles in communicating people of different generations, the stories of Lord Rama and Ravana, which has great cultural value in Indian society.

### *Krishna Leela Party*

This is also a traditional cultural agency of communication which communicates the characters of cultural hero, Lord Krishna right from birth of Lord Krishna to death of Kansa, the king of Mathura and maternal uncle of Lord Krishna.

### *Rasa Leela Party*

It is one of traditional cultural agencies of communication which communicates messages related to Lord Krishna as herd boy, flute players and performing dances along with Radha and Gopis of Gokula and Vrindavana. This party also stages play of Lord Krishna during childhood and adolesant period. This party organises plays on the request of villagers. They stage plays in simple and folk manner so that folk and peasants could understand the communication of *Rasa Leela.*

### *Mahabharata Party*

This is also a traditional cultural agency of communication which communicates the story of great *Mahabharata* war with Lord Krishna as supreme captain and charioteer of Arjuna. This party organises play on stages, when they are requested to perform the story of *Mahabharata.* For this they are paid food grains and money when the final play is over from each family of the village.

### *Traditional Dress Sewing Party*

This is also one of traditional cultural agencies of communication which is famous for sewing traditional dresses on the occasion of marriage and festivals. They get order for making traditional dresses to be worn during marriage rituals.

***Traditional Ornament Making Party***

This is a traditional cultural agency of communication which makes communication related to traditional ornaments and jewellery to be worn and purchased on the occasion of marriage. They get order from the people to make traditional jewellery for the purpose of marriage.

***Food Cooking Party***

This is a traditional cultural agency of communication which communicates messages related to cooking food items and making sweet meets of various varieties to be served on the occasion of birth, marriage and death feasts. They are requested to take order for cooking food items and sweets. They are paid in cash and kind both.

***Food Serving Party***

This is a traditional cultural agency of communication which communicates the cultural messages of serving breakefast, food and tea to guests with hospitality and respect. They are paid for the work.

***Folk Art Party***

This is a traditional cultural agency of communication which communicates the messages related to decorating marriage site, house, worship place in folk art manner with the help of leaves, branches, bamboo, flowers and grasses. They also paint beautiful designs in Kohvar house at the time of marriage. Walls of houses and courtyard are also decorated with various designs, drawings and painting. This group consists of young males and females of the village or of relatives' villages.

***Domkach Dance Party***

This is a traditional cultural agency of communication which communicates messages about a particular type of dance performed by females in the house of bridegroom when all male members go to the village of the bride as *barat* party. In this dance all female relatives of the bridegroom perform different roles and dance along with musical instrument for the whole night.

### *Bhajan Kirtan Party*

This is a traditional cultural agency of communication. This agency communicates *Bhajan Kirtan* songs which are sung to please Gods, Goddesses and other super human powers. For the purpose males and females have separate groups. Each group has its own musical instruments like *Dholak, Jhal, Kartal,* harmonium etc. The *Bhajan Kirtan* party plays significant cultural role in communicating prayer songs to the people and also from one generation to the next.

### *Kajari Geet or Jhula Geet Party*

This is a traditional cultural agency of communication which communicates cultural messages related to *kajari* song or *jhula geet.* These songs are sung in the month of *srawan* by married women. They play swing in their houses or in trees situated in front of their houses. They decorate their hands, arms and hairs with *Mehandi* (herbal dye) and play swing and sing geet. This makes the environment sweet and pleasant.

### *Sohar Geet Party*

This is also a traditional cultural agency of communication related to sending messages of *sohar geet* among the people and also from one generation to the next. The *sohar geet* is a kind of *geet* sung by the females of villages on the birth of a child. These songs communicate pains suffered by the mother of the child during pregnancy and delivery of child, care taken by family members, jokes cut by joking relatives and also *Gali* songs. The culture of *sohar geet* is communicated by *sohar geet* party.

### *Vivah Geet Party*

The occasion of marriage(*Vivaha*) brings performance of a series of rituals right from the settlement of marriage to the departure of bride in bridegroom's father house. The series of rituals are performed amidst singing ritual *geet*. For this purpose all female relatives form a *geet* party. They sing marriage *geet* in group by playing musical instruments. On this

Now, let us discuss about these traditional economic agencies of communication one by one.

### Family

Family is the unit of production and consumption in simple and peasant society. It performs economic function to fulfil various economic needs of the family members. For example food, cloth, shelter, medicine, play equipments, journey, education and so on. Each family has its own traditional occupation in which all members contribute in production and all members share in consumption. The messages related to family occupation, income, expenditure, saving, exchange, market and loan are communicated among members of the family by the head. The head of family also shares these economic news with his relatives, neighbour and friends. In this way, family is very important traditional economic agency of communication. The messages related to division of labour are also communicated in the family.

### Lineage Group

Like family, lineage group is also an important traditional economic agency of communication. The families belonging to same lineage share messages related to their family occupation, income, expenditure, exchange, market, saving, loan and so on. They are corporal kin group. They maintain reciprocal relation through exchange of service, gift, invitation and loan. The lineage, thus, contributes significantly in communicating economic news among lineage members.

### Clan

The families belonging to same clan reside together and cooperate each other during miseries. They have common occupation. They share common economic messages such as occupation, income, expenditure, saving, loan, exchange, market, gift, hospitality and reciprocity. Thus, a clan group works as a traditional economic agency of communication.

### Friend Group

The friend group which generally belongs to same occupation group also works as traditional economic agency of communication. They communicate with each other about their occupation, production, income, expenditure, saving, market, loan and credit. They also communicate with other to solve problems related to their occupation.

### *Priesthood*

Priesthood is also a traditional economic agency of communication. The village priest works as guide to economic activities carried out by the folk and peasant societies. He declares the date and auspicious time for beginning of agricultural works. At each stage of agricultural operation, the supervision of priest is required. For this purpose, the priest is paid a fixed share in the agricultural produce from each household.

### *Jajmani System*

It is a social economic system of Indian society in which different castes are functionally related to each other castes through service and payment. This system communicates messages to members of each caste what is its traditional occupation, how it is socially and economically related to other and what kind of payment will be made for rendering traditional occupational services. In this way, *Jajmani* system functions as a traditional economic agency of communication. As different functional castes such as Brahmin, barber, carpainter, potters, blacksmith, washerman are functionally related to land owning castes of own as well as neighbouring villages, they works as a traditional social-economic agency of communication.

## Middle Man/Trader/Shopkeeper

The middleman, also termed as trader or shopkeeper, is a traditional economic agency of communication. The middle man purchases grains, forest produce and other commodities from folk and peasant societies. They communicate significant messages related to rate of sell and purchase of commodities, which they purchase from peasants, and supply salt, spices, oil, sugar, loat sugar and other to local purchasers. Thus, middlemen have been traditional economic agent of communication.

### *Local Haat-Bazaar*

The local *haat-bazaar*, also known as weekly *haat*, is a traditional economic agency of communication. This economic institution works as economic agency of communicating news related to days, time, place of market, sellers, buyers, mode of transport, commodities sold and purchased, bargaining, hagling, price list, credit and loan. Thus, local market communicates a number of such messages which are of economic value. This agency is communicating economic messages to the people since time immemorial.

### *Cattle Fair*

Cattle fair is also a traditional economic agency of communication which is communicating messages related to time, place, days and date of occurring cattle fairs, varieties of cattle sold and purchased, cattle traders, bargaining, fixing price, sale and purchase of cattle, since time immemorial. These cattle fairs occupy significant place for cattle rearers.

### *Cattle Rearers*

Cattle rears are those castes whose economy is fully or partly based on cattle rearing. Cattle rearers domesticate animals like cow, ox, buffalo, goat, sheep, dog, horse. Cattle rearers generally belong to folk society and peasant society. Some landlords and *Zamindars* also domesticate tiger, lion, elephant, horse, camel and so on. But in peasant and folk societies only those cattle are domesticated which provide milk, meat and assist in agricultural work. Cattle rearers communicate messages among themselves regarding defective cattle, auspicious and inauspicious cattle and their body parts, diseases of cattle, nutrition of cattle, feed of cattle, sale and purchase of cattle and cattle fair. In this way, cattle rears are traditional economic agency of communication.

### *Craftsmanship*

There are some communities which are involved in craftmanship since time immemorial. For example iron smeltor, blacksmith, copper smith, bronze smith, carpainter, basket-makers, cloth weavers and cloth stickers. These communicate significant economic messages related to raw materials of their crafts, process of making, exchanging, trade, market, income, expenditure, saving, credit loan and problems these communities are facing.

### *Band Leader and Hunting Gathering*

Band is the earliest form of social organisation. Each band had a leader.

The band moved forest to forest in search of food and shelter. The economy of band was wandering based on hunting and gathering. The attempt has been made to make the band settled community. But they leave the settlement for gathering minor forest produce. Besides band, the tribal communities living in and around forest are still dependent on forest produce. Hunting has been banned. But gathering is continued.

The gathering community and the band leader work as a traditional economic agency of communication. This agency communicates messages related to availability of forest produce round the year and in which part of the forest.

### *Shifting Cultivation*

Shifting cultivation is a traditional economic agency of communication. It communicates messages related to the practices of shifting cultivation such as site selection, clearance, left for drying, burning to ash, sowing in first rain, weeding, watching, harvesting, thrashing and merry making. The communication of these processes of shifting cultivation goes on from community to community and from one generation to the next.

### *Settled Agriculturists*

The practice of settled agriculture also works as traditional economic agency of communication in folk and peasant society. This agency communicates messages related to the varieties of grains, oilseeds and vegetables in different seasons such as *Bhadai* crops, *Agahani* crops, *Rabi* crops and *Garma* crops. It also communicates messages related to dry cultivation and wet cultivation, and different processes like tilling land, manuring, sowing seeds, transplanting, weeding, using fertilizer, pesticides, watching, harvesting, thrashing, winowing, bringing grains in house and merry making.

It also communicates exchange and market of surplus grains produced. It sends messages of agricultural disease's and their treatment.

### *Labourer and Labour Market*

Labourers and labour market also work as an agency of communication. It communicates type of labour performer, working hours, rest, mode of payment, holidays, and labour markets where laburers go to sell their labour. It also communicates migration of labour for more wages and problems associated with them.

### *Reciprocity*

Reciprocity is a traditional economic agency of communication which communicates messages related to non-market and non-money exchange between friends and relatives who are of same status. It sends messages regarding types of reciprocity such as positive, balanced and negative and return of things obtained in reciprocity. It involves three actions to give, to receive and to repay. This is a traditional economic institutions found in folk and peasant society.

### *Redistribution*

This is also a traditional economic agency of communication. It communicates messages of non-market and non-money exchange between individual of different status. For example, the priest and villagers, the head and community members.

### *Folk Artists*

Folk artists also work as traditional economic agency of communication. There are a number of folk artists such as snake charmer, bearwala, monkey wala, *madari wala* and so on. They earn by the play of snake, bear, monkey and magic. They communicate messages related to their expertise in training snake and animals to perform dances. Traditional dress-makers also come under this category. Dance party and band party also come here.

### *Mason*

The mason are folk and peasant engineers who construct houses with brick, mortar and cement. They also act as traditional economic agency of communication.

### *Cottage Industry*

The cottage industry is also a traditional economic agency of communication. It communicates messages related to the practices of cottage industries such as oil industry, rice industry, flour industry, leaf sugar industry, things produced, exchange, market and problems associated with them.

***Medicine Man***

The medicine man also acts as economic agency of communication because they communicate messages related to sale and purchase of folk medicine prepared by them.

***Loan***

Loan is also a traditional economic agency of communication. It communicates messages related to credit and loan facilities available in the society. It communicates about traditional sources of loan, purpose of loan, interest on loan and repayment of loan. It communicates about traditional *Mahajani pratha* of loan and credit.

**Traditional Political Agency of Communication**

There have been a number of traditional political agencies which have played significant role in communicating political messages in the folk and peasant society. They are as follows:

- Village Pancha or Council of Elders
- Village head
- Village Panchayat
- Tribe leader
- Caste leader
- Inter-village head
- Inter-village panchayat
- Village priest
- Assistant to village head
- Assistant to inter village head
- Assistant to village priest
- Messenger of Zamindar
- Messenger of Raja and Maharaja

Now, let us discuss about there political agencies of communication one by one.

***Council of Elders or Village Pancha***

This is a traditional political agency of communication. This agency communicates messages to observance of village norms and values by members of community. It sends social controlling messages among members of the community. This council communicates messages related to maintenance of law and order in the society.

### *Village Head*

This is also a traditional political agency of communication. It communicates messages related to office and function of village head in maintenance of law, order and justice in village community.

### *Village Panchayat*

It is a traditional political agency of communication. It consists of all heads of all families living in a village. It is headed by the village head. The village panchayat takes decision related to disputes in family, divorce cases, conflict settlement, thefty, rape, gang rape, fire and so on. It also decides the nature of crime, punishment, compensation and conflict resolution. Thus, this traditional agency plays significant role in sending messages related to the office and functioning of the traditional village Panchayat.

### *Tribal Leader*

In each tribal village there are some persons who possess quality of guiding their community members during trouble and right decision-making. They are known as tribal leaders. The community members regard and obey them. They act as traditional political agency of communication. The political messages conveyed by them have much influence on community members. They play significant roles in conflict resolution and problem solving.

### *Caste Leader*

In caste village, there are some persons who possess the quality of guiding caste members in conflict resolution, decision-making and problem solving. They are known as caste leaders. The messages conveyed by them have much influence on caste members. Thus, they work as traditional political agency of communication.

***Inter Village Head***

This is a traditional political agency of communication functioning in tribal villages. The different tribal villages of a region have a common head, who performs significant role in inter village panchayat meeting. The time, date, day and place of meeting is conveyed by the inter village Head. The message conveyed by him bring much influence on the members of the community.

***Inter Village Panchayat***

This is also a traditional political agency of communication. It communicates messages related to inter village unity, office and function of inter village Panchayat. It is composed of all heads of villages under an inter village Panchayat. It is headed by the inter village head. It plays significant role in conflict settlement, crime determination, punishment, compensation and settlement.

***Village Priest***

The village priest is very honourable person of the village. Therefore, he is invited to attend the village Panchayat meeting. He plays significant role in oath taking ritual and purificatory ritual on the request of the village Panchayat. He functions as a traditional political agency of communication.

***Assistant to Village Head***

This is a traditional post of village official to assist the village head in communicating his decision of holding a village Panchayat meeting. The assistant to village head is regarded by all villagers. It is because he communicates the time, day, date, venue and agenda of village Panchayat meeting as a message bearer of the village head.

***Assistant to Inter Village Head***

This is a traditional political agency of communication found functioning in tribal villages forming an inter village Panchayat. He assists the inter village head in communicating to village heads of Panchayat and both parties the decision of holding inter village Panchayat. The date, time, day, place and agenda are communicated to members and parties by him.

### *Assistant to Village Priest*

This is a traditional political agency of communication which communicates significant messages related to oath taking, purificatory and feast ritual to the villagers on behalf of the priest.

### *Messenger of Zamindars*

During *Zamindari* period each *Zamindar* has his own messenger. The messenger used to communicate messages conveyed by *Zamindar* to the people. He was termed as messenger of *Zamindar*. This institution, now, has become the thing of past.

### *Messenger of Raja and Maharaja*

During *Zamindari* period *Raja* and *Maharaja* titles were created. Those *Raja* and *Maharaja* have their own messenger to communicate messages to another *Raja* and *Maharaja* and also people. This institution is also, now, not in existence.

## Traditional Religious Agency of Communication

There are a number of traditional religious agencies which are contributing significantly in communication of religious messages among the people since time immemorial. People still have deep faith on messages provided by them. They are as follows:

- Village Priest
- Religious symbols
- Religious festivals
- Religious processions
- Religious fairs
- Pilgrimage
- Religious plays
- Religious Texts
- Religious songs
- Religious preachers and their preaching
- *Yagya* and sacrifice
- *Puja patha*
- Ancestral worship
- Rituals

- Religious organisations

Now, let us discuss about these religious agencies of communication one by one.

***Village Priest***

In each village there is a religious post of village priest. The village priest is communicating significant religious messages to the people since time immemorial. Therefore, he is recognised as traditional religious agency of communication. The village priest communicates messages related to religious Gods, Goddesses, texts, stories, festivals, fairs, pilgrimage, worship and so on. He is a mediator between God and Goddes at one hand and the people on the other hand. That is why a priest is regarded as the most important traditional religious agency of communication.

***Religious Symbols***

The religious symbols are also regarded as traditional religious agency of communication. The religious symbols such as Sarana trees, bamboo or wooden poles, megaliths, mud hills, old tree root, temple, mosque, *gurudwara*, church, *math*, religious texts, wells, ponds, streams, river, sea, animals, birds and flags communicate beliefs and practices associated with them. Symbols play significant role in communicating religious messages to Gods, spirits and people of concerned religion.

***Religious Festivals***

Religious festivals are also traditional religious agency of communication. They communicate messages of concerned Gods, Goddesses, spirit, ancestors and the practices related to their Gods, Goddesses and spirits. This sends message of unity among followers. They also communicate messages related to cleanliness of house, dress, environment, wearing new dresses, cooking delicious food items, meeting friends and relatives, wishing best complements to each other, dancing, singing and playing musical instruments. In this way, religious festivals perform role as a traditional religious agency of communication.

***Religious Procession***

Religious procession also works a traditional religious agency of communication. In order to celebrate festivals, images of Gods and Goddesses are established and worshiped in auspicious period. When the worship is over, next day *Bidai* (departure) ritual is offered and images are drowned in ponds, rivers, streams, sea or any other water sources with a request to come again next year. This ritual is known as *visarjan* ritual. In *visarjan* ritual religious processions are also orgainised in which followers carry religious flags and weapons. They make journey in procession amidst singing and dancing. Such religious procession can be seen in *Sarhul* festival, *Durga puja*, *Ramnavami*, *Gurunanak Jayanti*, *Guru Govind Singh Jayanti*, *Mahavir Jayanti*, *Muharum* and so on. The religious processions communicates messages among followers regarding joy, dance, musical instruments, war weapons, singing songs or playing records, shouting religious slogan, regard and unity among followers.

## *Religious Fairs*

Religious fairs are also traditional religious agency of communication. Religious fairs are organised to cater various kinds of needs of devotees and followers. In fairs there are a number of shops related to different items such as festive dress, festive food, general dress, general food, items of worship, religious symbols, religious amulets, domestic articles and tools, shoes, slippers, duplicate ornaments, bangles, decorative items and plays and games of children. Relgious fairs are organised on the occasion of festivals. The followers and devotees offer worship to Gods and Goddeses, meet relatives and friends, make marketing of articles and commodities, make entertainment, share foods and come back home. There are several famous religious places where local, regional, national and international level religious fairs are organised. The religious fairs send messages of unity, pleasure, joy, worship, devotion, marketing, entertainment, meeting friends and relatives and sharing different kinds of messages among followers and people.

## *Piligrimage*

There are a number of national and international level famous places which are regarded as *Dham* (abode) of God and Goddesses on this earth. For example Badrinath, Kedar Nath, Gangotri, Yamunotri, are regarded as *Char Dham* of North India. Similarly, Puri, Dwarka, Rameshwaram, and Kedarnath are regarded as four *Dham* of India. Similarly, there are a number of regional and local level *Dham* such as Gaya, Varanasi,

Tirupati, Ayodhya, Mathura, Shirdi Ujjain, Omkareshwar, Trayambakeshwar, Bhima Shankar and so on. According to religious beliefs the visit of pilgrimage of these places brings benefit and prosperity in this life as well as a life after death or rebirth. Pilgrimage as a traditional religious agency communicates messages related to belief, ritual, journey, expenditure, benefits in this life and life after death.

***Religious Plays***

Religious plays also act as traditional religious agency of communication. On the occasion of worship and festivals, religious plays are organised in villages in simple manner. These plays are related to *Ramayana*, *Mahabharata*, *Ram Leela*, *Krishna Leela*, *Rasa Leela*, Lord Shiva, Vishnu, Brahma, Narada, Bhakta Prahlada, and a number of religious characters. Religious characters are staged which communicate among followers the characters of Gods, Goddesses, and divine powers.

***Religious Texts***

Religious texts are also traditional religious agency of communication. Each religions has its own sacred texts which are supposed to be composed by their Gods and Goddesses or divine incarnation. For example *Vedas*, *Puranas*, *Upanishads*, *Ramayana*, *Mahabharata*, *Quran*, *Bible*, *Gurugrantha* and so on. These religious texts or sacred texts communicate messages related to truth, honesty, morality, eternity, universality, sacrifice and brother-hood. The religious texts keep people united and adhered to the traditions established by Gods, Goddesses or their incarnation.

***Religious Songs***

The devotees have composed songs in praise of Gods, Goddess and their incarnations. These songs are known as *Bhajan, Kirtan Prarthana*. They are known together as religious song. For example Hindus sing religious songs in the name of Lord Shiva, Vishnu, Brahma, mother Goddess Durga, Lakshmi, Saraswati, Rama, Krishna, Hanumana. These songs convey messages related to divine characters of Gods and Goddesses, their super human work, universal visibility and giver of all kinds of pleasure and wealth, but destructor of joy and wealth when one gets deviated from the path of honesty, truth and morality.

### *Religious Preachers and their Preaching*

Each religious organisations organise religious speeches of their preachers or religious *gurus*. The religious preachers remain wandering from place to place for religious preaching to their followers. The day, time, place of preaching remain prefixed. All formalities are maintained by the organisers. Hearing the religious discourses or preachings of religious *gurus* followers become pleased and their faith in divine power becomes deep rooted. In this way, religious preachers and their preachings function as traditional religious agency of communication.

### *Yagya and Sacrifice*

For peace, prosparity and healthy life in society, the religious specialists perform *yagya* and sacrifice. The programme of *Yagya* continues 5 days, 11 days, a month or a month and quarter depending on the organisers and specialists. In *Yagya*, sacred specialists of different *maths* are invited to participate in special worship. At the end of *Yagya Hawana* is made. In the ritual of *Hawana*, *dhup*, rice, ghee, oat, leaf sugar, curd, sweet dry coconut, are sacrified to fire in the name of all Gods, Goddesses and *Nawagrahas*. With the performance of *Hawana* ritual, the *yagya* is over. Invited scholars and followers are offered *Prasad* and feast. The *Bidai* of each scholars and specialists is made by the organiser.

Aniamal sacrifice is also made at the end of a great worship to please the concerned deity. The sacrifice of he goat, he sheep, he buffalo, cock, egg, pegion are made in the name of deity The meat is cooked and shared as *Prasad*.

Thus, *yagya* and sacrifice communicates messages related to unity, ritualistic symbols, religious organisations, religious specialists, deities and expected benefit of joy, prosperity and health.

### *Puja-Patha*

*Puja-patha* is a traditional religious agency of communication. It includes daily, weekly, *Pakshiya*, monthly, half yearly and annual worship to Gods and Goddesses. Through worship, a follower makes communication with Gods, and divine power for good health, good wealth and good progeny. He/she demands peace, prosperity and healthy life for himself/herself and other family members. Thus, *Puja-patha* communicates messages related to wish fulfilment and peaceful prosper life in this world and *Moksha* after death.

***Ancestral worship***

Ancestral worship is a traditional religious agency of communication. It communicates beliefs, rituals, sacrifice, offering of *prasad*, *dan* and others to please the ancestral Gods and Goddesses. Their worship brings prosperity in the family.

***Rituals***

Rituals are also one of traditional religious agency of communication. On the occasion of birth, *mundana*, name giving, ear-boring, marriage, and death and also at the time of performing worships and festivals, a series of rituals are performed by a family with the help of village priest. Thus, rituals work as religious agency of communication. Rituals communicates messages related to Priest, *Jajman*, functional castes, invitation to kins, friends, guests and other and also performance of rituals.

***Religious* Organisation**

Religious organisations such as *Durgapuja Samiti*, *Lakhsmi Puja Samiti*, *Saraswati Puja Samiti*, *Chhath Puja Samiti* and so on function as traditional religious agency of communication. They celebrate festivals and perform worship in organised way. These organisations perform significant religious functions. They communicate messages of religious unity among the people.

**Traditional Health Agency of Communication**

There are a number of traditional health agencies of communication. They send significant messages related to health and hygiene. The important traditional health agencies of communication are as follows:

- Family
- Lineage
- Clan
- Medicineman
- Village Priest
- Vaidya
- Bone Setters
- Massage doer

- *Jharphuk* doer
- *Jari-buti* provider
- White magician
- *Dagarin* or *Kusarain*
- *Yoga* expert
- *Hakim*
- Homoeopathy Doctor
- Dietician
- Snake bite doctor
- Scorpion bite Doctor
- Food prescriber
- Dog bite doctor
- Jaikal bite doctor

Now, let us discuss about these traditional health agencies of communication one by one.

### *Family*

Family is a traditional health agency of communication. It communicates health related message to all members. Its is because family is basic unit of health activities and maintenance. It is said that mother is doctor of family. She takes care of health of all family members. She provides nourishment to all family members. In family health of newly born child, children, adult, aged, pregnant woman, lactating mother, diseased person and so on are taken care. The mother takes care of health of each and every family members. Family communicates messages related to good food habit, timely going to bed and getting up, going to ease, washing hand, mouth, bathing, breakfast, launch and dinner, wearing clean dress, keeping house, court yard, water source, kitchen, latrine quite clean. It also communicates messages related to diseases—general, age based and sex based and primary treatment of diseases.

### *Lineage*

Lineage is also a traditional health agency of communication. The lineage includes families descended from four or five generations above ancestor from the present descendants. The lineage is a corporeal kingroup. The lineage has we feeling. When a member of lineage fell ill all members become serious and attempt to cure his/her health by proper food, medicine and rest. They discuss health problems and bring medicine from different places. In this way, lineage contributes significantly in communicating health messages among its members.

### *Clan*

Clan is group of families having common mythical ancestor. The members of clan help each other in maintenance of health.

### *Medicine Man*

In tribal villages, medicine man is found since time immemorial. The medicine man has knowledge of diseases and herbal medicine available in the environment particularly forest. He also prepares medicine from *Jari-buti* collected from the forest. The medicine man functions as a traditional health agency of communication. He communicates messages related to diseases and their treatment from herbal medicine.

### *Village Priest*

The village priest also has knowledge of diseases and treatment from herbal plants found in the environment. He also possesses knowledge of *Jhar-Phuk* method. He communicates messages to the people that ill health is caused by superhuman power, evil spirits and black magic. But it can be cured by herbal medicine, worship to Gods and Goddesses and *Jhar-phuk* method.

### *Vaidya*

*Vaidya* is a folk doctor who cures diseases from Ayurvedic medicine prepared by himself. He functions as a traditional health agency of communication. He prepares medicine from the mixture of different ingredients prescribed in Ayurveda. He works as a communicator of Ayurvedic medicine for different kind of diseases.

### *Bone Setters*

In tribal and peasant villages, there are some persons who possess knowledge of setting broken or dislocated bones. They function as traditional health agency of communication. The persons suffering from the diseases of bone dislocation and fracture go to them for treatment. The bone setters set the dislocated bones or fractured bones and tie the spot with bandage. They provide some herbal medicine and oil to be applied over the spot after opening of bandage. In the mean time, the patient is adviced to take rest and do not exert pressure on the affected area. They communicate messages of setting bones by folk method. They also set bones of domestic animals.

### *Massage Doer*

In folk and peasant village, there are some persons expert in doing body massage. The patient suffering from body pain pay a visit to massage doers. The massage doers message the body with oil and the body pain is relieved. The massage doers communicate messages that the body pain can be removed by body massage therapy.

### *Jhar-Phuk doer*

In folk and peasant villages, there are some persons who are expert in doing *Jhar-phuk* treatment. They cure the diseases by *Jhar-phuk* method. They are known as, *Ojha, Guni, Bhagat* and *Bhagatin*. They please the evil spirit with worship and then remove the evil spirits by *Jhar-phuk* method from the body. After *Jhar-phuk* method, the patient is cured. Thus, *Jhar-phuk* doers work as a traditional health agency of communication. They communicate messages that ill health caused by evil spirits and black magician can be cured by *Jhar-phuk* method.

### *Jari-buti Provider*

In folk and peasant villages, there are some persons who possess knowledge of *Jari-buti*. They do not prepare medicine from *Jari-buti*. Rather they provide *Jari-buti* in raw form and ask the patient to use them raw, boiled, roasted on cooked. They provide services free of cost.

### *White Magician*

In folk and peasant villages, there are some persons who work as white magician to remove evil spirits and cure diseases. They touch the body of the patient, enchant some *mantra* and provide an amulet to be held in neck or arm. White magician communicates messages to the people that diseases can be cured or controlled by holding amulet. Thus, they work as a traditional health agency of communication.

### *Dagarian or Kusarain*

In folk and peasant villages, there are some senior woman of the community who are expert in delivery and taking care of mother and child in delivery room till *chhathi* ritual. They are locally known as *Dagarin* or *Chamain* or *Kusarain*. They function as a traditional health agency of communication.

### *Yoga Expert*

In villages, there are some persons who are expert in *yoga*. They train the people in performing *yoga* and exercises. They also function as a traditional health agency of communication.

### *Hakim*

In villages, some persons are also known as *Hakim*. They cure diseases by *Unani* method and medicine. They act as a traditional health agency of communication.

### *Homoeopathy Doctor*

In villages, there are some persons, who cure diseases by Homoeopathy. They provide homoeopathy medicine to the patient suffering from diseases. They also work as a traditional health agency of communication.

### *Dietician*

In folk and peasant villages, there are some persons expert in curing diseases by food control. They are known as dietician. They communicate messages that diseases can be controlled by controlling diet.

### *Snake Bite Doctor*

In folk and tribal villages, there are some persons who cure the patient suffering from snake bite. They do treatment by *Jhar-phuk* and *Jari-buti*. They convey messages that snake bite can be cured by *Jhar-phuk* and *Jari-buti* method.

### *Scorpion Bite Doctor*

In villages, some persons cure scorpion bite by *Jhar-phuk* and *Jari-buti.* They function as traditional health agency of communication. They communicate messages to the people that scorpion bite could be cured by *Jhar-phuk* and *Jari-buti.*

### *Food Prescriber*

In villages, there are some persons expert in prescribing the quality and quantity of food to patients suffering from different diseases. They act as traditional health agency.

### *Dog Bite Doctor*

In villages, there are some persons expert in curing dog bite. They cure dog bite by *Jhar-phuk* and *Jari-buti.* They function as a traditional health agency of communication.

### *Jaikal Bite Doctor*

In villages, some persons are expert in curing Jaikal bite. They cure Jaikal bite by *Jhar-phuk* and *Jari-buti.* They also function as a traditional health agency of communication.

## Traditional Sports and Entertainment Agency of Communication

There are a number of traditional sports and entertainment agencies which are contributing significantly in communication of messages related to sports and entertainment since time immemorial. They are as follows:

- *Lathi* play trainer
- Spear play trainer
- Sword play trainer
- Mace play trainer
- Folk Gymnasium
- Folk Gymnastic Competition
- Youth Dhumkhuria
- Archery Trainer
- Pallet bow Trainer

- Cock fight
- Sheep fight
- Bull fight
- Kabaddi Play

### *Lathi Play Trainer*

In villages, there are some persons who are well versed in the art of *lathi* play. They play *lathi* in such a way that no body can beat them with soil pieces, brick or stone pieces or even other *lathi* and spear. As they are expert of *Lathi*, so young men go to them to acquire training in playing *lathi*. They communicate messages related to *lathi* play and its training. Thus, they work as a traditional sport agency of communication.

### *Spear Play*

In folk and peasant villages, some persons are expert of playing spear. They play spear in such a way that no body can cause harm to them with another spear and *lathi*. They provide training to young people in handling spear play. They communicate messages that spear play is essential for the safety. They work as traditional sport agency of communication.

Some experts of spear play are found in villages. They act as traditional sports agency of communication. They provide training to rural youth in play of spear. They also train the learners in the art of attacking with spear on enemies and to encounter the spear attack of enemies. They communicate messages to learners that spear can be played as sports, but it can also be played for encountering the attack of enemies and also for making an attack on enemies.

### *Sword Play*

Some men of villages are expert in the play of sword. They play sword in such an expert manner that no body could cause harm to them with an another sword. They provide training to youth in sword play, how to make attack on enemy and how to save themselves from the attack of enemies. Thus, sword play communicates messages related to play of sword to make an attack with sword and to save from the attack of enemies. In this way, sword play is a traditional sports agency of communication.

### *Mace Play*

This is also a traditional sports agency of communication. It communicates messages related to recreation with mace play and to attack with mace and to save from mace. The folk trainer provides training to youth in playing spade (mace), attacking with spade and saving from spade.

### *Folk Gymnasium*

In folk society and peasant society one finds a place dedicated to gymnasium where the village youth perform excercises under the supervision of a senior member of the community. They also receive training in gymnastic. A gymnastic competition is also organised on the occasion of festivals. The winner of the competition receives prize.

### *Folk Gymnastic Competition*

In villages, folk gymnastic competition is organised on the occasion of festivals. Young people take part in it. The winners get price.

### *Youth Dhumkhuria*

*Dumkhuria* is a youth organisation where unmarried boys and girl spend night in separate houses under the supervision of a senior male member and a senior female member. They learn sports in Dhumkhuria. Dumkhuria is Oraon Youth Organisation. In different tribes it is known by different names. The Munda call it as Gitiora and the Gond call it Gothul. This youth organisation communicates messages among young members of the community regarding training of folk sports and other cultural activities.

### *Archery Training*

In youth organisation, some senior male members of the community provide training of archery to young members. Archery competition is also organised and the winner gets a prize.

### *The Pellet Bow Trainers*

In villages, there are some persons expert in pellet bow. They provide training of pellet bow to young of the community. A competition of pellet bow is also organised. The winner gets a prize.

### *Cock Fight Play*

In tribal areas, cock fight play is organised on weekly *Haat* day. The people come in the market with cock trained in fighting. Knife is tied in the legs of both cocks who come for fight. The victory is taken as good and defeat is taken as bad. The owner of victorious cock is entitled to get the meat of defeated cock. The crowd of people assembles encircling the place of cock fight. They enjoy with fighting scene. Cock fight play acts as a traditional sports agency of communication.

### *Sheep Fight Play*

In rural areas, fairs are held on different religious occasions. In fairs, the play of he sheep fight is organised. Two owners with their well decorated sheep come in the fray. Both owners have their supporters. The fight between two sheep starts. The owner of winner sheep gets prize. The victory is regarded as status symbol. Thus, sheep fight acts as a traditional sports agency of communication.

### *Bull Fight*

On festive occasion, bull fight play is also organised for the purpose of entertainment. It is taken as a symbol of victory for the owners of the bull. Two decorated bulls of two owners are brought in the field and allowed to fight. The bull which runs away from the field is made runner and the bull which remains in the field for fight is declared winner. The people remain around the field to see the play of bull-bull fight. Thus, bull fight works as a traditional sports agency of communication.

### *Kabaddi Play*

This play is very much famous in rural areas. In this play the youth are divided in to two groups. A competition is held between both team. The victorious team is given prize. Thus, the play of *Kabaddi* acts as a traditional sports agency of communication.

## Traditional Educational Agency of Communication

In folk and peasant villages, some traditional educational agencies of communication are found working to impart traditional education. They teach people about social-cultural values and religions of their community. They are not concerned with modern education. They are as follows:

- Family
- Neighbourhood
- Village community
- Kin groups
- Friend group
- Occupation group
- Priest
- Temple and *Math*
- *Sadhu*

Now, let us discuss about these traditional educational agencies of communication one by one.

### *Family*

The family is regarded as traditional educational agency of communication. The mother is regarded as the first teacher of this traditional institution. The family teaches its member about good habit, good food, good environment, clean dress, bathing, toilet training and social qualities like sympathy, pity, morality respect, sacrifice and cooperation. With the social qualities, an individual is able to lead social life in peaceful manner.

### *Neighbourhood*

The neighbourhood also plays significant role in controlling the bad habits of individuals. It makes advice frequently to children of families living together that they should not follow bad habit and anti-social behaviour. Thus, neighbourhood communicates educational messages of good habit, social quality and social value.

### *Village Community*

The village community is also a traditional educational agency of communication. The village community has council of elders and village head. These institutions impart the education of social-cultural traditions.

They provide social control by imparting educations of social-cultural tradition. Thus, the village community plays significant role in sending messages related to traditional education of the community concerned.

### *Kin Groups*

The role of kin groups in sending messages related to traditional education of culture and value is of great important. The kin group communicates messages related to kinship and maintenance of tradition of social relationship, reciprocity, hospitality, gift and presentation and their social value. Thus, kin groups play significant role in communicating traditional education.

### *Friend Groups*

The friend groups also communicate messages related to tradition of reciprocity, gift, presentation, hospitality and the value of friendship.

### *Occupation Groups*

The people working in the same organisation and of same occupation play significant role in communicating traditional education related to work values, production, consumption, exchange, trade and market. They also impart traditional education of maintaining social relation and social values.

### *Priest*

The villages priest also plays significant role in communicating religious messages among the people. He is mediator between God and the people. The temples are God's abode on this earth and the priest his representative. All rituals are performed by him. He uses to inform about festivals, rituals and worship to the people. He cures the people from the attack of black magician. He also provides some *Jari-buti* for curing diseases. He prepares horoscope of the individual. Thus, the village priest acts as a traditional educational agency of communication.

### *Temple and Math*

Temple, or other religious organization like *math*, *gurudwara* and others also work as traditional educational agency of communication. Here followers are taught regarding religious traditions and Gods and Goddesses.

***Sadhu***

There are a number of *sadhu* who remain visiting from one place to another preaching the people about Gods, Goddesses and benefits from their worship. They also teach the people about social-cultural values. Thus, they work as a traditional agency of educational communication.

**Modern Agency of Communication**

With the passage of time, we have developed modern agency of communication. The modern communication agencies have more and more developed means of communication. They communicate news not only of a region, but of whole nation and also the whole globe through press, print, electronic and satellite media. For the purpose of study, we can divide modern agencies of communication in to following types:

- Modern Social Agency of Communication
- Modern Cultural Agency of Communication
- Modern Economic Agency of Communication
- Modern Religious Agency of Communication
- Modern Political Agency of Communication
- Modern Educational Agency of Communication
- Modern Health Agency of Communication
- Modern Sports Agency of Communication

Now, let us discuss about there modern agencies of communication one by one.

***Modern Social Agency of Communication***

There are a number of modern social agencies of communication. They communicate social messages to members of the society. They are as follows:

- Gram Panchayat and officials
- Mukhia
- Village assembly
- Ward member
- Ward assembly

- Village elite
- Caste/tribe elite
- Tribe/caste leader
- Women and Child Development Ministry
- Ministers of Social Justice and Empowerment
- Ministry of Law
- Ministry of Tribal Affairs
- Bureaucrates
- Voluntary organisations
- Non-Governmental Organisation
- Radio
- Newspapers
- Journals
- Books
- Bulletins
- T.V.
- Cinema
- Phones
- Cell phones
- Hand set or Tablets
- Social media

Now, let us discuss about these modern social agencies of communication one by one.

### *Gram Panchayat and Officials*

Gram Panchayat is modern social agency of communication. It is a union of villages. Panchayat officials are elected on the basis of election. They consist of *Mukhia*, *Sarpanch* and their members and a government-official called Panchayat Sewak or Panchayat mitra who assists the Panchayat elected officials to have a village assembly meeting for deciding social and development issues in villages. Thus, this modern institution functions as a modern social agency of communication.

### *Mukhia*

*Mukhia* is head of Panchayat. It is he/she who officiates the village assembly meeting and decides with the help of village assembly members the development of children, women, aged, widow, SCs, STs, poor and so on. The beneficiaries of social development programmes are finalised in the meeting. Thus, *Mukhia* as head of the village assembly plays significant roles in communication of modern social development programmes and their beneficiaries.

### *Village Assembly*

As referred earlier, Panchayat is a union of villages. Each village has an assembly known as village assembly. The village assembly has all adult members who are voters in the village. The village assembly meets time to time under the chairmanship of *mukhia*. In village assembly matters related to village development and beneficiaries of social development, such as widow pension, unemployment bonus, old age pension, poor housing scheme, MNREGA beneficiary etc., are decided. Thus, village assembly plays significant role in communicating modern social development and welfare programme.

### *Ward Member*

A village is divided in to wards depending upon the population of the village. Each ward has an elected ward member. The ward member communicates families living in a ward about social welfare, poverty alleviation and social security programmes of the Government. He/she also plays significant role in selection of beneficiaries under different welfare and social security programmes.

### *Ward Assembly*

Ward assembly is union of all adult members of a ward to discuss and decide areas of social development, ward development, village development and social security beneficiaries. Thus, this assembly communicates significant social welfare and social development messages to the members of ward assembly. This assembly is chaired by the ward member.

### *Village Elite*

There are some educated and service doers in the village. The have knowledge about social welfare and security programmes of the Government. They are respected and regarded by the people of the village. They also play significant role in settling marriages and social problems. They work as an agent of modern social communication agency.

***Caste/Tribe Elite***

In a multi ethnic villages, families belonging to different castes and tribes live together. Each caste and tribe has its own elites. The elites of different caste and tribes play significant role in communicating messages related to social welfare, social security and social problems. Thus, they act as a modern agent of social communication.

***Tribe/caste Leader***

In multi ethnic village, tribes and caste live together. But each caste and tribe has its own leader who guides the behaviour of caste/tribe members. The tribe/caste leaders communicate tribe/caste members related to social welfare, social development, social security and other social problems.

***Women and Child Welfare Ministry***

This is a modern agency of social development. This Child Welfare Ministry communicates the masses related to women and child welfare programmes, family welfare programmes, maternity benefit programme, social security programmes of women and children. It broadcastes its programme through All India Radio, Television and other news agencies, social media, bulletin, posters and survey.

***Ministry of Social Justice Empowerment***

This is a modern social agency of communication. It communicates messages related to social justice of S.Cs, S.Ts, OBCs, deprived, oppressed and exploited persons of the society. The social justice news of the ministry is broadcoasted through Radio, T.Vs, Print media, electronic media, satellite media to the masses. Thus, it acts as a modern social agency of communication.

***Ministry of Law***

Ministry of law is a modern social agency of communication. It communicates messages related to social legistation, acts, statutes and other legal social aspects through its broad casting, T.V. Channels, Print media, Press media, electronic media, satellite media and social media. Thus, this department plays important roles in communicating news of social laws and reforms.

### *Ministry of Tribal Affairs*

It is also a modern agent of social communication. This Ministry looks after the tribal affairs. It communicates messages to members of tribal communities that what are acts, statutes and legislation for them as per Indian Constitution. It sends messages related to tribal development and tribal welfares programmes. Thus, it plays significant communicative role in social upliftment of tribals.

### *Bureaucrats*

Bureaucrates are modern social agency of communication. They implement programme of social development. With the help of other Government officials, they make public aware of social development programmes.

### *Voluntary Organisation*

Now-a-days, a number of voluntary organisations are working to make the people aware towards their rights, gender biasness, social discrimination, social problems and other as their voluntary work. In this way, voluntary organisations are functioning as modern social agency of communication.

### *Non-Governmental Organisations*

A number of Non-Governmental Organisations are functioning in society to make people educated towards their rights and duties. They are also launching awareness compaign for protection of daughters, safety of women, security of aged and children, gender biasness, social discrimination, exploitation, deprivation and oppression. They have been able to send a number of positive social messages to the people. They have also been able to send messages of not discriminating girls in education, food, clothes, treatment and health. In this way, non-Governmental organisations function as a modern agency of communication.

### *Radio*

Radio is an important modern agent of social communication. Social programmes are broadcasted from All India Radio related to social pathology, anti-social behaviour, social quality, social problems, social discrimination, social security, social welfare and social unity. Thus, a number of social messages are communicated to the people through All India Radio Programmes.

### News Papers

A number of local, regional, national and international news agencies are publishing daily news papers. The educated people wait eagerly to know different kinds of news published in the papers in the early morning. For some news readers, news paper reading is followed by morning tea after tea till reading is not ever. The news papers contain a number of news related to social pathology, anti-social behaviour, kith and kin killing, rape, murder, acid attack and so on. The reading of news papers communicates the readers about different types of social behaviour prevalent in our society. Thus, news papers act as a modern social agents of communication.

### Journals

In Journals different social thinkers and social scientists write essays and articles for publication. These articles communicate messages related to social problems and their remedies. Thus, they function as a modern social agent of communication.

### Books

A number of thinkers, social scientists and academician write books based on researches related to social problems and suggestions to solve those problems. They communicate meaningful messages of social significance and way to solve them. Thus, books work as a modern social agency of communication.

### Bulletins

A number of bulletins are published by different research institutes, voluntary organisations and non-Governmental organisations. They contain a numbers of social messages for the people and scholars. They act as modern social agent of communication.

### *Televisions*

A number of T.V. Channels show serials on social problems, social pathology, social inequality, social discrimination, gender bias and so on. Daily news analysis are also shown before T.V. viewers containing violence, rape, thefty, dacoity, acid burning, dowry death, foeticide, infanticide, human rights and so on. Thus, T.V. Channels play significant role in communicating messages to societies which are valuable for understanding social problems and attempting to curb them.

### *Cinema*

A number of social value and social problem based cinemas are prepared and shown to viewers for communicating social behavioural messages. The cinemas are shown to public in cinema halls. Thus, they act as modern social agent of communication.

### *Phones*

Phones are also a modern social agent of communication. Phone makes communication of a number of social messages to receivers and receivers to senders. Thus receivers and senders both become aware of social behaviour, problem, solution and so on.

### *Cell Phones*

Cell phones are also a modern social agency of communication. With the help of cell phones communication of social news can be made orally or through sms. Cell phones play significant role in sending social messages like birth, marriage and death news to relatives and friends situated far away.

### *Hand set or Tablets*

Hand set or tablets are cells phones with internet facilities. By loading different apps, hand set make communication of social messages verbally, but also written and visually. It is also possible to send messages on e-mail of the person known. In fact hand set is cells phones with computer and internet facilities. It is not necessary to carry laptop every where. But now-a-days, hand set holders fulfil all needs related to communication.

### *Social Media*

In the era of satellite communication revolution, a number of social media sites have come in to existence. They are googles, facebook, twiter, you-tube, Apps of different types. On these social media sites problems related to social behaviour are communicated. Reactions and counter reactions are also obtained. Thus, social media are now-a-days, a modern social agency of communication.

### *Modern Cultural Agency of Communication*

There are a number of modern cultural agencies involved in communicating cultural messages to the people. They are as follows:

- Ministry of art and culture
- Modern dance party
- Modern Rama Leela party
- Modern Rasa Leela party
- Modern Krishna Leela party
- Modern Mahabharata party
- Modern Poets and Poetries
- Modern story writer
- Modern noval writer
- Modern song singers
- Modern Bhajan-Kirtan Singers
- Modern drama academy
- Modern T.V. Serials
- Modern Marriage Adverting Agency
- Modern Marriage hall Agency
- Modern Videography Agency
- Modern Court marriage
- Modern Radio programme
- Modern cattering Agency
- Modern restaurant Agency
- Modern Branded dresses
- Modern hospitality culture
- Modern Jewellers
- Modern band party
- Internet
- Newpapers
- Cinemas

- Clubs
- Journals
- Books

Now, let us discuss about these modern cultural agencies of communication one by one.

### *Ministry of Art and Culture*

It is a modern cultural agency of communication. This modern agency communicates messages to the people related to cultural laws, laws related to promotion of art and culture, laws related to preservation of culture and art, prize distribution to modern artists and classical artists and a number of other messages. Thus, this institution functions as modern cultural agency of communication.

### *Modern Dance Party*

This is a modern cultural agency of communication. This modern agency communicates messages to the people about dances in modern manner having sound arrangement, light arrangement, modern musical instruments and modern dances. This party stages dance on the request of organiser on the payment of charges demanded by the party. This party acts as a modern cultural agency of communication. It stages dances only in urban and semi-urban areas. The viewers have to pay charges of ticket to see dances of this party.

### *Modern Rama Leela Party*

This is also a modern cultural agency of communication. This organisation has modernised the play of *Ramayana* with modern actors, actress, modern light and sound decoration of stage, modern musical instruments and their players. This party stages Rama Leela in modern ways on the request of cultural organisers. This party demands charges for playing Rama Leela in modern way. In this way, modern Rama Leela party play a role of modern cultural agency of communication.

### *Modern Rasa Leela Party*

This is also a modern cultural agency of communication, which communicates the culture of Rasa Leela done by Lord Krishna in his adolescence period with Radha and Gopis in modern way. This modern cultural agency of communication has modern actors, modern actress, modern dresses, modern music, musical instruments, musical instrument players, light and sound decoration and modern stage. This is organised only in urban and semi-urban areas where light and sound system functions properly and where viewers are controlled with formal institutions. The viewers have to pay charges to buy ticket for entry.

### *Modern Krishna Leela Party*

This is a modern cultural agency of communication which communicates the culture of Krishna Leela from birth to the killing of Kansha, maternal uncle and the king of Mathura, who had prisoned his parents and Grandfather Agrasen through modern technology and means. This play is organised in urban and semi-urban areas with the permission of the administration. The viewers have to buy ticket for seeing modern Krishna Leela which is organised by modern artists with modern light and sound system.

### *Modern Mahabharata Party*

This is a modern cultural agency of communication, which communicates the story of *Mahabharata* through modern actress, actors, music, sound and light system. This is organised in urban areas with the permission of administration. The people have to pay cash for buying ticket and entering in the hall or open air theatre. This agency communicates *Mahabharata* through quite new technology which attracts more and more viewers.

### *Modern Poets and Poetries*

Modern poets and poetries are also modern agencies of communication. Modern poets compose modern poetries, which are quite different from classical or old poetries. The modern poetries are full of modern complexities. But they communicate messages related to modern complex social life and its problems.

### *Modern story writers*

Modern story writers also functions as a modern cultural agency of communication. The modern story writers write stories based on modern complex social life and social relationship. They highlight modern complex family life, marital relation, rearing and caring of children, neglect of aged, problem of widow, gender biasness, live in relationship, surrogacy and so on. In this way, they play significant role in communicating complexities of social, familial and marital life of modern time.

***Modern Novel Writers***

Now-a-days, a number of novel writers have come in to existence who are writing novels in modern manner having stories of modern society, modern relationship and modern social behaviour with modern characters.

***Modern Song Singers***

Now-a-days, a number of modern song singers have come in to existence who sing song in modern tones, manners, styles with modern musical instruments. They prepare cassettes of their songs. The cassettes of such modern songs are played on the occasion of marriage and festivals. They are played with record players and electronic devices. They communicate a number of messages through their recorded songs.

***Modern Bhajan-Kirtan Singers***

Now-a-days, a number of modern *Bhajan-Kirtan* singers have come into existence. They sing songs in modern manner with modern musical instrument players. The entire procedure of singing is recorded. The cassettes of recorded songs are sold and purchased. Cassettes are played with electronic technology like VCR and computer. *Bhajan-Kirtan* songs are also down loaded. They are available in satellite media. Thus, modern *Bhajan-kirtan* songs communicate messages related to Gods, Goddesses and other devine power. They are preferred by young generations.

***Modern Drama Academy***

This is a modern cultural agency of communication. This institution communicates messages to the people by organising cultural drama in modern ways. Theatre is decorated in modern ways. The actors and actress follow moderate dialogue written by dialogue writers along with body language. The drama are staged with light and sound arrangement.

The songs and dances are performed to attract audience. The actings performed by different actors and actress communicate cultural messages among the drama viewers who come to see the drama staged by modern artists with the help of modern technology. Thus, this institution functions as a modern cultural agency of communication.

### *Modern Television Serials*

Different television agencies are found functioning as a modern cultural agency of communication. They show cultural practices, cultural values, cultural heroes, cultural programmes organised by cultural institutes and other cultural organisation in their cultural channels. The T.V. viewers are able to know the cultural customs, cultural institutions and cultural practices of not only own communities, but also communities living on different parts of nations and the globe. In this way, T.V. Serials function as a modern cultural agency of communication.

### *Modern Marriage Advertising Agency*

In place of traditional marriage settlers, now-a-days, modern marriage advertising agency has come in to existence, which communicates messages related to bride and bridegroom through their advertisement. Newspapers are modern marriage advertising agency. Marriage advertisements are also available in satellite media. There are sites like shadi.com , Jeevan Sathi and a number of others available in satellite media. These media help in selection of marriage mate online. Thus, on line mate selection agencies communicate significant messages related to mate selection.

### *Modern Marriage Hall Agency*

Now-a-days, a number of modern agencies have come in to existence, which communicate news related to the availability of modern marriage halls in urban and semi-urban areas. In metropolises, cities and towns, there are a number of marriage hall agencies. They provide marriage halls for the performance of marriage rituals. For this, they charge some fees to the parties. In fact, these halls are hired on payment of fees for one or two days. These halls have modern amenities, well decorations, light and sound system and, cattering facilities, security and parking space. In this way, this agency functions as a modern cultural agency of communication.

### *Modern Videography Agency*

Modern Videography is also a modern cultural agency of communication. It communicates messages that entire cultural processes like birth celebrations, marriage rituals, festival celebration, death rituals and other can be recorded audio-visually and can be recorded in casseettes. The cassettes can be played anywhere with the help of electronic technology.

### *Modern Court Marriage*

This is a modern cultural agency of communication, which communicates messages among the people that marriage could be held in court in less expenses. It also sends messages that court registration of marriage is essential for spousal visa.

### *Modern Radio Programme*

This is a modern cultural agency of communication, which communicates messages related to modern methods, modern innovations and modern technology, which are being adopted culturally by the people.

### *Modern Cattering Agency*

This is a modern cultural agency of communication. This agency communicates massages to the people regarding the culture of cooking different food items and serving them to the guests invited by the invitee concerned. The service of this modern cultural agency is hired by the people on the occasion of conferences, seminars, workshops, birth party, marriage party, festive occasions and so on.

### *Modern Restaurant Agency*

This is also a modern cultural agency of communication. This agency communicates messages among the people about availability of varieties of sweet and salty food items. This agencies supplies ready made food items on demand of the people. The food items can be purchased and served to the guests any time at short notice from morning to late night.

***Modern Branded Dresses***

Now-a-days, there are a number of modern dress agencies involved in supplying modern branded dresses in market. These agencies communicate messages to the people regarding best quality and all types of branded readymade gents, ladies and children wear. They function as modern cultural agency of communication.

***Modern Hospitality***

Now-a-days, a number of five stars, three stars, A.C. hotels, non-A.C. hotels, guest houses, have come in to existence. They send messages to the people regarding hospitality facilities available in their hostels, and guest houses. They provide comfort to their guests and tasty food items are served to them. They regard visitors not as a customer, but as a guest so that more and more guests could pay a visit in their guest or rest houses.

***Modern Branded Jewellers***

Now-a-days, a number of branded modern jewelers have come in to existence who claim their brand as most modern and superior in quality. They communicate messages related to the culture of jewellery. People are attracted in these shops for marketing of ornaments of males and females respectively.

***Modern Band Party***

Now-a-days, a number of band parties have come in to existence, which communicate cultural messages regarding playing modern musical instruments on the occasion of birth, marriage and festivals. They are hired on hour basis. They play musical instruments wearing modern dresses and performing modern dances.

***Internet***

Internal is a modern cultural agent of communication. It communicates a number of cultural messages to the people who have linked themselves with the globe through internet.

### Newspapers

Newspapers also function as a modern cultural agencies of communication. Newspapers contain advertisements related to modern dances, modern drama, modern songs, modern fashionable dresses, modern jewelleries and modern arts. Thus, they play significant role in sending cultural messages to the people.

### Cinema

Cinema works as a modern cultural agent of communication. In cinema, modern cultural items like dress, fashion, footwear, beauty cream, body fitness, good health, park, tourists spots, water falls, natural scenes, and photograph are presented through audio-visual means in cinema hall, or at any places with the help of cassette player. Thus, cinemà are modern cultural agents of communication.

### Clubs

The clubs are modern cultural agents of communication. In club, fashion competition, song competition, beauty competition, are held time to time. Modern dance competition, is also held. Modern drama is also staged. Conference of humer poetry is organised. Children show is also held. Actors and actress are invited to organise play. Thus, a number of cultural programmes are organised in clubs. Thus, clubs function as modern cultural agent of communication.

### Books

Books written on culture changes act as modern agents of communication. They communicate significant messages related to modern trends of culture.

### Journals

There are a number of journals which communicate cultural news to the people. They serve as modern cultural agent of communication. They consist of news related to beauty context culture, beautiful fashionable dresses, fashionable cream, powder, body fitness, facial expression and body language. Thus, cultural journals communicate significant news regarding dress, fashion, cream, footwear, body fitness, health and age management news.

### *Modern Economic Agency of Communication*

Now-a-days, a number of agencies have come in to existence which are playing significant role in communicating modern economic and business news to the people. They are as follows:

- Modern agricultural technology
- Modern animal husbandry
- Modern housewares industry
- Modern furniture and room-decoration industry
- Modern dress industry
- Modern jewellery industry
- Modern food industry
- Modern medicine industry
- Modern occupations
- Modern service
- Modern Fertilizer Industry
- Modern pesticide and weedicide industry
- I.T. Industry
- Multinational companies
- Management institutes
- Modern cinema industry
- Modern sex industry
- Flower growing industry/Modern Floricultue
- Ministry of Finance
- Ministry of Commerce
- Ministry of Textiles
- Decoration, Play and Games industry
- Publication industry
- Entertainment industry
- Staff Selection Commission
- Railway Employment Board
- Shiping industry
- Defence industry
- Different Service Commissions
- Vehicle and Transport industry
- Restaurant, hotels and guest houses
- Newspapers
- Television

- Radio
- Agricultural colleges
- Agricultural Research Institutes
- Vaterinary colleges
- Forestry colleges
- Modern Cottage Industry
- Modern Electrical Appliance Industry

Now, let us discuss about these modern economic agencies of communication one by one.

**Modern Agricultural Technology**

Modern agricultural technology functions as a modern economic agency of communication. The modern technology includes tilling of land with tractors, using patent HYV seeds, chemical fertilizer, pesticides, insecticides, weedicites, use of harvestor for cutting, harvesting, thrashing, winnowing, marketing, agricultural crops grains to food corporation of India through PACS and cooperative societies on prices fixed by the Government time to time. Thus, modern agricultural technology communicates a number of messages to agriculturists regarding entire agricultural processes from tilling to harvesting and marketing. It also sends messages related to agricultural loan and subsidy.

***Modern Animal Husbandry***

This is also a modern economic agency of communication. This economic agency communicates economic messages related to rearing cattle by modern technology such as domesticating cows, buffalo, goat, pig, poultry, duckery and so on of high breed variety. It also sends messages related to vaterinary services and marketing. Besides it conveys messages related to loan facility.

***Modern House Wares Industry***

This modern economic agency which communicates messages related to modern house ware industries such as ceramic, bone china, brass, bronze, copper, steel, glass and plastic, which are beautiful, attractive and economic. These house wares industries communicate messages to the people regarding production, sale, purchase and utility of different types of wares. They make advertisement to attract the people in newspapers, workshops, fairs, on line messages and so on.

### *Modern Furniture Industry and Room Decoration Industry*

Now-a-days, a number of modern furniture industries have come in to existence. They are communicating messages related to different types of modern furnitures such as bed, sofa, almirrah, bed room set, drawing roomset, bath room set, kitchen set and so on. They are made up of wood, plywood, steel, plastic and so on. They send messages about utility, sale and purchase of them.

### *Modern Dress Industry*

A number of modern dress industries have come in to existence. They have their branded name. They sell not only clothes, but also readymade dresses of gents, ladies, boys, girls and children. They make advertisement regarding quality, marketing and discount news to the people through newspapers, T.V., radio and sms. Thus, modern dress industries communicate modern economic news to the people.

### *Modern Jewellery Industry*

Now-a-days, a number of modern jewellery industries have come in to existence, which function as a modern economic agency of communication. They send message to the people regarding production, sell and marketing of different jewelleries prepared by different branded company. They make advertisement of their products. They assure guarantee of quality, purity and durability. They also make advertisement of discount on their products. They include ornaments of gold, silver, diamond, platinum and gems.

### *Modern Food Industry*

Now-a-days, a number of modern food industries have come in to existence, which produce varieties of readymade food items in various branded names. They sell not only readymade food items, but also branded raw food items like rice, wheat, pulses, spices, salt, loafsugar, sugar, oil, refine, ghee and so on. They make advertisement in newspapers, radio, televisions regarding their products and their sale and purchase. They claim their quality as superior to other brands. Thus, modern food industries act as modern economic agent of communication.

### *Modern Medicine Industry*

Modern medicine industries also function as modern economic agency of communication. A number of medicine companies have come into existence which produce modern medicines to be prescribed by specialist doctors for different kinds of diseases. They have medical representative who move doctor to doctor for prescribing their products. They also make advertisement in newspapers, radio, televisions, medicine, journals and on the cover of the medicine. Thus, modern medical industries play significant role in communicating people regarding the use of modern medicines in different kinds of diseases.

### *Modern Occupations*

Now-a-days, modernisation of traditional occupations like carpentry, blacksmithy, pottery, copper smithy, bronze smithy, basketry has taken place. As a result, traditional occupations have also acquired modern beautiful and attractive look.

A number of career-oriented occupations have also come in to existence like teacher, Professor, engineer, clerk, doctor, health staff, university staff, post office staff, department staff and so on. A number of new career oriented and other types of business and trade have also come into existence such as private tutors, coaching institutes, private hospitals, nursing home, school, colleges, university, law university, management and engineering institutes. Thus, modern occupations function as modern economic agency of communication.

### *Modern Service*

A number of modern services in private and public sectors have come in to existence such as computer operators, computer business, internet business, city manager, city squard, the professionals, knowledge traders, knowledge workers and so on. In fact, in every departments and sectors I.T. professionals have been hired to provide online services.

### *Modern Fertiliser Industry*

This is also a modern economic agency of communication. This agency communicates messages related to use of chemical fertilisers among the people for agricultural, floriculture, vegetable cultivation and spray of their solutions on crops for increasing fertility and assured yield. In this way, fertiliser industries work as modern economic agency of communication.

### *Modern Pesticide and Weedicide Industry*

This is also a modern economic agency of communication. This agency communicates messages related to use of pesticides and weedicides for assured yield of grains and vegetables to the people.

### *I.T. Industry*

This is also a modern economic agency of communication. This industry communicates messages among youth to select career as I.T. professionals and earn good packages from multinational companies. This industry also sends messages related to the production of means for information technology like computer, laptop, hand set, internet, software, hardware and so on. A good number of traders have come in to existence who make trade of hardware and software technology. Thus, I.T. industry is modern economic agency of communication.

### *Multinational Companies*

Now-a-days, a number of multi-national companies have come in to existence, which provide employment opportunities to I.T. Engineer and management professionals on good packages with chance of visiting foreign countries. With the emergence of multinational companies, knowledge employer, knowledge workers, knowledge trade and knowledge market have emerged globally. Thus, multinational companies make significant contribution as modern economic agency of communication.

### *Management Institutes*

Now-a-days, a number of management institutes have emerged which are producing management professionals. Youth are attracted towards management institute to opt career as management professionals. They are getting placement on a handsome packages with opportunities to visit abroad. Thus, management institutes are functioning as modern economic agency of communication.

### *Modern Cinema Industry*

Now-a-days, a number of modern cinema industries have come in to existence which are communicating messages among youth related to the career in modern cinema industry. Youth are getting opportunity to work in modern cinema industry in different capacity. They are also getting good packages. Thus, modern cinema industry is contributing significantly in communicating messages among youth for career and handsome packages.

### *Modern Sex Industry*

Now-a-days, sex has become a problem for the Government. It is related to continuous population growth, abortion, mother mortality, infant and child mortality and spread of sexually transmitted diseases. To have safe sex relation and for family welfare programme, a number of sex industries have come in to existence. These industries are communicating messages among people regarding family welfare and safe sex relation.

### *Modern Floriculture*

Now-a-days, horticulture has emerged as a modern source of income. A number of people are cultivating flowers not only for beauty and attraction, but also for earning money by supplying flowers regularly in the market. Thus, it makes contribution in the communication of earning by horticulture. A number of nurseries have come into existence which supply varieties of seedlings of crops.

### *Ministry of Finance*

This institution also functions as a modern economic agency of communication which Communicates a number of economic messages to the people relating to income tax structure, saving, service tax, educational tax, road tax and so on. The people have to follow the direction of Finance Ministry.

### *Ministry of Commerce*

This is also a modern economic agency of communication. This institution communicates messages related to import and export of commodities, trades, markets and other economic messages related to business and commerce.

***Ministry of Textiles***

This Ministry also functions as a modern economic agency of communication. This communicates economic messages related to production, trade and market of textiles which are valuable informations for traders involved in the business of textiles.

***Decoration Play and Games Industry***

There are a number of industries involved in the production of items of house decoration, plays and games. They communicate messages related to sale and purchase of decorative items, games and play items.

***Publication Industry***

There are a number of publication industries which are involved in the publication of books, journals, brouchures, booklets, bulletin and so on. They act as a modern economic agency of communication. They send messages of publication industry as a trade and business. The message related to royalty are also communicated to the author. The price of book is communicated for the buyers.

***Entertainment Industry***

Now-a-days, a number of entertainment industries have come in to existence as a modern economic agency of communication. They are involved in production of VCR, VCP, C.D. Cassette, record-players, computers, internet and musical instruments, which are used as means of entertainment. Entertainment goods are produced, sold and purchased in the market. Thus, entertainment industry functions as a modern economic agency of communication.

***Staff Selection Commission***

This agency also functions as a modern economic agency of communication. It invites applications for different posts for which examinations are taken, results are published and interview are held. Then selection of the staff is made. This commission communicates messages among the people regarding obtaining good service on good payment of salary. Thus, it functions as modern economic agency of communication.

### *Railway Employment Board*

This is also a modern agency of economic communication. It communicates messages related to employment in railway on different posts. The selection of candidates is made by this board on the basis of written examination and interview. The selected candidates are appointed to work in railway on different posts.

### *Shipping Industry*

This is also a modern economic agency of communication. It communicates messages related to employment in shipping corporation of India. The appointment is made on the basis of written test, and interview on different posts. The selected candidates make their joining and get salary in scale fixed by the Government time to time.

### *Defence Industry*

This is also a modern economic agency of communication. It communicates messages related to productions of arms ammunition and other defence related products. The appointment is held on the basis of written test and interview by the commission.

### *Different Service Commissions*

Different service commissions also function as an agency of modern economic communication. For appoint of Government jobs, there are a number of service commissions at state level and at national level. For example, Finance Service Commission, Defence Service Commission, Engineering Service Commission, Medical Service Commission, University Grands Commission, State Service Commission, University Service Commission, College Service Commission and so on. Through these service commissions, selection of the candidates is made on the basis of PT, written tests and interview. The successful candidates get appointment letter and they have to make joining against their posts. These commissions communicate messages related to competitions for prestigious appointments and opportunity to work on handsome salary on significant posts.

### *Vehicle and Transport Industry*

This is also a modern economic agency of communication. It communicates messages related to production of different types of vehicles such as two-wheelers, three-wheelers, four-wheelers, different types of cars, different types of trucks and good careers and their parts. This also communicates messages of selling prices, discounts, loan facilities and so on.

### *Restaurants, Hotels and Guest Houses*

Now-a-days, a number of restaurants, hotels and guest houses have come in to existence which are functioning as modern economic agency of communication. They have AC and non-AC rooms. These agencies communicate messages related to their charges of rooms, facility available and food items available.

### *Newspapers*

There are a numbers of newspapers published daily in local, regional, national and international languages. Newspapers play significant role in communicating different types of news. Economic news are also one of them. Thus, newspapers function as a modern economic agency of communication. They make people aware about economic activities of Government, trade and markets.

### *Television*

Television channels make us aware of different types of economic activities such as employment, production, consumption, trade, market, exchange, loan and so on. In this way, televisions function as a modern economic agency of communication.

### *Radio*

Radio is also a modern economic agency of communication. With the help of radio, economic news such as employment, production, consumption, exchange, trade, market, market price, loan facility are provided to the people.

### *Agricultural Colleges*

Now-a-days, a number of agricultural colleges have come in to existence where students are taught regarding carrying out agriculture with modern education. Getting graduation degree in agriculture, candidates get appointment as agricultural officer and agricultural scientists. Thus, agricultural colleges function as a modern economic agency of communication.

### *Agricultural Research Institutes*

A number of agricultural research institutes have came into existence which are functioning as modern agency of communication. The agricultural research institutes have a number of research scientists who are doing researches in different areas of agriculture to increase yield. HYV seeds, chemical fertilizer, pesticides insecticides are the result of their researches. They are also contributing significantly in processing and preserving processes of agricultural produce.

### *Vaterinary College*

This is also a modern economic agency of communication. It communicates messages regarding modern technology of domesticating animals and live stocks. There are a number of vaterinary colleges where teaching and researches in vaterinary sciences is done. After getting graduation degree in veterinary science, candidates get appointment as vaterinarian or vaterinary scientist. They also earn money as private praticener.

### *Forestry College*

There are a number of forestry colleges where teaching of forestry is done. After getting graduation degree, the candidates get appointment as forest scientists. They do researches in collection, preservation, processing, marketing and trade of forest produce. They act as a modern economic agency of communication.

### *Modern Cottage Industry*

Modern cottage industry functions as modern economic agency of communication. It communicates messages related to production, trade and marketing of goods produced by cottage industries.

### *Modern Electrical Appliances Industry*

Now-a-days, a number of electrical appliances industries have came in to existence which produce and sell electrical appliances in markets. They make advertisement of their electrical appliances and attract customers for purchasing their electrical goods. Thus, they act as a modern economic agency of communication.

### *Modern Political Agency of Communication*

In modern time, a number of political agencies have come in to existence which are known as modern political agency of communication. They are engaged in communicating political messages to the people. They are as follows:

- Ward member
- Ward assembly
- *Mukhia*
- Village assembly
- Village panchayat
- Panchyat or Prakhand Samiti
- Zilla Parishad
- Municipality
- Municipal corporation
- MLA
- MLC
- Assembly
- Lok Sabha
- Rajya Sabha
- Ministers
- Chief Minister
- Prime Minister
- Governor
- President
- Election Commission
- Parliamentary Committees
- Political Parties
- Different Commissions
- Newspapers

- Radio
- Internet
- Television

Now, let us discuss about these modern political agencies of communication one by one.

***Ward Member***

Ward member is a political representative of ward of a village. The ward member is responsible for communicating political decisions of the Government related to various village development programmes, poverty alleviation programmes, and selection of beneficiaries under different welfare and social security programmes. In this way, ward member acts as a modern political agent of development communication.

***Ward Assembly***

Ward assembly is also a modern political agency of development. The ward assembly decides ward development programmes and beneficiaries of welfare and social security programmes. It communicates messages related to a number of development programmes for the people. In this way, it functions as a modern political agency of development.

***Mukhia***

*Mukhia* is political head of all villages which come under the jurisdiction of a modern Gram Panchayat. He/she communicates messages related to development of villages and selection of beneficiaries for social security and welfare. Thus, he/she functions as a modern political agent of communication.

***Village Assembly***

The village assembly is a modern political agency of development communication. Each village coming under the boundary of one modern Gram Panchayat has a village assembly. Mukhia officiates this assembly meeting. In this assembly meeting, the future programmes of village development are discussed and priority areas are decided. Beneficiaries of different social welfare and security programmes are discussed and selected finally on the basis of unanimous decision. In this way, this assembly makes significant contribution in the communication of political news among the villagers.

### *Gram Panchayat*

Gram Panchayat is a Panchayat of all villages coming under the jurisdiction of Gram Panchayat. In fact, it is an inter village Panchayat. *Mukhia* and its executive members are elected through election. The elected person becomes the *mukhia* or head or chairman of the Panchayat. He/she represents all villages of his/her Panchayat in Panchayat Samiti meeting. All development and welfare programmes run under his/her supervision. The Gram Panchayat has Panchayat sewak and now panchayat mitra. He/she keeps record of all Panchayat meetings and village assembly meetings.

### *Panchayat Samiti/Prakhand Samiti*

This is also a modern political agency of communication. It communicates political messages to the people regarding allocation of funds for development programmes of different Panchayat. The *mukhia* of different Panchayats are its member. One of them is elected as chairman of Panchayat Samiti. He/she officiates the meeting of Panchayat Samiti. Prakhand Vikas Padadhikari is also member of this Samiti. It communicates news related to development of all Panchayats coming under the jurisdiction of a Prakhand.

### *Zilla Parishad*

This is also a modern political agency of communication. It communicates messages related to elections and functions of Zilla Parishad. The development of district and development budget of each Prakhand are discussed and decided in this meeting in presence of D.C. or D.M.

### *Municipality*

This is also a modern political agency related to the development of towns. This agency communicates political messages related to its election and functions in maintaining the cleanliness of the town.

### *Municipal Corporation*

This is also a modern political agency of communication. It communicates messages related to elections of ward members and mayor and the development work it performs for the cities.

### *MLA*

An MLA is a political head of an MLA constituency. He/she is elected on the basis of election which is held after each five years or in mid term in certain unavoidable condition MLA can also become a Minister in State Ministry formed under a Chief Minister. He/she functions as a political agent of development communication. He communicates messages regarding various development programmes which are going on in his/her constituencies.

### *MLC*

This is also a modern political agency of communication. MLC represents upper house. The acts, statutes passed by state assembly are sent to the members of legislative council for discussion and final decision. Thus, MLC acts as a modern political agency of communication. An MLC is also a political agent of development communication. He/she is not elected directly, but indirectly by elected members. He/she communicates political messages to development communication.

### *Assembly*

It is a place where Chief Minister, Ministers, and all elected MLA sit together under a chairman to discuss different political issues. Ruling and opposition parties share their views in assembly. Acts and statutes are formulated, discussed and passed in the assembly. This assembly acts as a modern political agency of communication.

### *Lok Sabha*

It is a very important political agency of communication. It communicates messages related to election and formation of Lok Sabha, Prime Minister, Council of Ministers, Chairman, Opposition Leader, members and discussions on various issues of national interest. All acts, statutes, policies, planning are formulated here for implementation.

### *Rajya Sabha*

This is upper house of policy formulation and enactment of acts and statutes. The bill passed by Lok Sabha is sent to Rajya Sabha for final decision. Thus, it acts as a modern political agency of communication.

### *Ministers*

State and Central Ministers also act as a modern political agents of communication. They play significant role in communicating messages related to development programmes of the Government. As a part of Government, they play significant role in communicating development policies, plans and programmes of the Government.

### *Chief Minister*

The Chief Minister is head of the State Assembly and the people. He is respected and obeyed by all. He/she makes development journey in the different parts of the state and communicate significant news related to development plans and programmes of the state and the people.

### *Prime Minister*

Prime Minister is head of Council of Minister of a country. He/she makes development journeys in different parts of the state. He/she also makes address to the people in which he/she communicates significant messages to the people regarding his planning for the development of the country and the people.

### *Governor*

The Governor is the first citizen of the state. Without his/her signature, no bill, act, ordinance and statute can be taken as passed. He/she is the final authority of the state. He/she can suspend the Government, can recommend for the Governor's rule or re-election of assembly. In this way, Governor acts as a modern political agency of communication.

### *President*

Hon'ble President is Head of a nation. No bill or act is taken as passed useless he/she signs on it. He/she invites the Chief of political parties in majority to form a Government and prove majority at the floor of House.

He can impose President rule during emergency. Thus, as a Head of nation he/she commands respect and regard of all citizens. He/she acts as a modern political agency of communication.

***Election Commission***

The election commission is the most powerful body during election period. It provides symbols to political parties and independent candidates. It decides code of conduct for candidates and political parties during the period of election. It keeps vigil on income and expenditure of funds of candidates and political parties. In this way, election commission functions as a modern political agency of communication.

***Parliamentary Committees***

The Parliament constitutes a number of committees for recommendation on different political issues. The recommendation of the committee is discussed in parliament before final decision. Thus, different parliamentary committees function as modern political agency of communication.

***Political Parties***

In democracy, there are a number of political parties with different names and different political symbols. Each party has its own agenda and election manifesto. They communicate the agenda and manifesto to the people for casting votes in their favour. Thus, political parties function as a modern political agency of communication.

***Different Commissions***

There are different political commissions, for example Human Rights Commission, Woman Commission, OBC Commission, S.C. Commission, ST Commission, Minority Commission and so on. These commissions function as a modern political agency of communication. They convey messages related to human rights protection, social security, protection from exploitation, oppression, deprivation of concerned sections of the society. Thus, they play significant role in communication of political messages.

### *Newspapers*

A number of newspapers are published daily in local, regional, national and international languages. These newspapers communicate news to their readers regarding different social, economic, political, religious, health, ethnic, national and international issues. Readers have communication among themselves on different issues which are happening in and around in world. Thus, newspapers act as a modern agency of communication.

### *Radio*

Radio is also a modern political agency of communication. It communicates news related to political issues, political decision, political events, in local, Hindi and English languages to the people. People hear radio programmes and news vary eagerly. It includes news readers, news editor and news writers.

### *Internet*

Internet is the most modern political agency of communication. Different political parties and leaders have their account on social media sites. They communicate political messages for the people. They also communicate their opinions, reactions and counter reactions related to political development.

### *Television*

Television also works as a modern political agency of communication. Different televisions have their news channels. In news channels, news related to political development in state, nation and world are presented. They communicate political messages among the people regarding political issues and development taking place in our country and in the world. It includes news writer, editor and reader, besides news reporters.

### *Modern Educational Agency of Communication*

Now-a-days, a number of modern educational institutions have come in to existence which claim themselves as modern educational agency of communication. They are as follows:

- School
- Teacher
- College and University
- Professor
- Technical Institutes
- Management Institutes
- Secondary Education Board
- Intermediate Council
- College Service Commission
- University Service Commission
- University Grants Commission
- Human Resource Development Ministry
- Research Institute and Research Centres
- Books
- Journals
- Library
- Lecture Notes
- Special Lecture
- Seminar
- Newspapers
- Television
- Internet
- e-book
- e-library
- e-lecture

Now, let us discuss about these modern educational agencies of communication one by one.

***School***

School is one of modern educational agencies of communication. It communicates messages related to admission in school, teaching in school, teachers of the school, class work, homework, examination, result and promotion from K.G. to class 9 and board examination in class 10. The students and parents have to follow these messages for the purpose of school education. The school may be nursery, K.G., Primary, middle and secondary level, but they act as modern educational agency of communication.

***Teacher***

The teacher is also a modern educational agent of communication. He/she communicates about the value of modern education. He/she teaches in the class on the basis of which students get success in the class test and promotion from one class to the next and finally in board examination. The teacher not only teaches, but he/she also develops character and values in students. He/she contributes in the nation and society building. Thus, teacher plays significant role in communicating educational development, character building, incalculating national values and social values.

***College and University***

Colleges and universities are also modern educational agencies of communication. They communicate about the value of higher education from the point of the view of career. They also communicate messages related to admission process, admission fees, class attendance, examination and result. They also communicate messages about chances of getting pass for unsuccessful candidates. Thus, colleges and universities communicate significant messages related to modern education.

***Professor***

Professors are the most significant modern educational agents of communication. Through their classroom lectures, they communicate messages related to knowledge on the subjects taught. They share the responsibility to complete the syllabus and make students worthy of getting success. They take examination and evaluate answer book. They do tabulation work and prepare cross list. Thus, Professors play significant role in communicating messages of knowledge on the subject and career related suggestions.

The University professors are actively and dedicatedly engaged in researches. They guide Ph.D. research scholars to write Ph.D. thesis under their guidance. They also do their own researches, too. They do research projects and submit projects to concerned financing agency.

***Technical Institutes***

There are a number of technical research institutes which provide technical education and degree to the students who get admission there. The technical institutes are also known as Engineering colleges, Medical colleges, Ayurvedic colleges, Homoeopathy colleges and Polytechnic colleges. They communicate messages related to admission in technical courses, syllabus taught, fee structure, class attendance, resource persons, examination and results. Thus, technical institutes function as a modern educational agency of communication.

### Management Institutes

Now-a-days, a number of management institutes have come in to existence which are imparting education in financial management, human resource management, rural management, and public administration. Management institutes impart career-oriented courses. The students get placement on handsome package. Thus, management institutes functions as a modern educational agency of communication.

### Secondary Education Board

This is a modern educational agency of communication. It communicates messages related to secondary board examination such as filling up of forms, issue of admit card, examination on Scheduled dates, evaluation of answer books and publication of result with mark sheet and certificate. Thus, it performs significant role in communicating messages related to Secondary Board Examination.

### Intermediate Council

This is also a modern educational agency of communication. It communicates messages related to intermediate education between secondary education and college education. This communicates messages related to intermediate council examination schedules such as filling up of forms, issue of admit card, examination on scheduled dates, evaluation of answer books, publication of results, issue of cross list certificate and mark sheet to successful candidates. Thus, it plays significant role in imparting intermediate education and related message.

### College Service Commission

This is also a modern educational agency of communication. It communicates messages regarding employment of teacher and staff in affiliated colleges and budgetary provision of affiliated colleges.

### University Service Commission

This is a modern educational agency of communication. It communicates messages related to appointment and promotion of university teachers.

### University Grants Commission

This is a modern educational agency of communication. It communicates messages related to various kinds of funds to different universities of country under different items in each plan period. It also creates post of lecturer, reader and university professors in different departments of the universities. It provides doctoral research fellowships to S.Cs, S.Ts and minority students for a period of five years. It also provides post-doctoral fellowships to doctoral candidates. It sanctions research project grants to individual teacher concerned. It provides SAP and CAS to different Departments of Universities. In this way, UGC performs very significant role in communicating different types of educational messages to universities and colleges.

### Human Resource Development Ministry

This is very important modern educational agency of communication. This Ministry communicates budgetary provisions for primary, secondary, Intermediate, College and University education and also for different kinds of welfare programmes related to educational development. The Ministry launches several educational schemes, fellowship schemes, welfare schemes, foreign study schemes, establishment of colleges, Universiteis, research institutes, research centres and so on. Thus, it plays very significant role as modern educational agency of communication.

### Research Institutes and Research Centres

Government has established a number of research institutes and research centres for natural sciences, earth sciences, life sciences, social sciences, agricultural sciences, vaterinary science, forestry science, astrology, astronomy, atomic researches, defence researches, space research, medicine research, law research and so on. These research institutes and centres communicate significant messages related to activities of those research institutes and their significant outcomes.

### *Books*

Books are modern educational agency of communication. Research after research, study after study, new forms of knowledge appear. When new knowledge appears, the previous knowledge becomes old. The publication of books based on recent researches have brought a new knowledge in every discipline and subjects chosen for study. Thus, books act as modern educational agency of communication of different kinds of knowledge.

### *Journals*

Different University departments and research institutes publish journals containing articles of distinguished scholars on different themes and areas. Those journals make significant contribution in the field of knowledge and also for the benefit of society. They communicate research based knowledge among different scholars of different discipline.

### *Library*

Library is a place where one finds storage and preservation of books written by several scholars of different disciplines. It also consists of different journals published by different disciplines. It also makes collection of newspapers, periodicals, reports and so on. Thus, library functions as a knowledge centre. It communicates different kinds of knowledge among readers and scholars.

### *Lecture Notes*

Lecture notes given by different teachers on subject to be taught in classroom also function as a modern educational agency of communication. It communicates new accumulated knowledge of teachers among students.

### *Special Lecture*

In University departments and research institutes, a number of special lectures are organised on special subject in which eminent scholar of the subject is invited to grace the occasion by his/her speech. The audience of the special lecture are benefited by hearing speech of the expert scholars. They learn a number of new areas of knowledge on the subject. Thus, special lecture contributes in the communication of knowledge.

### *Seminar*

The University Departments and research institutes organise seminar, symposium, workshop and conferences on a special title to gather knowledge from different scholars. The different expert scholars present their views and knowledge on the subject concerned. The outcome of the seminar is published in the form of journal or book. The journal or book communicates knowledge among the scholars.

### *Newspapers*

Different newspapers have educational column in their paper in which they cover news related to schools, colleges, universities, research institutes and other educational issues. They also publish list and review of books published recently. Thus, newspapers act as modern educational agency of communication.

### *Television*

Television also functions as a modern educational agency of communication. Each television agency has its educational channel where educational news are presented audio-visually. The educational channel gives us news about the publication of books, author and book release functions and book review.

### *Internet*

Internet is a modern educational agency of communication. With the help of internet scholars are able to down load and study about different areas of study and research. It also provides readymade materials on different topics of syllabus and research. It also provides book lists on the topic concerned.

### *e-books*

Now-a-days, a number of books have been made available on line. The reader can study those books with the help of internet. Thus, it is a modern educational agency of communication.

### *e-library*

With the help of internet, one can get knowledge about e-library. Now-a-days, a number of libraries have been made on line. They give knowledge to a scholar on line about the books related to their topic in the library. Thus, it functions as a modern educational agency of communication.

### e-lecture

A number of scholars have made available their lectures on line for the readers. The readers down load those lectures for the purpose of study and research.

### *Modern Religious Agency of Communication*

There are a number of modern religious organisations which function as religious agency of communication. They communicate their religious agenda in modern way. They use not only oral media, but also press, print, electronic, satellite and social media. They are as follows:

- Religious meeting
- Religious conference
- Religious Guru
- Religious Saints
- Religious yagya
- Pilgrimage
- Religious fairs
- Religious Great baths
- Religious voluntary organisations
- Religious organisations
- Ministry of Culture
- Government and Administration
- Puja Samiti
- Mela Samiti
- Online worship
- Online Darshan
- Online death/funeral ritual

- Online Bhajan-Kirtan
- Radio
- Newspapers
- Televisions
- Books and booklets
- Religious Journals
- Internet

Now, let us discuss about these modern religious agencies of communication one by one.

### *Religious Meeting*

Now-a-days, the followers of different religions assemble at the place of their religious symbols and hold a meeting for the protection of their religious beliefs and practices. They hold meeting with modern means of communication and formal ways. The day, date and time of the meeting is predecided. They use modern sound system, and do recording of entire procedures of the meeting.

### *Religious Conference*

Now-a-days, the followers of different religions organise conference at regional, state, national and international level. The followers make their contribution for holding conferences. They also make contribution of funds to strengthen the organisation and do welfare to the needed community members. These conferences send messages to community members that they are not alone. They are united. They can fight against evil practices, fanatics and danger from other community. In this way, religious conference acts as modern religious agency of communication.

### *Religious Guru*

There are a number of religious *Guru* (preachers) in a religious sect. Again a religious sect is divided in to sub-sects and each sub-sects have its own *Guru*. The *Guru* moves from place to place to preach the religious norms, values, traditions, customs and morality to lead a healthy and wealthy life on this earth and life after death. The religious *Gurus* are respected by their followers. The followers meet expenditure of their visit, stay, accommodation and food. They also offer clothes, money and flowers to seek their blessings. Thus, religious Guru act as modern religious agency of communication.

### Religious Saints

There are a number of religious saints who have their stay at *Ashrama* or huts located on the bank of sacred rivers. They act as a modern religious agency of communication. They organise camp on the confluence of rivers on the occasion of greath religious bath. The followers get shelter in their *bari* (shelter). They also share food as *Prasad.* Followers pay some fund as contribution to run the *bari.* These religious saints also organise their preachings to followers. They also organise religious play of Rama, Krishna, Shiva, Hanumana, Surya, Narada, Indra and others at night with light and sound system.

### Religious Yagya

Different religious *Guru* organise their *yagya* on different religious occasions. They collect fund from followers to do *yagya* for the benefit and betterment of the community. They erect temporary *Ashrama* (hut) on the bank of river or on the confluence of rivers. The programme of *yagya* continue for a month. Daily worship, morning and evening *Aarati, Bhajan-Kirtan*, religious preachings, religious plays are held amidst light and sound system. Followers from different places come to participate in *yagya* and take benefit of other religious programme. At the end of *yagya*, the ritual of *Havan* (sacrifice) is made with rice, oat, *dhup*, *gugul*, black *til*, dry coconut and items of *Prasad.* The ritual of *Havan* marks the end of the *yagya.* After *Havan* ritual, distribution of *Prasad* and *Bhandara* (ritual of serving food) are done. In this way, religious *yagya* acts as a modern religious agency of communication.

### Pilgrimage

Pilgrimage acts as a modern religious agency of communication. There are a number of tour agency which visit village to village for having pilgrimage of four *Dhams* (abode of deities) and other *Dhams* situated in different parts of the country. People make pilgrimage of these places with great devotion for getting wordly achievements and *moksha* (liberation from rebirth) after death. In making pilgrimage, people use buses, cars, aeroplane and railways. They stay in *Dharmashala*, rest house, guest houses and hotels. They have bath in religious ponds, rivers and sea, offer worships to deities, put their desire before deity for wordly achievements and to get *moksha* after death.

### *Religious Fairs*

Different religious fairs take place on different religious occasions throughout the length and breath of the country. The people from neighbouring as well as distant places pay a visit in the religious fairs. They have bath, do worhship, visit fairs, do marketing and enjoy different plays. The advertisement regarding the day, date and administrative arrangements are made through oral, press, print, electronic and satellite media. Thus, religious fairs play significant role in communicating messages to the people regarding the value and significance of the religious fairs.

### *Religious Great Baths*

A number of religious great baths take place on the bank of rivers or confluence of rivers, or river and sea such as *Kumba Maha Asnana*, *Makar Sankranti Maha Asnana*, *Surya grahana* (solar eclipse) *Maha Asnana*, *Chandra Grahana Maha Asnana* and others. The people from different parts assemble on the bank of rivers, ponds, confluence of rivers, confluence of river and sea to have great bath on great religious occasion. Propaganda, announcement, broadcastings, and advertisements regarding those great bath occasions are made through media. The *Maha Asnana* acts as a modern agency of communication.

### *Religious Voluntary Organisations*

There are a number of voluntary organisations which come forward to extend welfare works to devotees and visitors on the occasion of pilgrimage, great bath, religious fairs, meetings, conferences and *yagya*. These organisations have their registration number and the list of voluteers with identity card. They remain 24 hours on duty to help worshippers, devotees, pilgrims, visitors and tourists. They make advertisement about their activities in newspapers, print media, electronic media and satellite media.

### *Religious Organisation*

The organisers of Great *Puja*, fair, *asnan*, *Kumbha*, *Chhath* worship meeting, conference and *yagya* also act as modern religious agency of communication. They make advertisements of their programmes and extend invitation for participation through card, paper, electronic media, print media and satellite media. Thus, they play significant role as modern religious agency of communication.

### *Ministry of Culture*

The Ministry of Culture also acts as modern agency of communication. It highlights the cultural and religious significance of pilgrimage, worship, fairs, great baths. It also advertises the programmes of religious importance and the role of Government in providing facilities to devotees, and visitors. Thus, it acts as a modern religious agency of communication.

### *Government and Administration*

The Government and administration act as a modern religious agency of communication. It is also duty of the Government and administration to provide safety to organisers, devotees and visitors. To provide travel facilities on pilgrimage, Great bath and great fair is also duty of Government and administration. With the order of Government police personnel and administrators are deputed for peaceful end of the religious occasions. Medical facilities, drinking water, electricity, food and other essential services are managed by the Government and administration.

### *Puja-Samiti*

On the occasion of festivals and great worship, bathing and pilgrimage, the local people form *Puja Samiti.* They extend help to the administration in successful completion of the festivals. Thus, *Puja samiti* works as a modern religious agency of communication.

### *Mela Samiti*

On the occasion of Great *Mela*, the local people form *Mela Samiti* to extend help to the people at one hand and the administration on the other hand. Thus, it plays significant role as modern religious agency of communication.

### *Online Worship and Darshan*

Now-a-days, online worship and *Darshan* facilities are available with the help of satellite media. The people can offer on line worship and make on line *Darshan* of the religious places and Gods and Goddesses.

### *Online Funeral Ritual*

Now-a-days, such agencies have come in to existence which arranges on line funeral ritual for those living in foreign countries, but like to do funeral of their parents or others at Manikarnika Ghat, Varanasi. They book dead body in plane and the agency received the body and on line funeral rituals are performed. The payment for ritual performance is also made on line by the person concerned.

### *Online Bhajan-Kirtan*

Now-a-days, on line *Bhajan-Kirtan* are available. People listen to them through internet.

### *Radio*

The religious programmes are announced with the help of radio by the administration. Through radio news people are informed about tour, health, food, stay, drinking water, medicine, safety, electricity arrangements made by the Government and administration.

### *Newspapers*

Newspapers are modern religious agency of communication. Newspapers provide messages to the readers regarding time, day and duration of occurring religious occasions and different types of arrangements made by the Government and voluntary organisations.

### *Televisions*

Televisions are also modern agency of religious communication. Televisions present *Ramayana*, *Mahabharata*, *Geeta, Puranas* through different serials. They also advertise the religious performances at different places in their serials. T.V. news communicates detail messages to the people regarding time, days, duration of great religious occasions and facilities and arrangement to be provided by the Government.

### *Interest Service*

The religious places, their values, great festivals, great fairs and great *mela* are available on internet sites. People visit internet sites for detail description, route detail, travel agency, accommodation facility and a number of other informations. Thus, internet service acts as modern religious agency of communication.

### *Online Priest Service*

In internet, online priest service is also available which is very modern arrangement.

### *Books and Booklets*

A number of books and booklets are available which communicate messages related to mysterious origins of religious places and benefits of offering worships there.

### Religious Journals

Religious books and Journals are also modern religious agency of communication. They have new and new informations regarding religious things.

## Modern Health Agency of Communication

Now-a-days, a number of modern health agencies of communication have come in to existence. They are communicating modern messages to the people. They are as follows:

- Village School Teacher
- Anganwadi Kendra
- Health Sub-Centre
- Primary Health Centre
- Extra Primary and Subsidiary Health Centre
- Community Health Centre
- Referral Hospital
- Sadar Hospital
- Government Medical College and Hospital

- Private Medical College and Hospital
- Nursing Colleges
- Private Nursing Hospitals
- Ayurvedic Medicine and Research Centre
- Homoeopathy Medicine Centre
- Unani Medicine Centre
- Acue Pressure Centre
- Electro-magnetic Centre
- Naturopathy Centre
- Siddha Medicine Centre
- Ministry of Health
- Medical Stores
- Ministry of Family Welfare
- Mobile Hospitals
- Medical Companies
- Medical Students
- Medical Books and Journals
- Media
- Free Check up Camp
- Free Cataract Operation Camp
- Paramedical Staff

Now, let us discuss about these modern health agencies one by one.

### *Village School Teacher*

The school teacher works as a modern health agency of communication. The school teachers not only teach books in schools and enhance knowledge ability of students, but they also teach about good habit, good food and cleanliness. Thus, they play significant role as a modern health agency of communication.

### Anganwadi Kendra

Anganwadi Kendra functions as modern health agency of communication. The staff of the Kendra take care of pregnant woman and lactating women and children. They communicate messages related to modern concept of health by regular health check up of pregnant woman, lactating mother and infants. This Kendra sends messages among rural people about woman, mother and infant health. The Kendra also provides nutritious diet and medicine to woman folk and children. It has played significant role in sending messages of mother health, pregnancy health, and safe delivery and vaccination of infants and children for protection from killer diseases. Anganwadi Sevika, Sahaika and *Dai* act as health communicators.

### *Health Sub-Centres*

Our Government has established health sub-centres by uniting several Panchayats. These centres have compounder, nurse, health workers and trained *Dai* as health communicators. Doctors pay a visit to these centres time to time. These health staff make survey of health status of the people by visiting door to door. They act as Government health messengers. They communicate news about different types of diseases, mother mortality, infant mortality, safe delivery, family welfare programme and cleanliness to the people. They communicate messages related to modern scientific concept of disease, medicine and treatment.

### *Primary Health Centres*

At each headquarters of a block, there is a primary health centre. Each primary health centre has four medical officers. Under each medical officer, there are nurse, *Dai* and health workers. All these staff are modern health communicators. They communicate messages that disease can be identified by modern methods of investigation and can be cured or controlled by modern medicine. They also communicate messages related to healthy life style, good nutritious food, exercise, timely checkup and regular use of modern medicine with the help of modern medical practicener. Thus, this health institution work as modern health agency of communication.

### *Extra Primary and Subsidiary Health Centre*

At each 20,000-30,000 population, an establishment of extra primary and subsidiary health centre has been done by the Government. Here, there are two medical officers. Besides, medical officers, there are nurses, compounder, *Dai* and health workers. All these staff act as modern health agency of communication. They communicate modern concept of health and healthy life style.

### *Community Health Centre*

At a population of 80,000 to 1,20,000, a community health centre has been established. The community health centre has medical officers, specialists in medicine, gynaecology and surgery, besides nurses, *Dai*, health workers. All staff of this institution function as modern health communicators. They communicate messages related to modern concept of health, disease, treatment and healthy life style.

### *Referral Hospital*

In this institution, there are four posts of expert doctors – child specialist, women disease specialist, surgeon and medicine specialist. Besides expert doctors, there are nurses, compounders, health workers and sweepers. All expert and staff work as modern health communicators. They convey messages related to modern scientific method of identifying diseases, treatment and medicine and healthy life style.

### *Sadar Hospital*

In each district, the Government has established a Sadar hospital. The Sadar hospital has a Chief Medical Officer and other expert doctors of different departments as medical officers. Besides, there are staff like compounders, nurses, health workers *dai* and sweepers. They work as modern health communicators. They convey messages related to modern scientific methods of diagnosis of diseases and their treatment.

### *Government Medical College and Hospital*

The Government has established Government Medical Colleges and Hospitals for teaching medical sciences to medical students and treatment of diseases of people. The doctors, teachers, students, paramedical staff, nurses, *Dai*, sweepers all functions as communicator of modern health, treatment of diseases and life style.

### *Private Medical Colleges and Hospitals*

A number of private medical colleges and hospitals have been established with the permission of Government to teach medical sciences to medical students and also for treatment of diseases and to enhance the concept of modern healthy life style.

### *Nursing Colleges*

A number of private and Government nursing colleges have been established to teach nursing science to students interesting in serving as nurses in hospitals and medical colleges. Nursing colleges have teachers, students and staff who work as modern health communicators.

### *Private Nursing Hospitals*

There are a number of private nursing hospitals where specialist doctors are available for the treatment of diseases with modern medicine. They also have nurses, *dai* and paramedical staff for assisting doctors in diagnosis and treatment of diseases. Thus, private nursing hospitals have worked as a modern communicator of health.

### *Ayurvedic Medicine and Research Centres*

In our country, there are number of Ayurvedic medicine and research centres which are contributing significantly in the treatment of diseases by making researches and repairing medicine with advanced researches and technology. Thus, Ayurvedic medicine and research centres are contributing significantly in communicating messages related to the treatment of diseases with Ayurvedic medicine.

### *Homoeopathy Medicine Centre*

This is also a modern communicator of treating diseases with the help of homoeopathy medicine. There are a number of colleges and research centres in homoeopathy medicine. The scholars after getting degree and doing researches are getting employment as homoeopathy doctor. They are communicating messages in the people that homoeopathy medicines are also alternative medicines for treating diseases.

### *Unani Medicine Centre*

There are a number of Unani Research centres where teaching and researches are done. The experts of Unani medicine are produced, which act as Unani medicine communicator. They communicate messages regarding Unani medicine as an alternative medicine for curing diseases.

### *Acue Pressure Centre*

There are a number of acue pressure centres in our country where training in acue pressure techniques are provided for curing different types of diseases. The centre communicates messages related to cure of diseases or control of disease by acue pressure.

### *Electro-magnetic Centre*

There are also a number of electro-magnetic centre where training in curing diseases by electro-magnetic method is provided. This method is used for curing a number of diseases. This system communicates messages that diseases can be treated with this technique. It can be adopted as an alternative method of curing diseases.

### *Naturopathy Centre*

In our country there are a number of naturopathy centres which provide training in curing or controlling diseases by nature. Here, natural things like water, soil, air, mud, wind, ash, and others are used for curing diseases. It takes time. But it can be adopted as an alternative method of curing diseases.

### *Siddha Medicine Centre*

In south India, there are a number of Siddha medicine centres, where treatment of diseases with Siddha medicines is done. This method communicates messages that it can be used as an alternative method of treating and controlling diseases.

### *Ministry of Health*

The Ministry of Health Communicates a number of messages related to health promotion schemes, opening medical colleges, hospitals and family welfare programmes. It communicates messages through announcement, radio, T.V. news papers and satellite media. Thus, it acts as a modern agency of communication.

### *Medical Stores*

In order to sell medicines, there are a number of medical stores where medicines are sold and purchased. They act as modern health agency of communication.

### *Ministry of Family Welfare*

This is a modern health agency of communication which conveys messages related to family welfare.

### *Mobile Hospitals*

Now-a-days, our Government has established mobile hospitals to provide health services at door. This is modern agency of communication.

### *Medical Companies*

There are a number of medical companies which produce medicines in the name of their companies. They want to sell their products in markets. For this purpose, they have their medical representatives, who visit from doctor to doctor to prescribe medicines of their companies. Thus, they act as modern agency of health communication.

### *Medical Students*

The students doing study and internship in medical colleges also act as modern agency of health communication. They communicate messages related to modern health concept, disease and treatment.

### *Medical Books and Journals*

There are a number of books and journals related to medicine. They are useful guide for the medical students in medical courses examination. They also act as modern health agency of communication.

### *Media*

The media like press, print, electronic and satellite also work as modern agency of health communication. They communicate messages related to modern methods of treatment and inventions of modern medicine. They also inform about super speciality hospitals, health checkup camps, health survey and health indicators.

### *Free Health Check up Camp*

A number of specialist doctors organize free health check up camp in the name of social welfare. They check up the patient and give suggestion. They also give free medicine to patients.

### *Free Cataract Operation Camp*

A number of NGOs organise free cataract operation camp where catract patients are admitted for operation. They are treated and free lenses are provided along with dress and blankets.

### *Para Medical Staff*

There are a number of paramedical staff who are contributing significantly in medical colleges and hospitals, private hospitals. They are also providing private services. They are X-ray technician, ultra-sound technician, blood test, stool test, urine test and other kind of test technician. They are contributing significantly in spread of modern medical services and treatment. Thus, they are working as modern health communicator.

## Modern Games and Sports Agency of Communication

There are a number of modern games and sports agencies, which are contributing significantly in communication of modern games and sports. They are as follows:

- Cricket match
- Football match
- Hockey match
- Table tennis match
- Badminton match
- Running competition
- Cycling competition
- Kabaddi competition
- Long jump competition
- High jump competition
- Boxing competition
- Wrestling competition
- Weightlifting competition

- Archery
- Ministry of Youth Affairs
- Ministry of Sports
- Media

### *Cricket Match*

A number of cricket matches are organised at regional, state, interstate and international level by different cricket organizations. Those matches are shown on T.V. screen. Commentaries are also herd on radio. Press and print media also highlight them. Thus, cricket matches act as modern games and sports agency of communication. They communicate messages regarding rules, regulations, cricket team, stadium and other informations to youth and children. Children are found playing cricket even in remote villages.

### *Hockey Match*

Like cricket matches, hockey matches are also organised at regional, state, interstate and international level. They communicate messages among youth regarding hockey team, rules of play, play materials, dresses and so on. Thus, hockey matches contribute significantly in communicating messages regarding hockey play.

### *Football Match*

Foot ball matches are also organised at regional, state, interstate, national and international level. The organisation of these matches sends messages among youth towards playing the foot ball in team and to know the rules related to it.

### *Table Tennis Match*

Table tennis matches are held at regional, state, interstate national and international level. These matches communicate rules and regulations of playing this match of table tennis.

### *Badminton*

This play is also popular among children and youth. They play it with bat and cork. Its matches are organised at state, national and international level. Matches are broadcasted.

### *Running Competition*

Running competition is organised at regional, state, national and international level. The winner gets prize. This competition sends messages among youth that they should also join this competition and win the competition.

### *Cycling Competition*

Cycling competitions are also organized at regional, state, national and international level. They send positive messages to youth towards joining this competition and coming out as victorious.

### *Kabaddi Competition*

Kabaddi competitions are organised at regional, state, interstate, national and international level. This competition also acts as a modern agency of sports and games. This competition encourages youth to take part in this competition and to know rules of the play.

### *Long Jump Competition*

Long jump competitions are also held at regional, state, interstate, national and international level at different times. This competition also acts as a modern agency of communication. This competition sends positive messages towards youth to take part in the competition and win the races.

### *High Jump Competition*

This competition also acts as a modern sports agency of communication. This communicates messages related to enthusiasm in youth towards such competition. This also communicates messages related to winning prizes.

### *Boxing Competition*

This competition also acts as modern sports agency of communication. It communicates messages related to boxing as a competitive game. It also sends messages of winning the prize. Youth interested in this competition, receive training from the coaches.

### *Wrestling Competition*

This sports competition also acts as a modern games and sports agency of communication. It communicates messages related to wrestling as a competitive match. The winners are awarded with prizes. It sends positive messages towards this sports competition.

### *Weightlifting Competition*

This is also a modern sports agency of communication. If encourages youth to take part in this competition. For this, they receive training under coach. It sends messages towards receiving prizes after winning the competition.

### *Archery Competition*

This is also a modern sports agency of competition. This communicates messages related to archery as a competitive sports. It also sends messages related to getting prizes after victory. It also provides rewards by the Central and State Governments.

### *Ministry of Youth Affairs*

The Ministry of Youth Affairs also works as modern sports agency of competition. It sends different kinds of sports messages to youth. Thus, it acts as communicator of sports messages.

### *Ministry of Sports*

Ministry of Sports also work as a modern agency of communication. It sends messages related to different kinds of sports in which youth can take part. Thus, it is very useful communicative agency of sports.

### *Media*

Media are the communicators of news about organizations of different kinds of plays, games and sports in different parts of state and country. It also highlights messages related to games and sports which are played between different countries of the globe at different places. Each type of media press, print, electronic and satellite have a space in the name of games-sports. Sports lovers read those news, hear those news or see and hear those news with great interest. Thus, media are most significant agency of sports communication.

## International Agency of Communication

Now-a-days, we have a number of international institutions which are contributing significantly as international agency of communication. They are as follows :

- Red Cross Society
- CARE
- UNICEF
- UNESCO
- World Bank
- World Health Organisation (WHO)
- UNO
- ILO
- FAO
- IAEA
- IMF
- IFC
- UNHCR
- UNIDO
- UNFPA
- ADB
- UNEP

### *Red Cross Society*

It is an international agency of communication. It communicates messages to extend all possible help to international community during wars, refugees, care of disabled, flood affected, earthquake affected and epidemic victims. It sends special message for health, suffering and elimination of diseases. Thus, it functions as an international agency of communication.

### *CARE*

The full form of care is Cooperative for Assistance and Relief Everywhere. It is an international agency of communication. It communicates messages related to mother and child health promotion in international community, specially the developing countries. In India, it communicates messages related to ICDS (Integrated Child Development Programmes), National Health Nutrition Programme (NHNP), and Kishori Yojana. It sends messages regarding extension of services during war, flood, epidemic, earth quakes and cyclones.

### *UNICEF*

Its full form is United Nations International Children's Emergency Fund. It is an international agency of communication. It communicates messages related to nutritional goods for children, trained nurses and mid-wives for maternity aids, sanitation schemes, safe drinking water in rural and urban areas, equipments for health centres, health subs-centres, special health centres, community health centres and referral hospital and also assistance to flood and cyclone victims.

### *UNESCO*

Its full form is United Nations Educational, Scientific and Cultural Organisation. It is an international agency of communication. It communicates messages related to promotion of peace and security in international community through education, science and culture of cooperation. It communicates messages against any kind of discrimination. It sends messages related to translating rare manuscripts, preserving national monuments, rare manuscripts and archaeological heritages.

### *World Bank*

It is also known as International Bank for Reconstruction and Development (IBRD). It functions as an international agency of communication. It communicates significant messages related to promotion of social and economic progress in developing nations.

***World Health Organisation (WHO)***

It is an international agency of communication. It communicates messages of maternal and child health, nursing, blindness, tuberculosis, malaria, Kalajar, cholera, AIDS, cancer, and heart diseases and sanitation.

***UNO***

United Nations Organisation is the full form of UNO. It is an international agency of communication. It communicates messages related to international peace and security, cooperation and friendly relations in world nations, respect for human rights and fundamental freedom, international problems of human, social, economic, and cultural character and social and economic advancement of all people of world community.

***ILO***

Its full form is International Labour Organisations. It is an international agency of communication. It communicates messages related to promotion of labour conditions, raising living standard, and promoting economic and social stability.

***FAO***

Its full form is food and agricultural organisation. It is also an international agency of communication. It communicate messages to world community regarding raising standard of living, improving food quality, fight against hunger and malnutrition.

***IAEA***

Its full form is International Atomic Energy Agency. It is also an international agency of communication. It communicates messages related to contribution of atomic energy to peace, health and prosperity throughout the world.

***IMF***

Its full form is International monetary fund. It is also an international agency of communication. It communicates messages related to promotion of international monetary cooperation, expansion and balanced growth of international trade, exchange stability, establishment of multilateral system of payment and elimination of foreign exchange restrictions.

### *IFC*

Its full form is International Finance Corporation. It is an international agency of communication. It communicates messages related to encouraging investment of private capital in productive capabilities in less developed areas of the world.

### *UNHCR*

Its full form is United National High Commission for Refugees. It is an international agency of communication. It communicates messages related to legal protection and material assistance to refugees.

### *UNIDO*

Its full form is United Nations Industrial Development Organisation. It is an international agency of communication. It communicates messages related to promotion of industrialization in developing countries.

### *UNFPA*

Its full form is United Nations Fund for Population Activities. It is an international agency of communication. It communicates messages related to promotion of population programmes and sustainable population assistance to developing countries. It also sends messages dealing with population problems.

### *ADB*

Its full form is Asian Development Bank. It is an international agency of communication. It communicates messages related to lending funds, promoting investment and providing technical assistance to Asian and Pacific region countries.

**United Nations Environmental Programme (UNEP)**

This is also an international agency of communication. It communicates messages related to conservation of soil, water, air, and forest. It also sends messages related to sustainable development. It also communicates messages related to green house effect.

# 10

# Media of Communication

Media are those news agencies, which act as mediators of different kinds of news among people at one hand and the Government on the other hand. Media are regarded as fourth pillar of democracy. The other three pillars are executive, legislative and judiciary. Thus, media occupy very significant place in democracy. They are news providers. They communicate news to public, Government and people living in different parts of the country and the globe. Media communicate news to the public daily. They cover such aspects as welfare programmes, development programmes, functioning of the Government, election processes, election campaign, election rally, *Dharana*, *Pradarshan*, flood, earth-quakes, drought, starvation, social pathological problems, public opinions, storms, fire, epidemic, games, sports, cinemas, education, examination, employment, unemployment, entertainment, business, trade, market, exchange value, crime, family welfare and so on. In fact, they attempt to cover almost all aspects of our society and day-to-day events. Thus, media and communication are interdependent, interrelated and maintain their co-existence. Media have their own news reporters. The news reporters visit different places, meet with the people and collect news. They send news to the editor for announcement or publication. Different organizations also prepare news related to their special activities and communicate them to media for proper coverage. Media are of different types. Main types of media are as follows :

- Oral media
- Press media
- Print media
- Electronic media
- Satellite media

- Social media

These media may broadly be divided in to two categories:

- Folk media
- Mass media

***Folk Media***

Folk media are those media, which act as news providers in folk societies. Folk society is such a society which is small in size, members have face-to-face relation, members know each other by name, face and place. Illiteracy, magic and religion prevail. Their technology is very simple, and there is very simple specialisation of labour. In these societies, means of communication is very simple. As these societies have oral traditions, that is why they have oral media. Oral media is also known as folk media. Folk society has its own news reporters and news communicators. News reporters are members of their own community and the news communicators are also members of own community. They use different kinds of symbols and codes for the purpose of communication. They do not have developed means of communication. But they use their own means of communication.

***Types of Folk Media***

Folk media may be divided in to two types which are as follows:

- Traditional folk media
- Modern folk media

***Traditional Folk Media***

The traditional folk media are of following types:

- Family head
- Village head
- Village Panchayat
- Village Priest
- Village Magician

- Village Medicine man
- Inter village Panchayat
- Inter village Panchayat head
- Caste Panchayat
- Village Chaukidar (watchman)
- Dhumkhuria (Youth Organisation)
- Festival organising committee
- Fair organising committee
- Folk dance performers
- Folk dramatist
- Folk poets
- Folk story tellers
- Folk song singers
- Folk musicians
- Folk barker
- Folk washerman
- Folk carpenter
- Folk black smith
- Folk potters
- Folk sweet makers
- Folk cloth weavers
- Animal dance performers
- Cock fight organiser
- Sheep fight organiser
- Goat fight organiser
- Bull fight organiser
- Folk mason
- *Chaiti* Dance (*Nach*) organiser
- Folk *Kirtan-Bhajan* organiser
- Holi song organiser
- Folk shopkeeper and middle man
- Folk *Haat-bazar*
- Folk sports competition
- Folk delivery expert
- Puppet show organiser
- Folk cattle medicineman
- Folk leaders
- Cultural programme organising committee

Now, net us discuss about these traditional folk media one by one.

### *Family Head*

Family head acts as media of communication. He/she communicates family level news to the other families living in neighbourhood, village community and among relatives living in different villages. He/she acts as family level news provider for members of the society. He/she communicates news orally.

### *Village Head*

In tribal villages, there is traditional post of village head. The village head acts as media for the members of tribal villages. He communicates different types of news among community members. He communicates news related to venue and date of meeting of village Panchayat. For communicating news orally, he takes help of his assistant. His assistant moves door to door to convey messages on behalf of the head. The village head acts as media for the whole village in inter village panchayat meeting.

### *Village Panchayat*

The Village Panchayat also acts as media of communication. In this Panchayat, all family heads living in the village take part. They sit together, discuss together and reach at consensual decision. The news of consensual decision is communicated by the head to all members of the community.

### *Village Priest*

Village priest also performs functions as media for members of community. He communicates messages and news to members related to time, day and date of village level worship and sacrifice on festive occasions.

### *Village Magician*

The village magician also acts as media for the members of village community. He performs white magic for good harvest, control of epidemic and cattle diseases. He communicates news related to day, time and date of magical performances.

### *Village Medicine man*

The village medicine man also performs functions as media for members of village community. He communicates messages to members regarding diseases and their cure by herbal medicine.

### *Inter Village Panchayat*

In tribal villages, inter village panchayat is found. This panchayat functions as media for members of inter village panchayat. It communicates news about the meeting of inter village panchayat and its agenda.

### *Inter village Panchayat Head*

Inter village panchayat head officiates the meeting of inter village panchayat. He communicates the day, date and time of meeting of inter village panchayat to all members with the help of his assistant.

### *Caste Panchayat*

In villages, caste panchayat functions as media for members of village community. The caste panchayat officials send news related to day, date, time and agenda of caste Panchayat meeting to all members of caste community.

### *Village Chaukidar (Watchman)*

The village watchman functions as media for members of village community. He communicates news related to thefty, dacoity, rape, loot, fire, epidemic in and around villages.

### *Youth Organisation*

In tribal villages, youth organisation is known as *Dhumkhuria, Gitiora* and a number of local names. This youth organisation functions as media for members of community. It communicates news related to family life, traditions, customs, music, dance, archery and sports among youth of the village.

### *Festival Organising Committee*

In folk society, there is organisation for organising festivals. This organisation functions as media for folk society. Its organisers communicate news regarding day, date, time and programme to be organised on the occasion of festivals among members of community.

### *Fair Organising Committee*

In folk society, fairs are organised on different occasions. For this purpose there is fair organising committee. The members of the committee communicate messages related to day, date and time of occurring of fairs and programmes to be organised on this occasion. Thus Committee functions as media for the members of folk committees.

### *Folk Dance Performer*

In folk society, there are folk dance performers. They perform individual dance and group dance. The folk dance performers function as media for members of folk society. They communicate news related to the day, date, time, place and programme of performing dance among members of folk communities.

### *Folk Dramatist*

There are folk dramatists in folk society. They function as media of folk society. They communicate news regarding day, date, time, place and programme of folk drama among members of folk community.

### *Folk Poet*

There are a number of folk poets in folk society. They create folk poetry and sing them on social, cultural, religious and political occasions. They act as media of communication among folk society. They communicate social, cultural, religious, political, educational and health related news among members of folk community through their poetries.

### *Folk Story Tellers*

There are folk story tellers. They tell different types of tales among members of folk society. They act as media in folk society. They communicate myths, legends, ferry tales, king tales, witch tales, deity tales, and so on through their story telling.

### Folk Song Singers

There are folk song singers in folk society. They communicate messages related to social, cultural and religious songs by singing them individually or in group. They act as media of communication in folk society.

### Folk Musicians

There are a number of folk musicians in folk society. They play musical instruments like Dholak, Jhal, Kartal, flute, whistle, harmonium and so on. They act as media of communication in folk society. They communicate message and news among members of folk community regarding playing of musical instruments on different occasions in the society.

### Folk Barber

For saving, hair cutting and nail cutting there are barbers in folk society. They move door to door and village to village for their work. They act as folk media. They communicate news of different families and different villages.

### Folk Washerman

There are washermen in folk society. They do the work of cleaning clothes of delivery, death, diseases and general dresses. They move village to village and door to door for this purpose. They work as folk media of communication. They communicate news of different villages and of different families.

### Folk Carpenter

In folk society, there are some families of carpenter. They work as folk media of communication. As they move from family to family and village to village for doing carpentry, they have several news of different villages and families. They communicate news of one village to another villages.

### *Folk Blacksmith*

In folk society, there are some families of blacksmith. They prepare iron tools with the help of their folk technology. People of different villages visit at the workshop of blacksmith for giving order of supply. When the iron tools are ready, blacksmith supplies them to the people. The folk blacksmith functions as folk media of communication. It is because people of different villages visit of his house and he also visits different families of different villages so he has a huge collection of news of different families and villages.

### *Folk Potters*

In folk society, there are some families of folk potteres. They prepare potteries of different types and sizes. People of different villages visit at his house for the supply of potteries on different occasion. He functions as folk media of communication. It is because he has huge collection of news of different families and different villages.

### *Folk Sweet Makers*

In folk society, there are some families of sweet makers. They prepare folk sweets and sell them in their own shop. They have contacts with families of different villages. It is because people of different villages come there to purchase sweets daily. They have huge storage of news of different villages. They share those news with different people. Thus, they function as folk media of communication.

### *Folk Cloth weavers*

In folk society, there are folk cloth weavers. They have contacts with people of different villages who come at his house to purchase clothes. As they meet people of different families and villages, they have collection of varieties of news. They share those news with people of different villages. Thus, they act as news providers. They function as folk media of communication.

### *Folk Animal dance performers*

In folk society, there are some animal dance performers. They have animals whom they train in performing dances. They are known as

*Bhaluwala*, *Bandarwala* and snake charmer. These animal dance performers move from village to village to show animal dances and earn in cash or in kind. As they move from one village to another, they function as folk media of communication. They communicate news related to entertainment by animal dances.

***Cock fight Organiser***

In folk *haat-bazaar*, there are cock fight organisers. They act as folk media of communication. They communicate news related to cock fight on market day. People visit with their trained cocks to take part in cock fight competition. Visitors also pay a visit to see the cock fight competition. Thus, cock fight organisers play the role of folk media of communication.

***Sheep fight Organiser***

In folk *haat-bazaar*, there are sheep fight organisers. They organise sheep fight competition. For this purpose, they act as folk media. They communicate news of sheep fight competition in neighbouring villages on the market day. People come in the market with their sheep to take part in competition. Visitors also pay a visit to take part in the competition.

***Goat fight Organiser***

In folk *haat-bazaar*, there are goat fight organisers. They organise goat fight competition. For this purpose they act as folk media. They communicate news of goat fight competition in neighbouring villages. People come with their goat to take part in competition. Visitors of different villages also pay a visit to see the goat fight competition.

***Bull fight organiser***

In folk haat bazaar, there are bull fight organisers. They organise bull fight competition. For this purpose, they act as folk media. They communicate news related to bull fight competition in neighbouring villages. The people come with their bull to take part in bull fight competition. Visitors also pay a visit to see the bull fight competition.

### *Folk mason*

In folk society, there are some people who do the work of mason. They play significant role in construction of houses in folk society. For this purpose, they move from village to village. As they work in different villages, they have huge collection of news. They share those news with people on different occasions.

### *Chaiti Dance (Nach) Organiser*

In villages, there are people who organise *Chaiti Nach* (dance). They organise a *Chaiti* dance competition between different groups. They fix the day, date and time of *Chaiti* dance competition. For this purpose, they act as folk media of communication. They communicate news related to *Chaiti* dance competition in neighbouring villages. People of different villages come to take part in the competition. People also pay visit to see the dance competition.

### *Folk Kirtan-Bhajan Organiser*

In folk society, there are some persons who organise *kirtan-bhajan* competition. For this purpose, they act as folk media. They communicate news of *kirtan-bhajan* competition. They invite people of different villages to take part in *kirtan-bhajan* competition. The competition continues for the whole night or whole day.

### *Holi song Organiser*

In folk society, there are some persons who organise *Holi* song competition in the month of *Holi*. For this purpose they act as media in folk society. They provide news related to day, date, a time and venue of *Holi* song competition among the people of neighbouring villages. Hearing such news, people come to take part in *Holi* song competition and to see the competition.

### *Folk shop keepers and middleman*

In folk society, there are some shopkeeper and middle man who are engaged in buying and selling of goods and commodities. They act as folk media. They communicate different types of news in local villages.

***Folk Haat-bazaar***

In folk society, *Haat-bazaar* takes place in one or two days in a week. In *Haat-bazaar*, buyers and sellers of neighbouring villages assemble at a place. They share news of different kinds. Thus, folk *Haat-bazaar* acts as a folk media of communication.

***Folk Sports Competition***

In folk society, a competition of folk sports is held. The folk sports competition organisers organise play of *Lathi, Bhala, Gadaka, Mugadar* and so on. They act as folk media of communication. They communicate news related to folk sports competition in neighbouring villages. People of neighbouring villages assemble at a place to participate in competition of folk sports.

***Folk delivery expert***

In folk society, there are some women who are regarded as folk delivery expert. They are known as *dagarin, chamain* and *kusarain.* They act as folk media of communication. They communicate news related to successful or unsuccessful delivery.

***Puppet show Organiser***

In folk society, puppet show is organised in fair. The puppet show organiser acts as folk media of communication. They communicate news related to puppet show in neighbouring villages. The people from neighbouring villages assemble to see puppet show.

***Folk Cattle medicine man***

In folk society, there are some persons expert in cattle diseases and medicine. They act as folk media of communication. They communicate news related to cattle diseases and their treatment.

***Folk leaders***

In folk society, there are some persons who act as leaders. They guide community members on different occasions and in different situations. They are regarded by all members of the community.

occasion of great festivals and gathering of people. The committee looks after travel, drinking water, health crime control. The committee acts as modern folk media of communication.

***Fair Management Committee***

In our country great fairs are organised on different religious occasions. In order to look after fair, fair management committee is established. This committee provides management of travel, accommodation, drinking water, health, food, commodities and other basic facilities of visitors. It also has eyes on crime doers. This committee also acts as modern folk media of communication.

***Election Campaign***

We have democratic country. We have democratic Government. In democracy we have been given voting right to choose the political parties to run the Government. In democracy, elections are held for M.P., MLA, Panchayat, and other local self-Governing bodies. The election campaign takes place. The election campaign follows rallies, meeting, slogan shouting, canvassing, door to door visit, poster stiching and so on. The election campaign acts as folk media of communication. It communicates several news to folk people regarding candidate, political party, leaders, symbols, voting rights, voters and others.

***Door to door canvassing***

Door to door canvassing also acts as modern folk media of communication. At the time of election, candidates and leaders visit door to door in villages. They meet each adult members of the village and ask to vote for them. Door-to-door meeting conveys a number of news among folk communities. The members of folk communities see their leaders with own eyes and hear them with own ears. This has great influence on election.

***Political Rallies***

Now-a-days, political rallies are organised by different political parties to show their strength among public. The rally organisers visit in villages and provide news related to the purpose of organizing rally. They also provide news regarding free travel, free accommodation, free food and

***Folk Haat-bazaar***

In folk society, *Haat-bazaar* takes place in one or two days in a week. In *Haat-bazaar*, buyers and sellers of neighbouring villages assemble at a place. They share news of different kinds. Thus, folk *Haat-bazaar* acts as a folk media of communication.

***Folk Sports Competition***

In folk society, a competition of folk sports is held. The folk sports competition organisers organise play of *Lathi, Bhala, Gadaka, Mugadar* and so on. They act as folk media of communication. They communicate news related to folk sports competition in neighbouring villages. People of neighbouring villages assemble at a place to participate in competition of folk sports.

***Folk delivery expert***

In folk society, there are some women who are regarded as folk delivery expert. They are known as *dagarin, chamain* and *kusarain.* They act as folk media of communication. They communicate news related to successful or unsuccessful delivery.

***Puppet show Organiser***

In folk society, puppet show is organised in fair. The puppet show organiser acts as folk media of communication. They communicate news related to puppet show in neighbouring villages. The people from neighbouring villages assemble to see puppet show.

***Folk Cattle medicine man***

In folk society, there are some persons expert in cattle diseases and medicine. They act as folk media of communication. They communicate news related to cattle diseases and their treatment.

***Folk leaders***

In folk society, there are some persons who act as leaders. They guide community members on different occasions and in different situations. They are regarded by all members of the community.

***Cultural Programme Organising Committee***

In folk society, there is a cultural programme organising committee. This committee organises cultural programme like song, dance, play, sports, drama on different occasions. They also lead cultural procession. It acts as folk media of communication. It communicates news of cultural programmes.

## Modern Folk Media

Now-a-days, modern media have also come in to existence in folk society. They are known as modern folk media. The modern folk media are of following types:

- Gram Panchayat
- Gram Sabha
- Gram Panchayat Mukhia
- Gram Panchayat officials
- School and school teachers
- Health Sub-centre and its Staff
- Anganwadi Kendra and its Staff
- Folk elite
- Folk leader
- Thana-police
- Block officials
- Festival management committee
- Fair management committee
- Election campaign
- Door to door canvasing
- Political rallies
- *Dharana-Pradarshan*
- *Band* and *Gherao*
- Morning prayers
- Light procession (*Mashal Julus*)
- Candle march
- Slogan shouting
- Announcement by loud speaker
- Wall writing
- Poster stiching

- Political meeting
- Development meeting
- Development fair (*Vikas mela*)
- Awareness campaign
- Visual show
- Cartoon show
- Voluntary organizations
- Non-Governmental organisations
- Local Radio

Now, let us discuss about these modern folk media of communication one by one.

### Gram Panchayat

Gram panchayat is a modern folk media of communication. It communicates the news of local self-government among folk people. All village development programmes are formulated and implemented through Gram Panchayat. Thus, it is most important modern media of communication. It is elected body. At the time of Panchayat election, the role of folk media becomes very significant. One finds the existence of door to door canvasing, announcement by loud speaker, meeting with people, slogan shouting, poster stiching, pamphlets distribution, rallies and picture show. These folk media communicate news of Panchayat election.

### Gram Sabha

*Gram sabha* is also a modern folk media of communication. It communicates news related to day, date, time and agenda of *Gram sabha*. In this *sabha,* all adult members participate. They discuss development and welfare matters in this meeting.

### Mukhia

The *Mukhia* is chairman of the Gram Panchayat. He/she officiates Panchayat meeting and village assembly meeting. He/she acts as modern folk media of communication. *Mukhia* communicates news related to village development and welfare programmes among the people of the Panchayat.

### *Gram Panchayat Official*

The Gram Panchayat has Panchayat officials like Panchayat Sewak and Panchayat mitra. They communicate news of development and welfare. They extend help to public in solving their problems. They are connecting link between Panchayat and the people. They play significant role as modern folk media.

### *School and School teacher*

The school and school teacher also function as modern folk media of communication. The school and school teacher communicate news related to enrolment of children for study, regular attendance, reading and writing materials, dresses, mid-day-meal scheme, hostel facility, syllabus, examination and class promotion. The school and teacher also communicate messages related to good habit, character building, good food, good health and sanitation. The school located in folk areas and teacher posted there work as folk modern media of communication.

### *Health Sub-centre and its Staff*

In folk areas, our Government has established health sub-centre. Health staff like compounder, nurse and health servant are posted there. Doctor also pays a visit there time to time. The health sub-centre and its staff function there as modern folk media. They communicate news related to modern concept of health, disease and treatment. They make health survey of each individual and try to find out diseases. They suggest them to visit centre and cure diseases with the help of modern medicine suggested by expert doctor. They have communicated news towards safe delivery, proper nourishment during pregnancy and lactation, control of pre-natel and neo-natal death, child mortality and mother mortality. With their help, folk people have come to know new concept of leprosy, Cholera, pox, diarrhoea, T.B., AIDS and cancer.

### *Anganwadi Kendra and its Staff*

In order to improve the health status of pregnant wonan, safe delivery, lactating women and infants and children, our Government has established Anganwadi Kendra. The Anganwadi Kendra has staff to monitor the health condition of pregnant women, lactating mother, infants and children. They do regular health check-up and provide medicine as per requirement. In serious condition, they suggest to visit health sub-centre, health centre, community health centre, referral hospital or Sadar hospital. Thus, Anganwadi Kendra and its staff function as modern folk media. They communicate a number of health news to the folk people. They have brought positive change towards folk health.

### *Folk Elite*

Now-a-days, some educated persons are found in folk society. They are known as folk elite. They communicate a number of news to members of the community. Their news provide members a knowledge base. The members regard them very much. The folk elites guide the people in several situations.

### *Folk Leader*

Due to democratic process, leaders have also come in to existence in folk society. They have contacts with MLA, M.P., *Mukhia*, Thana-police, B.D.O. and other at local levels. Some of them are also *Mukhia* and ward member. These folk leaders work as modern folk media of communication. They communicate various types of news and knowledge to community members.

### *Thana-Police*

Our Government has established Thana Police in folk areas from the point of view of administration. Thana-police have officials, police *mitra* and *chaukidar*. The police personnel acts as modern folk media of communication. They communicate news related to maintenance of law and order and control over crime.

### *Block officials*

Our Government has establishment blocks for implementing village development and welfare plans. Block officials like B.D.O., C.O., VLW, land revenue collectors visit from village to village and make people aware towards development and welfare programmes. They act as modern folk media of communication.

### *Festival Management Committee*

Our Government establishes festival management committee on the occasion of great festivals and gathering of people. The committee looks after travel, drinking water, health crime control. The committee acts as modern folk media of communication.

### *Fair Management Committee*

In our country great fairs are organised on different religious occasions. In order to look after fair, fair management committee is established. This committee provides management of travel, accommodation, drinking water, health, food, commodities and other basic facilities of visitors. It also has eyes on crime doers. This committee also acts as modern folk media of communication.

### *Election Campaign*

We have democratic country. We have democratic Government. In democracy we have been given voting right to choose the political parties to run the Government. In democracy, elections are held for M.P., MLA, Panchayat, and other local self-Governing bodies. The election campaign takes place. The election campaign follows rallies, meeting, slogan shouting, canvassing, door to door visit, poster stiching and so on. The election campaign acts as folk media of communication. It communicates several news to folk people regarding candidate, political party, leaders, symbols, voting rights, voters and others.

### *Door to door canvassing*

Door to door canvassing also acts as modern folk media of communication. At the time of election, candidates and leaders visit door to door in villages. They meet each adult members of the village and ask to vote for them. Door-to-door meeting conveys a number of news among folk communities. The members of folk communities see their leaders with own eyes and hear them with own ears. This has great influence on election.

### *Political Rallies*

Now-a-days, political rallies are organised by different political parties to show their strength among public. The rally organisers visit in villages and provide news related to the purpose of organizing rally. They also provide news regarding free travel, free accommodation, free food and

### *Development Meeting*

Now-a-days, block officials are organising development related meeting with folk people as a part of Government in the village programme. They act as modern folk media of communication. This meeting communicates messages related to development and welfare programmes among the folk people.

### *Vikas Mela (Development Fair)*

Now-a-days, Government officials are organising *Vikas Mela* in local *haat-bazaar* in which assets are distributed among the beneficiaries selected under development and welfare programmes. *Vikas mela* works as modern folk media of communication. This also communicates corruption free messages related to asset distribution among the people.

### *Awareness Campaign*

Now-a-days, awareness campaigns are being organised by Governmental and Non-Governmental agencies towards health, education, environment, sanitation and others. These campaigns work as modern folk media of communication. They communicate news related to awareness of different kinds—social, political, cultural, health, sanitation, poverty alleviation and environment.

### *Visual Show*

Visual shows related to family welfare, family planning method, health, sanitation, social problems, economic awareness and a number of social-cultural events also function as modern folk media of communication. They send a number of positive news among the people.

### *Cartoon Show*

Cartoon shows also act as a modern folk media of communication. Cartoon visual shows are organised in villages to communicate significant news among the folk people.

### *Voluntary Organisations*

Now-a-days, a number of voluntary organisations have come in to existence which function as modern folk media of communication. They organise awareness campaign, slogan shouting, wall writing, morning prayer and door to door canvassing. Thus, they are very much useful in communicating significant news among the people.

### *Non-Governmental Organisations*

Now-a-days, a number of Non-Governmental Organisation have come in to existence which are functioning for the upliftment and betterment of the people. They are functioning as modern folk media of communication. They communicate a number of development, welfare and awareness related news among the people.

### *Local Radio*

Now-a-days, a number of local radios have come in to existence which function as modern folk media of communication. There are programmes for folk people in local languages. The local radios communicate a number of news among folk people.

### *Mass Media*

Mass media are those news agencies which use developed technology for communication to masses. As they communicate news to masses with the help of developed technology, they are known as mass media. Mass media may be divided in to following types:

- Press media
- Print media
- Electronic media
- Satellite media
- Social media

### *Press Media*

Press media are very popular mass media in all countries of the world. They convey written messages to the masses on different issues. People wait press media eagerly along with morning tea. Newspaper vendors start moving door to door for supplying news papers in each houses. But press media are popular only among literate masses. Illiterate masses are totally dependent on oral media. They are not dependent on written media. The important press media are as follows:

- Daily Newpapers
- Weekly Newspapers
- Monthly Newspapers
- Employment Newspaper
- News letters/News bulletin
- Magazine and Journals
- Books and Booklets
- Papers/Articles
- Pamphlet/poster
- Brochure/syllabus
- Agenda and Minutes of Meeting
- Written speech
- Reports

Now, let us discuss about these press media one by one.

### *Daily Newspapers*

Daily newspapers are most popular press media in masses. Newspapers are published daily. They are published in local, regional, national and international languages. The newspapers are published in morning and evening. There is morning and evening edition of some newspapers. The newspaper agency has chief editor, deputy editor, assistant editor, chief manager, manager, news reporters, printing press and its workers. They work day and night to supply published news to masses. In our country newspapers are published in English, Hindi, regional and local languages.

### *Weekly Newspapers*

Some newspapers are published weekly. They consist of news covering the entire week. For example illustrated weekly, employment news and so one. Weekly newspapers are published media of communication. These media communicate news with the help of press and its workers.

*Monthly Newspapers*

Some newspapers are published once in a month. They are known as monthly news papers. They consist of important news covering the whole month. They have their own news readers. For example: employment news.

*Employment Newspaper*

This a monthly news paper which covers employment news of Central and State Governments. It communicates employment related news. Service seekers wait eagerly for it.

*News letters/News bulletin*

Different Governmental institutions publish their news letters or news bulletin. For example universities, health department, education department, medicine department, surgery department, law department, sports department, art and craft department and so on. The news letters or bulletin consists of news of the concerned departments.

*Magazines and Journals*

Magazines and Journals are press or published media of mass communication. Magazines and Journals are published by different departments, such as health, education, law, medicine, sports, culture, arts, communication, railway, finance, law, and others. The magazines and journals consist of news related to their departments concerned. They are regarded as valuable reliable source of communication. They are published or press media of communication.

*Books and Booklets*

Books and booklets are regarded as published media of communication. They consist of huge informations on the topic concerned. Books and booklets are preserved for future source of knowledge. There are a number of book publisher in our country. They publish books of different authors on different title. They are published in English, Hindi, regional and local languages to cater the needs of different readers.

*Papers/Articles*

A number of experts, professional and academicians publish their research or experience based papers/articles. They work as press media of mass communication. Papers/articles are published in Journals and edited books. They work as a source of knowledge not only for the readers of present generation, but also for the readers of future generation.

*Pamphlets/posters*

Pamphlets/posters also function as press media of mass communication. They are published source of information. They consist of different kind of news. People see and understand the news contained in posters and pamphlets.

*Brochure/prospectus*

Different educational institutions publish their brochure and prospectus containing specialities, admission process, examination and promotion, fee structure, hostel facilities, administration and so on. They are published source of information for admission seeker and parents. They work as press media of mass communication.

*Agenda and Minutes of meeting*

A number of organisations get published the agenda and minutes of the meeting held on different occasion. They work as published media of communication.

*Written speech*

A number of leaders, academicians and professionals get their speech published for mass communication. Thus, published speech work as mass media of communication.

*Reports*

A number of Governmental and Non-Governmental institutions get their annual reports and research reports published. They are circulated in different libraries and archieves. They work as press media of communication.

### *Print Media*

Now-a-days, we have a number of print media which act as an agency of communications. They are as follows:

- Photography
- Maps
- Chart
- Tables
- Invitation card
- Visiting card
- Price list
- Cartoons
- Diagrams
- Cover pages
- Name plate
- Vehicle No.
- Registration No.
- Forms
- Biodata
- Autobiography
- Playing cards
- Ludo
- Carom
- Puppet show
- Family planning symbols
- Railway crossing symbols
- Petrol pump symbols
- Hospital symbols
- Prohibited area symbols
- Drinking water symbols
- Tour and travel

#### *Photography*

This is very famous print media of communication. The media persons take photography of different occasions and of different places and publish them in daily newspapers for communicating to the masses. Now-a-days, photography has become very easy with the help of mobile phones. Phones have camera which can print photographs of persons, places and things anywhere and can be communicated to relatives, friends and others at any place in the world with mobile phones having internet facilities. Photography is very popular print media of communication.

*Maps*

Maps are also a print media of communication. Each country, each state, each town, each city, each metropolise, and each village has its own map. Maps are helpful in locating places and areas. Maps are also shown in different media to describe facts and figures.

*Chart*

Charts are also print media of communication. Different features are shown on charts while dealing with a problems. Charts are also found in press media to describe facts.

*Tables*

Tables are also print visual media of communication. Tables are printed and shown in reports, thesis, dissertation and books. Tables make presentation clear.

*Invitation card*

Invitations are also print media of communication. Innovation cards are printed and served to friends, relatives and well wishers to participate in different types of functions such as birth, marriage, inauguration, house worship and other occasions.

*Visiting card*

Different professionals have their visiting cards. They use it is as a medium to meet different authorities, officials, and professionals. Thus, visiting cards act as a print media of communication.

*Price list*

In different markets, malls and big shops, whole sale and retail price list of commodities to be sold is displaced. It works as print media of communication.

*Maximum retail price*

Maximum retail price is printed on the cover of medicine, branded clothes and other big shops. MRP (maximum retail price) works as print media of communication.

*Cartoons*

Cartoons also work as print media of communication. Cartoons showing different characters of society and political leaders are displayed through press and print media. Cartoons convey satirical messages to the people.

*Diagrams*

Diagrams also function as print media of communication. Diagrams of Gods, spirits, natural scenes, scenery are printed and displayed for conveying messages to the people.

*Cover pages*

Cover pages are print media of communication. Books, Journals, thesis, dissertation, research reports have cover pages. The cover page functions as print media of communication. They have attractive beautiful designs.

*Name plate*

Doctors, Engineers, professors, directors, D.C., D.M. and a number of authorities have their name plates on the entrance gate of house. The name plates are printed. They act as print media of communication.

*Vehicle Number*

Each vehicle has a number which is printed. This vehicle number acts as print media of communication. It communicates about the state and ownership of the vehicle.

*Registration Number*

Registration numbers of vehicles, examinees, and other candidates appearing for interview play significant role as print media of communication.

*Forms*

Examination forms and other kinds of forms act as print media of communication. They communicate messages required for the purpose of admission, registration, loan, treatment and others.

*Biodata*

Biodata of candidates work as print media of communication. Biodata is required along with application forms for suitable posts.

*Autobiography*

Autobiography is also a print media of communication. Some people write their auto-biography and get them published. Some researchers also write autobiography of eminent persons on the basis of their researches.

*Playing cards*

Playing cards also function as print media of communication. They communicate symbols of card and play rules.

*Ludo*

Ludo is also a print play media of communication. They symbols and rules of play are printed on board. The players follow the rules printed over the card.

*Carom*

Carom is also a print play media of communication. Its rules of play are printed over the board. The players play the games following rules printed over the board.

*Puppet show*

Puppet show is also a print play media of communication. Printed puppet show is displayed on screen for entertainment.

*Family Planning symbols*

Family planning symbols are printed for displaying to the masses. They are stiched on walls here and there. They are also distributed as pamphlets. The printed family planning symbols work as printed media of communication.

*Railway Crossing symbols*

Railway crossing symbols are displaced at the place of railway crossing. They convey printed messages to stop, watch and move after seeing properly. They act as print media.

*Petrol Pump symbols*

Petrol pump symbols are printed and displaced here and there on road to convey messages of location and direction of petrol pumps for vehicle drivers.

*Hospital symbols*

Printed hospital symbols are displayed on road which communicate messages regarding distance, direction and location of hospitals for the public.

*Hotel symbols*

Printed hotel, restaurant, lodge symbols are displaced throughout the length of road to communicate messages related to location and distance of hotels, restaurants and lodges where guest can get hospitality of food and accommodation.

*Prohibited area symbol*

In some cities and towns, there are some prohibited areas where common people do not get entry. The printed prohibited area symbols are displayed to communicate messages of no entry zone of the town or city.

*Water source symbols*

Symbols of water sources like tap, tank, river, chapakal, boring, wells are printed and displaced to convey messages to the people regarding availability of water sources.

### *Tour and Travel Symbols*

Tour and travel symbols of different places of pilgrimage are printed and displaced to communicate news to visitors and others. They work as print media of communication.

- Railway station symbol
- Bus stand symbols
- Bus stoppage symbols
- Speed limit symbols
- Accident prone area symbol
- Zoo symbols
- National park symbols
- Place direction symbols
- Train time table
- Aerodrum symbols
- Trade and business symbols

Now, let us discuss about these each print media of mass communication one by one.

*Railway station symbols*

Railway station symbols are printed and displayed to communicate messages to the people regarding ticket window, train name, platform name and others. They convey messages for the public.

*Busstand symbols*

Printed busstand symbols are displayed on roads near busstand. They act as print media of communication.

*Bus stoppage symbols*

Printed bus stand symbols are also displayed here and there. They convey messages related to stoppage. They act as print media of communication.

*Speed limit symbols*

Speed limit symbols are printed and displayed near bridges on roads. The vehicle drivers have to follow those rules, while they drive vehicle. Speed limit symbols act as print media of communication.

*Accident Prone area Symbols*

On surface roads, some areas are identified as accident prone due to nature of roads. In those areas, accident symbols are displayed. These symbols are printed. They act as print media of communication.

*Zoo symbols*

Zoo symbols are printed and displayed nearby the zoo area. These symbols convey messages related to existence of zoo. The zoo visitors follow those symbols and visit the zoo to enjoy with birds, animals, snakes, swimming pool, steamer etc.

*National park symbols*

Printed symbols of national park are displayed near the area on road. These symbols convey messages related to existence of national park.

*Place direction symbols*

On road crossing places called chalk printed symbols of directions of different places are displayed. They convey messages to vehicle driver about the direction of places.

*Train Time Table*

On railway station, printed time table and fares of different places are displayed. They convey meaningful messages to the passengers.

*Aerodrum symbols*

Aerodrum symbols are displayed on roads near by the aerodrum. They convey messages related to direction of aerodrum.

*Flight time table*

The time table of different flight are displayed at aerodrum. They are in printed form. They convey messages regarding arrival and departure of flights to air passengers.

*Trade and business symbols*

Each big business man or corporate house has its own brand symbol. The printed brand symbols are displayed on packets of different products. They convey messages and assure quality of different products.

***Electronic Media***

Now-a-days, we have a number of electronic media. They convey significant messages electronically. They act as electronic media of communication. They convey significant messages to masses with the help of electronic technology. The chief electronic media are as follows:

- Radio
- Cinema
- Computer
- Internet
- Electronic message
- Electronic name plate
- Electronic train time table
- Electronic display of train and platform
- Electronic display of station name
- Electronic display of hospitals
- Electronic display of medicine shops
- Electronic display of cricket match result
- Electronic voting machine
- Electronic display of election result
- Electronic display of hotels
- Electronic display of malls & market centres
- Electronic Display of Ramleela
- Electronic display of Mahabharata
- Electronic display of cartoons
- Electronic display of visual arts
- Electronic display of puppet show
- Electronic display of news

- Electronic print
- Electronic display of photographs
- Voice recording
- Electronic recording of views and news
- Electronic recording of cultural programmes
- Videography of marriage rituals
- Videography of Lok Sabha and Rajya Sabha proceeding
- Videography of assembly proceeding
- Videography of meeting
- Videography of conferences, seminars and workshops
- Electronic display of worship of different places.
- CCTV camera recording

Now, let us discuss about these electronic media of communication one by one.

*Radio*

Among all electronic media radio is very popular among masses even to-day. Now-a-days, radio is available in car and cell phones. In folk areas radio programmes of local nature is heard with great eager. Choupal programme is very popular. Similarly, war news, election results, earth quake, flood, epidemic starvation, Government related news and sports news are heard and discussed among the masses.

*Cinema*

Cinema is also a very popular mass media of communication. Cinema is shown in cinema halls. In fact, cinema is audio-visual media of communication. Cinema consists of social, cultural, economic, political, religious, pathological, war, business and foreign related news. Such news are conveyed through entertainment. People visit cinema hall for entertainment. They entertain themselves with moving pictures, scenes, scenary, song, dance, tragedy and comedy stories.

*Computer*

Computer is also a very popular electronic media of communication. It communicates news, entertainment and news related to different areas of society, culture, nation and foreign countries. The computer may be desktop, laptop, handset and others. But they are very useful electronic media of communication.

*Internet*

Now-a-days, internet is very useful and popular electronic media of communication. With the invention of WWW internet has brought communication revolution. It is because with the help of internet facility in computer, phones and cell phones, people have been connected to entire world. Now, distance is not a distance and place is not far off. Rather, they are in handset.

*Electronic messages*

Now-a-days, electronic messages are conveyed on mobiles by different companies, professionals and friends. Thus, cell phones act as electronic media of communication.

*Electronic name plate*

Now-a-days, electronic name plates are available. They display name of house owner and locality in the form of appearing and disappearing message.

*Electronic Train time table*

Now-a-days, train time table is displayed electronically on each railway stations. It acts as electronic media of communication.

*Electronic Train name and Platform number*

Now-a-days, train name, number and the platform number on which it will arrive are displayed electronically here and there on station and platform. They act as electronic media of communication.

*Electronic display of station name*

Now-a-days, name of each railway station is displayed electronically to the people. This acts as electronic media of communication.

*Electronic display of Hospital*

Now-a-days, name and different departments of a hospital are displayed electronically to convey messages to the people.

*Electronic display of medicine store and shop*

Now-a-days, name of different medical stores and shops are displayed electronically to convey messages to the people with the help of electronic media.

*Electronic display of cricket match and result*

Now-a-days, cricket matches and results are displayed electronically on T.Vs. and screens out side stadium.

*Electronic voting machine*

Now-a-days, we have invented electronic voting machines which convey messages related to candidates and their election symbols. The voters see name and election symbols of the candidate on voting machine and press the button to cast their votes in favour of a candidate.

*Electronic election result*

The election results are also displayed electronically on counting stations and in T.V. It conveys messages quickly to the people.

*Electronic display of hotel*

Now-a-days, names and facility available in a 3 stars, 5 stars or general hotels are displayed electronically on screen out side the hotels. They act as electronic media of communication.

*Electronic display of malls and market centres*

Now-a-days, there are a number of malls and big market centres. Their names and facilities are displayed electronically on each storey and out side walls of the shops.

*Electronic display of Ram Leela*

Now-a-days, *Ramayana* or *Ram Leela* is displayed electronically on screens, which acts as electronic media of communication.

*Electronic display of Mahabharata*

Now-a-days, stories of *Mahabharata* are displayed on screen electronically. They act as electronic media of communication.

*Electronic display of cartoons*

Now-a-days, different cartoons are displayed on screens. They act as electronic media of communication.

*Electronic display of Arts*

Now-a-days, different visual arts are displayed electronically. They act as electronic media of communication.

*Electronic display of Puppet show*

Now-a-days, a number of Guria dances or Puppet shows are displayed electronically. They act as electronic media of communication.

*Electronic display of News*

Now-a-days, daily special news are displayed electronically. They are related to special events of a day such as weather, temperature, earth quake, train accident, air crash and so on.

*Electronic print*

Now-a-days, electronic printers are available. They can print out the messages quickly. Messages can be made available on screen.

*Electronic photographs*

Now-a-days, electronic photography is done and photographs are displayed on screen.

*Voice recording*

Now-a-days, voice recording is done with the help of voice recorder. They are preserved and displayed on screen. They act as electronic media of communication.

*Recording of News and views*

Now-a-days, news and views are recorded from different areas and persons through recorder. They are preserved and displayed on screen.

*Recording of cultural programmes*

Now-a-days, whole cultural programmes are recorded and displayed on screen with the help of electronic visual aids.

*Videography of marriage rituals*

Now-a-days, videography of marriage rituals is done with the help of electronic aid. The videography is displayed on screen.

*Videography of Lok Sabha and Rajya Sabha proceeding*

With the help of electronic aid, the videography of Lok Sabha and Rajya Sabha proceeding is done and displayed electronically.

*Videography of assembly meeting*

Now-a-days, videography of assembly meeting is done and displayed on screen with the help of electronic aids.

*Videography of meetings*

Now-a-days, videography of different types of meetings such as social, cultural, business, political, religious spiritual and health are recorded with the help of videography camera and videographer.

*Videography of conference, seminar and workshop*

Now-a-days, videography of entire proceedings of conference, seminar and workshops is done and displayed on screen.

*Electronic display of worship*

Now-a-days, worships and rituals performed at several religious places are displayed electronically on screen outside religious centres.

*CCTV Camera*

Now-a-days, CCTV camera have been installed at several places in towns, cities, shops, malls, jewellery shops, houses to prevent crime and catch the crime doers. CCTV camera acts as electronic media of communication.

***Satellite Media of Communication***

Now-a-days, a number of satellite media have come in to existence. They convey different types of news with the help of satellite based devices. The chief satellite based media are as follows:

- Radio
- Computer
- Television
- Internet
- Cell phones

***Radio***

Satellite radio acts as satellite media of communication. Satellite radio communicates news obtained from the satellite from different countries of the world. Satellite radio is very significant medium of communication to the people of the globe.

***Television***

Television is also a satellite based medium of communication. It communicates a number of messages obtained from satellite on different channels. Different channels of television covers news of different aspects of the world.

### *Computer*

Computer is a satellite based medium of communication. It is of different types such as desktop, laptop, and hand tablet. It is very useful satellite communication. Messages from different parts of the globe can be obtained with the help of it.

### *Internet*

Internet is very important satellite medium of communication. With the discovery of w.w.w. internet has integrated the entire world and the people. Every type of informations are available on internet. People visit internet site to get infromations related to education, employment, business, trade, pilgrimage, train tickets, plane ticket, market and a number of other aspects. Now-a-days, it has been proved a very useful media of communication.

### *Cell Phones*

Cellular phones are also very useful satellite medium of communication. With the help of cell phones, all individuals of the globe living in different parts are connected and inter related. Each cell phone owner has its own number. With the help of number they are connected to other persons living any where in the world. Cell phones, computer and internet have been able to provide a new definition of distance and time to visit there. Now, we are integrated to our world with the help of mobiles or cell phones.

### *Social Media*

Now-a-days, a number of social media site has come in to existence. Those media convey significant news related to views, reactions and opinions of individuals. To day, each individual has its own e-mail address. Each individuals has its own space in social media. In social media account, he/she shares his/her own views and reactions on a particular issue. Different scholars, professionals, technical experts, businessman, traders, leaders and Ministers have their own e-mail space and account which is used for the purpose of communication. The important social media sites are as follows:

- Google

- Facebook
- Twitter
- You-tube
- Whats App

Sometimes, news of social media gets viral. They attract attention of many media persons. Thus, viral individual news reaches to Government and other people.

# 11
# Communication Revolution

Today, we are living in an age of communication revolution. This age is also known as knowledge revolution age, information revolution age, media revolution age, digital revolution age, globalisation age and satellitisation age. The beginning of this age is invisibly taken as 1985 and visibly by 1990. Thus, this age is nearby three decade old. But during this short span of 30 years, it has influenced all individuals and all aspects of our life. Silicon valley project was established in New York City of America. The computer was invented, cell phones and internet were added to it. In order to integrate the entire world and the people w.w.w. (world wide websites) were invented. The invention of w.w.w. made world in the hand of people. This invention gave rise to communication revolution and information revolution throughout the world. Now global level messages were exchanged with the help of e-mail. With the help of internet global level social, cultural, educational, political, religious, health, business trade, market, entertainment, tourism, safety and hospitality messages were made available on different sites of internet. These sites can be visited with the help of desktop, laptop and tablets with internet facilities. Thus, internet presents before us huge storage of informations. By providing informations of various kinds internet sites enhance our knowledge. By obtaining knowledge we are empowered. It is because knowledge is power. The powerful is one who possesses knowledge. The communication revolution has made knowledge powerful. We become powerful in seconds by putting our fingers on computer and obtaining knowledge. This proverb is very popular today that one who possesses knowledge, lives as powerful in the society.

## Impact of Communication Revolution

We can divide the impact of communication revolution in to following sub-headings for the purpose of study and description:

- Impact on Society
- Impact on Culture
- Impact on Economy
- Impact on Education
- Impact on Banking system
- Impact on Entertainment
- Impact on Food and Breakfast
- Impact on Employment and Service
- Impact on Tour and Tourism
- Impact on Politics and Political system
- Impact on Administrative system
- Impact on Media and Communication
- Impact on Talk and Conversation
- Impact on Urbanization
- Impact on Youth
- Impact on Woman
- Impact on Scheduled Castes
- Impact on Scheduled Tribes
- Impact on OBCs
- Impact on Children
- Impact on Migration
- Impact on Aged

Now, let us discuss about these impacts of communication revolution in detail, one by one.

### *Impact on Society*

Communication revolution has influenced our society to a great extent. Due to its impact new termilogy for society has appeared in literature of researches. The society of today is known by the following names :

- Communication Society
- Information Society
- Media Society
- Drawing Room Society

- Knowledge Society
- Digital Society
- Computer Society
- Cellphone Society
- Internet Society
- e-mail Society

*Communication Society*

The society of today is known as communication society. It is because all members have developed means of communication. They spend much on communication. They maintain social relation with communication. Thus, communication has become focal theme for the members of society today. That is why today's society is known as communication society.

*Information Society*

Today's society is also termed as information society because its members are fully dependent on informations. They collect informations from satellite media and share information through satellite media.

*Consumption Society*

Now-a-days, consumption society has come in to existence due to communication revolution. Members of today's society believe in eat, drink and be merry. With the help of google and other sites, they are in a position to know about varieties of consumable goods. They order online and make payment online. They want to consume goods as early as possible. They do not do saving. They have debit card facility which they use for the purpose of consumption.

*Media Society*

The society of today is also known as media society. It is because its members consume what ever media convey them. Today, needs are created by media. Media convey news about dresses of different brands, *sarees* of different brands, jewellery, soap, shampoo, edible oils, detergent, m. oil, refine, vegetable oils, grains, spices and others of different brands. The members of society rely upon media. They start believing in hyper reality.

*Drawing Room Society*

The society of today is also known as drawing room society. Its members have drawing room. The drawing room has T.V., Internet, computer, phone, cell phones. The members of today's society sit in drawing room and see T.V. programmes on different channels. Thus, the concept of drawing room society has emerged today.

*Knowledge Society*

The society of today is known as knowledge society. Its members are powerful because they have knowledge through satellite media. They visit sites and get knowledge of different issues. The knowledge makes them powerful.

*Digital Society*

The society of today is known as digital society because its members are digitally literates. They put fingers on digits of computers or cell phones and get informations which they require.

*Computer Society*

Today's society is also known as computer society. It is because its members have computers through which they are interrelated.

*Cell Phone Society*

The society of today is also known as cell phone society. It is because its members have cell phones through which they maintain their relationship in society.

*Internet Society*

The society of today is known as internet society because its members maintain relationship through internet.

*e-mail Society*

Due to communication revolution, e-mail society has come in to existence today. In this society, each numbers has its own e-mail address. They maintain relationship through e-mail. They also have their own social media site.

***Impact on Culture***

Due to communication revolution, different forms of culture have come in to existence today. The impact of communication revolution on culture can be discussed under following headings:

- Communication Culture
- Information Culture
- Consuming Culture
- Media Culture
- Drawing room Culture
- Knowledge Culture
- Digital Culture
- Computer Culture
- Cell Phone Culture
- Internet Culture
- Advertising Culture
- Restaurant Culture
- Dating Culture
- Chating Culture
- online mate Selection Culture
- online Marriage Culture
- online Divorce Culture
- Live in relation Culture
- Surrogacy Culture
- Same Sex marriage Culture
- Cultural corporation Culture
- Cultural merchant Culture
- Cultural Organisation Culture
- Culture Market Culture
- Pop or Popular Culture
- Fast Food Culture
- Beauty Contest Culture
- Naked and semi-naked Culture
- Nursing Home Culture
- Old Age Home Culture
- Cashless Culture

Now, let us discuss about these cultural forms, which have emerged due to communication revolution today one by one in detail.

*Communication Culture*

Due to communication revolution, communication culture has come in to existence today. This culture is marked by developed means of communication like computer, cellphones, internet, T.V. and so on.

*Information Culture*

The communication revolution has created information culture today. The culture of today is characterised by informations obtained through internet and other kinds of media. The communication revolution has brought before us information culture.

*Consuming Culture*

Consuming culture has come in to existence due to media. Media have created this culture. We consume whatever media fell us to consume.

*Media Culture*

The communication revolution has created media culture. The different kind of media play significant role in culture of today. That is why it is known as media culture.

*Drawing Room Culture*

Communication revolution has created drawing room culture. In drawing room, all members of a family sit together and see different channels together.

*Knowledge Culture*

The communication revolution has created knowledge culture. Knowledge culture has emerged due to developed means of communication.

*Digital Culture*

The communication has created digital culture. Computer, internet and cell phones have created digitally literate people. Digitally literate people use digital numbers for the purpose of communication.

*Computer Culture*

Due to communication revolution, computer culture has come in to existence. This culture is characterised by producing, selling, buying and using computers by the people for various purposes.

*Cell Phone Culture*

Communication revolution has given rise to cell phone culture. This culture is characterised by producing, selling, buying and using cell phones for various purposes by the people.

*Internet Culture*

Due to communication revolution, the internet culture has been created. This culture has great value for internet. It is characterised by producing, selling, buying and using internet technology for various purposes by the people.

*Advertising Culture*

The communication revolution has given rise to advertising culture. The culture of today has become thing of advertisement. They are being advertised by different media.

*Restaurant Culture*

Communication revolution has given birth to restaurant culture. Now-a-days, there is no division of labour for cooking food. There are a number of restaurants, 3 stars and five stars hotels and standard canteen. They providing food. People have started buying food in place of cooking food.

*Dating Culture*

The communication revolution has given birth to dating culture. Dating culture can be seen in internet café or on own cell phones or computers with internet facilities. They fix date for chating.

*Chating Culture*

The communication revolution has given birth to chating culture. On own cell phones or computers with internet facility or in internet café, young boys and girls are found chating with their friends of same sex or of opposite sex.

*Online mate selection Culture*

Now-a-days, a number of shadi.com sites or matrimonial sites have come in to existence due to communication revolution. The desirous boys and girls visit the matrimonial sites for selecting mates of own choice. Now-a-days, internet is playing significant role in mate selection. It is acting as a marriage mediator.

*Online marriage and divorce Culture*

Communication revolution has given rise to online marriage and divorce culture. Thousand and thousands of marriages are held onlines and thousands and thousands of online divorce are taking place daily.

*Live in Relation Culture*

The communication revolution has given rise to live in relation culture. Now-a-days, young and adult unmarried males and females are living together in relation without marriage. They are neither married nor unmarried. They live like married couple. They enjoy sex but do not want to produce children. If child is born, it is thrown as commodity or kept in orphanage. If woman wants to keep child, live in relation is broken. Some compensation is paid.

*Surrogacy Culture*

The communication revolution has brought surrogacy culture before us. Now, this culture has emerged in all countries of the world. Well to do couples do not want to reproduce children. But they want to have child from a surrogate mother.

*Same Sex Marriage Culture*

The communication revolution has brought before us, same sex marriage culture. Some individuals of same sex prefer to marry with each other. Thus, in place of hetero sexual marriage, homosexual marriages have come in to existence.

*Cultural Corporation Culture*

The communication revolution has brought before us the culture of cultural corporation. The cultural corporates are involved in sale and purchase of culture. They have made culture as a commodity to be sold and purchased.

*Cultural merchant Culture*

The communication revolution has brought before us the culture of cultural merchants. The global cultural merchants have come in to existence. They are involved in cultural trade and business.

*Cultural Organisation Culture*

Due to communication revolution, cultural organisation culture has come in to existence. Now, global cultural organisers have emerged. They organise cultural contest. The winner is awarded by cultural organisation.

*Beauty Contest Culture*

The communication revolution has brought before us the culture of beauty contest. This contest is organised in the name of culture. The cultural organisation has brought before us beauty queen contest at global, national, regional and state level.

*Cultural Market Culture*

The communication revolution has brought before us the culture of cultural market. Now, ethnic markets are available in the global markets.

*Pop Culture or Popular Culture*

The communication revolution has brought before us pop culture or popular culture. The pop culture is characterised by same type of global dresses, songs, cinemas, dances, and food.

*Fast Food Culture*

The communication revolution has brought before us fast food culture. This culture is characterised by ready made food items packed in different types of packets.

*Naked and Semi-naked Culture*

The communication revolution has brought before us the culture of nakedness and semi-nakedness. Inner and thinner dresses are being used. Such dresses are also being sold and purchased which keep the body half naked. All these are being done in the name of culture.

*Nursing Home Culture*

The communication revolution has brought before us the culture of nursing home. Children are not reared in the house. Rather, they are being reared in nursing home.

*Old Age Home Culture*

The communication revolution has brought before us the culture of old age home. Old persons are not being looked after in houses, but they are being kept in old age home.

*Cashless Culture*

The communication revolution has brought before us cashless culture. This culture has influenced people to use cashless transaction.

***Impact on Economy***

The communication revolution has brought great impact on economy. The impact of communication revolution on economy can be discussed under the following headings:

- Knowledge economy
- Knowledge worker
- Knowledge trade

- Knowledge trader
- Knowledge market
- Day-night market
- World as a market complex
- World Trade Organisation
- Intellectual Property Right
- Patent law
- Home delivery of goods
- Home cashless payment facility
- Online Trade and Business
- Online Payment
- ATM card & Debit card
- Multinational companies
- I.T. Professionals and Management Professionals

Now, let us discuss about these economic impact one-by-one.

*Knowledge Economy*

Due to communication revolution, knowledge economy has come in to existence. This economy is characterised by knowledge worker, knowledge traders, knowledge trade and knowledge market.

*Knowledge Worker*

The communication revolution has created knowledge workers. The workers of knowledge economy are IT Engineers and management professionals.

*Knowledge Trade*

The communication revolution has created knowledge trade. Now, IT and management professionals are involved in trade of knowledge.

*Knowledge Trader*

The communication revolution has created multinational companies as knowledge traders.

*Knowledge Market*

The communication revolution has created knowledge markets where sale and purchase of knowledge takes place.

*Day-night Market*

Due to communication revolution day-night markets have emerged. In these markets, sale and purchase take place round the clock because this market is open day and night.

*World as a Market complex*

Due to communication revolution, world has emerged as a market complex. Now, marketing can be done anywhere at any time.

*World Trade Organisation*

The communication revolution has brought before us the concept of world trade organisation. This organisation has been formed by knowledge traders who are also known as multinational company.

*Intellectual Property Right*

The communication revolution has brought before us the concept of intellectual property right. The knowledge traders are also intellectual property owner.

*Patent Law*

The knowledge revolution has also brought before us the concept of patent law. Now, knowledge traders are patenting their product or intellectual products.

*Home delivery of Goods*

The communication revolution has brought before us the home delivery of goods and products. Different companies deliver their products at home address of the customer.

*Home Cashless Payment Facility*

The communication revolution has brought before us the practice of home cashless payment facility. Companies deliver their products at home address and receive cashless payment from the customer.

*Online Trade and Business*

The communication revolution has brought before us the practice of online trade and business. Now, products are supplied on online demands.

*Online Payment*

The communication revolution has brought before us the practice of online payment. The knowledge traders supply their products on online order and receive payment online.

*ATM card and Debit card*

The communication revolution has brought before us the practice of payment and withdrawal by ATM card and Debit card.

*Multinational Companies*

Communication revolution has brought before us multinational companies. These MNC have their business and trade across countries. That is why they are termed as multinational companies.

*I.T. Professionals and Management Professionals*

Communication revolution has brought before us the concept of IT professionals and management professionals. They are expert knowledge workers and traders.

***Impact on Education***

The communication revolution has influenced our education to a great extent. We can discuss the impact of communication revolution on education under following sub-headings:

- Impact on classroom
- Impact on syllabus
- Impact on teaching
- Impact on admission
- Impact on attendance
- Impact on study
- Impact on fee payment
- Impact on filling up forms
- Impact on examination
- Impact on evaluation system
- Impact on exam result
- Emergence of corporate in education
- Emergence of e-knowledge centre
- Emergence of e-library
- Emergence of e-books
- Emergence of e-Journals

Now, let us discuss about these impacts of communication revolution on education one by one.

*Impact on Classroom*

The communication revolution has brought before us the practice of smart class room. The smart class consists of A.C. class room with latest teaching aids like computer, multi-media, projector and screen. The concept of smart class room has also emerged even in rural areas where there is electricity supply. In order to generate electricity, generator has also been installed.

*Impact on Syllabus*

The communication revolution has also influenced the syllabus of teaching from schools to universities and technical institute. Even in school education teaching about computer and its parts has been started. The courses go on changing in higher classes, colleges, universities and technical institute. Computer and computer application curriculum has been made a must for education from lower to higher level.

*Impact on Teaching*

The communication revolution has also influenced the method of teaching. Now-a-days, teaching is done with the help of new developed teaching aids such as computer, projector, C.D., multimedia and others. Thus, in place of oral and written teaching methodology, visual teaching methodology has come in to existence.

*Impact on Admission*

The communication revolution has also influenced the admission system in schools, colleges, universities and institutes. Now, facility of online admission is available. Even cash payment is computerized. Cashless admission process has also been started.

*Impact on Attendance*

The communication revolution has also influenced the attendance system. The teachers have to follow biometric attendance. The attendance of student is recorded through computer.

*Impact on Study*

The communication revolution has also influenced the study of students. The students are now using internet for the purpose of study. They are not dependent only on classroom teaching, teacher and books. But they are also studying reading materials available on internet and satellite media.

*Impact on Fee Payment*

The communication revolution has also influenced the fee payment processes from schools to universities. The fees can be paid online by using internet.

*Impact on Filling up forms*

The communication revolution has influenced the process of filling up of examination, employment and other kinds of forms in schools and universities and commissions.

*Impact on Examination*

The communication revolution has influenced the examination system.

The examinations are held online. Results are being published online.

*Impact on Evaluation System*

The communication revolution has also influenced the evaluation system. The help of computer is taken in evaluation of answer sheet. In evaluation of answer sheet of competitive examination, the help of computer is being taken.

*Impact on Result*

The communication revolution has influenced the publication of examination results. Now-a-days, educational institutions load the exam results on their websites. The students downloads the result.

*Emergence of Corporates in Education*

The communication revolution has brought the emergence of business corporate in education. Multinational companies and business corporate are purchasing lands, establishing schools, colleges, universities, technical institutes and management institutes.

*Emergence of e-knowledge centre*

The communication revolution has brought before us the emergence of e-knowledge centres. Here students and scholars are skilled in e-learning technology and skill.

*Emergence or e-library*

The communication revolution has brought before us the emergence of e-library. Now, libraries are available on their internet sites. The students and scholars visit e-library to find out names of books available there.

*Emergence of e-books*

The communication revolution has brought before us the emergence of e-books. Now, entire books or parts of a book are available online. The students and researchers visit the site and download those parts of book.

*Emergence or e-Journals*

Due to communication revolution e-Journals have come in to existence. The students and scholars visit the e-Journal sites to consult articles published in e-Journals.

***Impact on Banking System***

The communication revolution has influenced our banking system to a great extent. The impact of communication on banking system can be discussed under following headings:

- Plastic money
- ATM card
- Debit card
- e-banking
- Online transaction message
- Cashless transaction

*Plastic money*

The communication revolution has brought before us the emergence of plastic money. ATM card and Debit card are plastic money. They are helpful in cashless transaction.

*ATM card*

Due to communication revolution, ATM card has come in to existence. The ATM card is such a card through which money can be withdrawn anywhere from any bank. It is a plastic money always with us.

*Debit card*

Due to communication revolution, bank ATM card also functions as debit card. This card is also used for cashless payment anywhere.

*e-banking*

Communication revolution has brought before us the existence of e-banking system. The e-banking system is helpful in transaction of money from one bank to another.

*Online transaction message*

The communication revolution has brought before us the transaction messages on cell phones and handsets.

*Cashless transaction system*

The communication revolution has brought before us the system of cashless transaction. The cashless transaction is attaining attention even in rural areas.

***Impact on Entertainment***

The communication revolution has influenced our entertainment to a great extent. The impact of communication revolution on entertainment can be discussed under the following headings:

- Online entertainment channels
- T.V. Channels
- Cable Channels
- Five star hotels
- Three star hotels
- Cinema houses and cinemas
- Eyelex
- Entertainment clubs
- Online dance, music and songs
- Online informations about Picnic spots
- Online information about parks and sanctuaries
- Online broad casting of matches
- Online information about scene and scenery
- Online Railway and air ticket
- Online hotel reservation
- Online taxi/car reservation
- Information about different types of Games

Now, let us discuss about these impacts of communication revolution on entertainment one by one.

*Online entertainment channels*

Due to communication revolution, entertainment channel sites are available online. They give us different informations about entertainment and entertainment channels.

*T.V. channels*

The communication revolution has brought before us different entertainment channels on television. Those channels can be used for the purpose of entertainment.

*Cable channels connection*

The communication revolution has brought before us the cable channels connection in T.V. for entertainment purposes. We have to pay charges for cable channels connection.

*Five Star hotels*

The communication resolution has brought informations before us regarding the existence of five star hotels. In these hotels well to do persons visit for entertainment and enjoyment.

*Three star hotels*

The communication revolution has brought before us the information regarding three star hotels where well to do people visit for entertainment.

*Cinema houses and cinemas*

The communication revolution has brought before us informations regarding different cinema halls and the cinemas they were showing. People visit these cinema halls to see pictures. They get cinema ticket online.

*Eyelex*

The communication revolution provides us informations about different eyelex and cinemas being shown there.

*Entertainment clubs*

Communication revolution provides us detail informations about entertainment clubs, their fees and programmes.

*Online dance, music and songs*

Due to communication revolution, it has become possible to enjoy music, dance, songs and drama online.

*Online Informations about Picnic spots*

People visit different picnic spots for entertainment. They get informations about those picnic spots online.

*Online Information about Parks and sanctuaries*

Informations about parks and sanctuaries are available on sites. People visit those sites and get detail informations about those parks and sanctuaries.

*Online information about scene and scenery*

The communication revolution has brought before us online information about different scenes and scenery of different areas.

*Live broad casting of matches*

Due to communication revolution, it has become possible to see and hear live broadcasting of cricket matches, football matches, badminton match, table tennis match, kabaddi and athletic matches.

*Online Railway and Air Ticket reservation*

Due to communication revolution, it has become possible to reserve advance railway and air ticket with the help of internet.

*Online Hotel reservation*

Due to communication revolution, it has become possible to reserve rooms in hotels in advance with the help of internet.

*Online Taxi/Car/AC Buses Reservation*

The communication revolution has provided us opportunity of online reservation in Taxi/Car/A.C. buses for visiting different sites.

*Informations about different types of games*

Due to communication revolution, we can get informations on different types of games by visiting game sites.

***Impact on Food and Drinks***

Communication revolution has influenced our food and drink to a great extent. The impact of communication revolution on food and drink can be discussed under following headings:

- Informations about hotels and restaurants
- Informations about country food
- Informations about fast food and packed food
- Informations about vegetarian food
- Information about non-vegetarian food
- Information about healthy food
- Information about nutrients and nutritious food
- Informations about different types of fruits
- Informations about price of food and fruits
- Information about regional food
- Information about local food and ethnic food
- Online order supply of food
- Online payment of food bill
- Online information of local drink
- Online information of regional drink
- Online information of national drink
- Online information of foreign drink
- Informations about caterers and catering

Now, let us discuss about these impacts of communication revolution one by one.

*Informations about Hotels and Restaurants*

Due to communication revolution, we are, now, in a position to know list of hotels and restaurants of the area, where we want to visit for breakfast, lunch and dinner. Knowing branded hotels and restaurants people are able to enjoy the taste of luxury food items.

*Informations about country food*

Due to communication revolution, people are in a position to know country based food items even in Foreign countries. The list of country food and hotels, where they are being sold and purchased, is available on website. The website users visit those sites with the help of internet. This information is very much useful for the foreign visitors.

*Information about fast food and packed food*

Informations related to availability of fast food and packed food items are also available on websites. The customer visit the websites of the area and find out the name of malls, big shops, hotels and restaurants. This has become possible due to communication revolution.

*Information about non-vegetarian food*

Informatons related to the availability of non-vegetarian food items are available on websites of the area or place concerned. The internet users visit the area site and find out the list of non-vegetarian food items available in a hotels or restaurant. This has happened due to communication revolution.

*Informations about vegetarian food items*

On websites of an area, the list of hotels and restaurants where vegetarian food items are sold and purchased, is available. The websites user visits the site and find out the list of vegetarian food times for order. Communication revolution has made this possible.

*Information about non-vegetarian food*

On websites of hotels and restaurants, the list of non-vegetarian food items are available. The website users visit the site for home delivery order.

*Information about healthy food*

On websites of health, a list of healthy food items is made available. This includes not only grains, but also edible oils, ghee, refine, dry fruits and others. The website users visit websites and try to find out the list for order or purchase. This has become possible due to communication revolution.

*Information about nutrients and nutritious food*

Due to information revolution, it has become possible to know list of nutrients, vitamins and other diets with the help of websites. On websites list of nutrients, vitamins and nutritious food available in the market is available. The website users visit websites, find out list and order for home delivery. They make payment online. All these facilities and informations are available due to communication revolution.

*Information about different types or fruits*

The list of different types of fruits are now available online with price list. The users visit the site for home delivery.

*Informations about price of food and fruits*

Online, informations about price of different food items and fruits of different regions and countries are now available due to communication revolution.

*Information about regional food*

The list of different regional food is available online in hotels and restaurants of the area. The users visit the site for order and home delivery.

*Information about local food and ethnic food*

The list of local and ethnic food is available on sites of hotels and restaurants. The users visit the site for order and home delivery.

*Online order for supply of food*

The website visitors visit the sites of hotels and restaurants of the area and make order for home delivery of food items they need. This has become possible due to communication revolution.

*Online payment of food bill in Hotel*

Due to communication revolution, it has become possible not only to make online order of food item, but also to make online payment to hotels.

*Online information of local drink*

Online informations of local drink are available. The website users visit the websites, order for home delivery and make online payment. This has become possible due to communication revolution.

*Online information of regional drinks*

On websites online informations of regional drinks are available. The website users visit the site, order for home delivery and make online payment.

*Online informations of national drinks*

On websites online informations of national drink are available. Website users visit the websites, order for house delivery and make Online payment.

*Online informations of foreign drinks*

On websites informations about foreign drink are available. The website users visit the site, make order for home delivery and online payment.

*Online informations of caterers and catering*

Informations about catering and caterers are available on websites. The website users visit the websites, make order of food items to be served on birth, marriage and other parties and make payment online. All these have become possible due to communication revolution.

***Impact on Service Occupation***

The communication revolution has brought influential change on service occupation. This revolution has opened new areas of service. This impact of communication revolution on service occupation can be discussed under following sub-headings:

- Rise of Software companies
- Rise of Hardware companies
- Online Joining Report
- Rise of multinational companies
- Rise of IT and management professionals
- Offshoring and outsourcing business
- Package in place of salary
- Online advertisement of jobs
- Online application form of jobs
- Online interview of candidates
- Online declaration of result
- Online joining report
- Online work
- Online payment of package
- Online job shifting
- Online transfer of P.F. and other benefits.

Now, let us discuss about these impacts of communication revolution on service occupation one by one.

*Rise of Software companies*

The communication revolution has opened job opportunities in software sectors. Software IT professionals are appointed to create softwares from the point of view of business. Thus, communication revolution has opened chances of jobs to IT engineers and management professional in softwares company.

*Rise of Hardware company*

The communication revolution has brought before us IT and management professionals. As a result, hardware companies have come in to existence. They produce hardware products and do their business.

*Rise of Multinational Company*

The communication revolution has given rise to multinational company. The multinational companies have established hardware and software business all over the world.

*Rise of IT and Management professionals*

The communication revolution has given rise to IT and management professionals. Those I.T. and management professionals work in hardware and software multinational companies.

*Offshoring and outsourcing business*

The communication revolution has given rise to offshoring and outsourcing business by multinational companies.

*Package in place of salary*

The communication revolution has given rise to a new term package in place of salary. Now, IT engineers and management professionals are appointed on annual packages in lacs.

*Online advertisement of jobs*

The communication revolution has given rise to online advertisement of Jobs. Different multinational companies make online advertisement of jobs on different posts.

*Online application form of Jobs*

Due to communication revolution IT and management job seekers are in a position to fill up online application form against the post advertised.

*Online Interview for selection*

Due to communication revolution, the candidates have been able to appear at an inter view online.

*Online declaration of result*

Due to communication revolution, it has become possible to declare result of interview and selection list online. The candidate visits the site and download the result.

*Online joining report*

Due to communication revolution, it has become possible to submit joining report online.

*Online work*

In multinational company, it has become possible to work online due to communication revolution.

*Online payment of package*

Due to communication revolution, it has become possible to make online payment of package to I.T. professionals and management professionals.

*Online job shifting*

Due to communication revolution, online shifting of job has become possible.

*Online transfer of P.F. and other benefits*

Due to communication revolution, online transfer of P.F. and other benefits has become possible.

***Impact on Tour and Travel***

The communication revolution has brought a number of impacts on tour and travel pattern of people. Impact of communication revolution on tour and travel can be discussed under following headings:

- Online information about distance and mode of travel to a place
- Online ticket booking in plane, train, ship and bus
- Online return of ticket

- Online booking of car and taxi
- Online booking of hotel and lodges
- Online supply of food
- Online payment of bill
- Online conversation with friends and relatives

Now, let us discuss about these impacts of communication revolution on tour and travel one by one.

*Online information about distance and mode of travel to a place*

The communication revolution has brought before us, informations related to distance and mode of travel to a place. Now, informations regarding distance and plane, train, ship, bus, car and taxi connectivity are available on sites. The website visitors visit websites to find out these informations in detail.

*Online ticket booking in plane, train, ship and AC buses*

Due to communication revolution, it has become possible to book tickets in plane, train, ship, A.C. buses in advance according to travel plan individually or in a group.

*Online return of ticket*

The communication revolution has brought before us online facility of returning ticket, if travel plan gets fail due to some unavoidable reason.

*Online booking of Car and Taxi*

Communication revolution has brought before us the facility of booking taxi or car on-line. Details of taxi or car agency and fares are available online.

*Online booking of hotels and lodges*

The communication revolution has brought before us the facility of online booking of hotel, lodge, *Dharmashala* and other place of accommodation at tour places. The room rent charges, food facilities and other facilities are also available online.

*Online supply of food*

Due to communication revolution, it has become possible to supply desired food materials in room on online order.

*Online payment of bills*

Communication revolution has provided us the facility of online payment of bills of hotels and hospitality.

*Online conversation with friends and relatives*

Due to communication revolution, it has become possible to have online photographic messages and conversation with friends and relatives.

***Impact on Health Tourism***

Communication revolution has influenced health tourism to a great extent. Now, we are in a position to tour different places of countries and abroad for treatment of diseases and recover health. The impact of health tourism can be discussed under following sub-headings:

- Online information about super speciality hospitals
- Online information about multi speciality hospitals
- Online appointment with doctor
- Online advice of doctor
- Online advice information of medicine
- Online order of medicine
- Online bill payment
- Online ambulance facility
- Online advice of alternative medicine
- Online reservation of accommodation
- Online complaint against hospital authority

Now, let us discuss about these impacts of communication revolution on health tourism one by one.

*Online information about super speciality hospitals*

Communication revolution has provided list of super speciality hospitals in the country and abroad on websites. The website users visit the website to find out the names of super speciality hospitals.

*Online information about multispeciality hospitals*

Due to communication revolution, list of multispeciality hospitals are available on websites along with expected expenses. Patients or their guardian visits websites and get those information.

*Online appointment number with doctor*

Communication revolution has provided facility to patient to get appointment number with doctor online.

*Online advice of doctor*

Communication revolution has provided facility for online advice of doctor after first visit.

*Online advice information of medicine*

Communication revolution has provided facility for online advice of medicine or change in previous medicine.

*Online order of medicine supply*

Due to communication revolution it has become possible to place online order of medicine supply at home.

*Online bill payment*

Communication revolution has provided facility for online bill payment before or after home delivery.

*Online ambulance facility*

Communication revolution has provided facility for booking ambulance during emergency by visiting website of hospitals or by contacting through phones or mobiles.

*Online advice of alternative medicine*

Communication revolution has provided facility of alternative medicine advice from alternative medicine institutes.

*Online Reservation of Accommodation*

Due to communication revolution, it is possible for reserving room for accommodation of patients and guardians.

*Online complaint against hospital authority*

Communication revolution has provided facility of lodging online complaint against hospital authority in case of negligence of duty or misbehaviour with patient or his/her attendants.

***Impact on Political System***

Communication revolution has also influenced our political system. The impact of communication revolution on political system can be discussed under following sub headings:

- Online information of modern law
- Online information of primitive law
- Online concept of good Governance
- Information about forms of Government
- Impartiality in Governance
- Concept of e-Governance
- Online election campaign
- Online political reactions
- Online conversation between PM and public
- Online conversation between CM and public
- Online conversation between Ministers and Public
- Online conversation between leaders and public
- Online account of different Ministries
- Use of voting machine for casting votes
- Online political news
- Online election results
- Video conferencing of political leaders

Now, let us discuss about all these impacts of communication revolution on political system one by one.

*Online informations of modern law*

Due to communication revolution, information about modern laws, acts, statutes, amendments is possible online.

*Online informations of primitive law*

Communication revolution has also provided informations of primitive law prevalent in different parts of the world.

*Online information of good Governance*

Due to communication revolution, we have informations and concept about good Governance online.

*Informations about forms of Government*

Due to communication revolution, we are in a position to know the forms of Government prevalent in different countries of the globe.

*Impartiality in Governance*

Communication revolution has brought before us impartiality in Governance.

*Concept of e-Governance*

Due to communication revolution the concept of e-Governance has come in to existence. Now, Governance is available on websites.

*Online election campaign*

Communication revolution has brought before us the facility for online election campaign. The leaders have opened their accounts on social media like facebook, twitter, YouTube and WhatsApps. They make election campaign by visiting their sites and expressing reactions on social media sites.

*Online political reaction*

The political reactions of different leaders and political parties appear on social media sites. This has become possible due to communication revolution.

*Online conversation between P.M. and Public*

The communication revolution has brought before us the online conversation between PM and public. The PM shares *Man ki Baat* (message of heart) with public online. This is very much useful in formulating different policies and programmes by the Central Government.

*Online conversation between CM and Public*

Communication revolution has brought before us the online conversation between CM and public. This has also become significant for formulation of policies of development by State Government.

*Online conversation between Ministers and Public*

Due to communication revolution direct online conversation between different Ministers and public has started. This is very helpful in knowing the reactions of public by different Ministers of Central and State Governments.

*Online conversation between leaders and public*

There are a number of leaders who are not elected as MLA, MLC, M.P., Ministers and so on. But they are mass leaders. Communication revolution provides a chance to public for having a direct conversation with such path showers, whom people regard very much.

*Online budget account of different Ministries*

Due to communication revolution, it has become possible to get online budgetary provision account. The public can also get pattern of expenditure of different departments.

*Use of voting machines for casting votes*

Communication revolution has provided us chance to cast votes through voting machines. We are also moving towards e-voting.

*Online political news*

Due to communication revolution, we are able to get daily and minuts to minuts political news online through e-news paper and live broadcasting on T.V.

*Online election results*

Due to communication revolution, we are in a position to get election results online.

*Video conferencing of different political leaders*

Due to communication revolution we are in a position to have video conferencing of different political leaders on an issue.

***Impact on Administrative System***

Communication revolution has brought significant impact on present day administrative system. The impact of communication revolution on administrative system can be discussed under following headings:

- Computerisation of all administrative organisations
- Online informations of administrative arrangements
- Online allotment of work duty
- Bio metric attendance
- Online F.I.R.
- Online crime report
- Online report of action
- Online punishment information
- Online suspend order
- Online discharge order
- Online bail petition
- Online Court judgement
- Online leave petition and leave sanction
- Online payment

- Online complain against officials
- Online information of corruption
- e-administration

Now, let us discuss about these impacts one by one.

*Computerisation of all administrative organisations*

Due to computer revolution, it has become possible to computerise all administrative organisations of State Government and Central Government. Now, list of all state and national level administrative organisations is available on websites. The website users can visit those sites for any type of irregularities, complaints and justice.

*Online information of administrative arrangements*

On the occasion of Parliament Session, assembly session, visiting leaders, fairs, flood, earthquakes, epidemic, public health and safety of public, description of administrative arrangements is given online. The website visitors get acquainted with those informations by approaching the websites of administration.

*Online allotment of work duty*

Due to communication revolution, it has become possible to allot duty of police personnel and other officials online.

*Biometric attendance*

Due to communication revolution, biometric attendance system has been implemented in all Government institutions. Employees have to mark biometric attendance at the time of coming and leaving the institution.

*Online F.I.R.*

Due to communication revolution, it has become possible to lodge F.I.R. against crime.

*Online crime report*

Due to communication revolution, it has become possible to provide crime reports online.

*Online report of action taken*

Due to communication revolution, it has become possible to report on action taken at websites.

*Online punishment information*

Due to communication revolution, it has become possible to provide informations regarding punishment given.

*Online suspend order*

The communication revolution has provided opportunity to send and to receive suspend order.

*Online discharge order*

Due to communication revolution, it has become possible to send and receive discharge order.

*Online bail petition*

Due to communication revolution, it has become possible to file bail petition online.

*Online Court Judgement*

Due to communication revolution, it has become possible to communicate judgement online to the parties concerned.

*Online leave petition and leave sanction*

Due to communication revolution, it has become possible to apply online for leave and to communicate sanction of leave online.

*Online payment of salary*

Due to communication revolution, it has become possible to send and receive salary payment online.

*Online complaint against officials*

Due to communication revolution, it has become possible to lodge complaint against officials to higher authorities.

*Online information of corruption*

Due to communication revolution, it has become possible to provide information of corruption online to the concerned authorities.

*e-administration*

The communication revolution has brought before us the concept of e-administration.

***Impact on Media and Mass Communication***

Communication revolution has brought impact on media and mass communication to a great extent. The impact of communication revolution on media and mass communication can be discussed under following headings:

- Online news reporting
- Live news broadcasting
- Continuous news broadcasting
- Breaking news facility
- e-newspaper
- e-news bulletin
- e-news Journals

Now, let us discuss about these impacts one by one.

*Online news reporting*

Due to communication revolution, it has become possible to report news online to media. The media reporters and other institutional news reporters, now-a-days, report news on websites of media for media coverage.

*Live news broadcasting*

Due to communication revolution, live news broadcasting has become possible on satellite and electronic media.

*Continuous news broadcasting*

Due to communication revolution, it has become possible to broadcast news continuously on the occasion of election results or on the occasion of great event.

*Breaking news facility*

Due to communication revolution, breaking news is provided time to time to T.V. viewers in course of continuous news broadcasting.

*e-newspaper*

Due to communication revolution e-newspaper has come to existence. Newspapers are available on websites. In order to read news, people visit websites.

*e-news bulletin*

Due to communication revolution, concept of e-news bulletin has come in to existence on websites. The website visitors visit the site of e-news bulletin to read news published in e-news bulletin.

*e-news Journals*

Due to communication revolution, e-news Journals have come in to existence on websites. The news readers visit the websites to study articles published in e-news Journals.

***Impact on Conversation and Message Sending***

Communication revolution has brought influencing impact on conversation pattern. The impact of communication revolution on conversation can be discussed under following sub-headings:

- Conversation at distant places
- Conversation in few seconds
- Conversation in time limit
- New conversation terminology
- Conversation on Telephones
- Conversation on mobiles
- SMS on mobiles
- Communication through facebook
- Communication through twitter
- Communication through WhatsApps
- Communication through YouTube
- Communication through e-mail address
- Communication through cell phones with photographs
- Communication through websites

Now, let us discuss about these impact of communication revolution on conversation and message sending one by one.

*Communication at distant places*

Communication revolution has provided facility of conversation between friends and relative staying at different distant places, even in foreign countries. The communication has provided a new definition of distance.

*Conversation in few minutes*

Due to communication revolution, conversation between friends and relatives staying at different distant places has become possible in few seconds. Thus, communication revolution has also provided a new definition of time along with distance. Now, distance is not a barrier of communication. Distantly located persons can make conversation in few minutes.

*Conversation in time limit*

Due to communication revolution, communication takes place in time limit. It is because we have to pay charges for communication. Therefore, communication is made in limited words. The people have to select limit words for the purpose of communication.

*New conversation terminology*

Communication revolution has brought before us new communication terminology such as hello, O.K. bye, hai and so on. Similarly, new terminology for computer, its, parts, and language has come into existence.

*Conversation on Telephones*

Communication revolution has made it possible to make conversation on phones. For this purpose people have own phone set and phone number. The phones have local, regional, STD and ISD facilities.

*Conversation on mobiles*

Communication revolution has made possible conversation between friend and relatives through mobiles. For this purpose, each individuals has his/her own mobile number, and set.

*SMS on mobile*

Communication revolution has given us occasion to send message in SMS form to a known persons or institutions.

*Communication through facebook*

Due to communication revolution, we are in a position to have our own a face book account. Communication through facebook account is made.

*Communication through twitter*

Due to communication revolution, it has become possible to make communication through twitter.

*Communication through WhatsApps*

Communication revolution has provided us facility for communication through different WhatsApps.

*Communication through YouTube*

Due to communication revolution, it has become possible to communicate messages through YouTube.

*Communication through e-mail address*

Due to communication revolution, it has become possible to communicate on e-mail address.

*Communication through Cell phones with photographs*

Due to communication revolution, it has become possible to make communication with seeing photographs of each other.

*Communication through websites*

Communication revolution has given us an opportunity for communication through websites. Each agencies has its own websites. In order to communicate something, we have to visit websites.

***Impact on Urbanisation***

Communication revolution has brought a great impact on the process of urbanisation. The impact of communication revolution on urbanisation may be discussed under the following sub-headings:

- Online informations about towns and cities
- Online informations about mode of travel
- Online informations about urban administration
- Online informations about hotels, lodges, restaurants and *Dharmashala*
- Online information about transport agency
- Online information about expansion of towns and cities
- Online information about educational institutions of towns and cities
- Online information about hospitals and nursing houses
- Online information about old age home
- Online information about petrol pumps
- Online information about markets, malls, big shops
- Online information about Government offices

- Online information about post office
- Online information about bank
- Online information about builders and contractors
- Online informations about sale and purchase of land
- Online information about sale and purchase of flats
- Online information of parks, cinema halls, and eyelex
- Online information of tourist and religious places
- Online information of technicians

Now, let us discuss these impacts of communication revolution on urbanisation process one by one in detail.

*Online information about towns and cities*

Due to communication revolution, it has become possible to get online informations about each towns, cities and metropolises and their available maps from websites.

*Online information about mode of travel*

Due to communication revolution, online informations about mode of travels of each towns and cities are available. Following the information, people are free to choose any one mode such as air ways, surface ways, water ways and others.

*Online information about urban administration*

Due to communication revolution, it has become possible to get information about urban administration of each town, cities and metropolises.

*Online information about hotels, lodge, restaurant, Dharmashala*

Communication revolution has given us opportunity to know about hotels, lodges, restaurants and *Dharmashala* located in each town, city and metropolis.

*Online information about transport agency*

Communication revolution has provided us online information about transport agency of each town, city and metropolise.

*Online information about expansion of town and cities*

Due to communication revolution, it has become possible for us to get online information about the expansion area of each town, city and metropolis.

*Online informations about educational institutions of towns and cities*

Due to communication revolution, it has become possible to know the educational institution of each town and city online.

*Online information about hospitals and Nursing homes*

Due to communication revolution, it has become possible to known list of hospitals and nursing homes of each town and city.

*Online information about old age home*

Communication revolution has given us occasion to know about—old age homes of each town and city.

*Online information about petrol pump*

Due to communication revolution, it has become to know about petrol pumps and their area of each town and city.

*Online information about markets, malls and big shops*

We are able to get online information about markets, malls and big shops of each town, and city.

*Online information about Government offices*

Now-a-days, we are in a position to get online information about Government offices of each town and city due to communication revolution.

*Online information about Post office*

Communication revolution has provided us opportunity to get information about post office/offices of each town, city and metropolis.

*Online information about bank*

Due to communication revolution, we are in a position to get online information about banks and their branches in each town, city and metropolis.

*Online information about builders and contractors*

Due to communication revolution it has become possible to know about builders and contractors of each town, city and metropolis.

*Online information about sale and purchase of land*

Communication revolution has given us knowledge about sale and purchase of land of each town, city and metropolis.

*Online information about Sale and purchase of flats*

Communication revolution has given us opportunity to know sale and purchase of flat and house online of each town, city and metropolis.

*Online information of park, cinema halls and eyelax*

Due to communication revolution, it has become possible to know about parks, clubs, cinema halls, and eyelax of each city and metropolis.

*Online information of tourist and religious places*

Communication revolution has given us opportunity and facility to know online about tourist and religious places of each town, city and metro.

*Online information of technicians*

Communication revolution has provided facility to know online about different types of technicians such as welder, fitter, plumber, carpenter, blacksmith, washerman, gardener, electrician, driver and others.

*Impact on Youth*

Communication revolution has influenced our youth to a great extent. The impact of communication revolution on youth can be discussed under following headings:

- Use of cell phones
- Use of computers
- Use of internet
- Use of internet café
- Use of dating and chating
- Use of Facebook
- Use of Twitter
- Use of WhatsApp
- Use of YouTube
- Follower of adoption of pop culture
- Adoption of global dress
- Use of entertainments channel at TV or internet
- Attraction towards costly travel
- Accommodation in costly hotels
- Meals of costly restaurants
- Interest in global matches of sports
- Study of e-news papers
- Use of e-library
- Visit to e-knowledge centre
- Study through internet
- Use of e-books and e-Journals
- Education in IT and Management institutions
- Service as IT and Management professionals
- Preference of foreign travel
- Service and settlement in foreign countries
- Settlement in foreign countries
- Thinking above caste, religion and language
- Intercaste marriage
- Rise of new classes
- Preference of class marriage
- Very late marriage
- Live in relationship
- No interest in procreation of child
- Procreation by surrogacy mother
- Always in search of new jobs.

Now, let us discuss about these impacts of communication revolution on youth one by one in detail.

*Use of cell phones*

Communication revolution has made urban and rural youth both users of cell phones. They are found using cell phones continuously. They remain busy in operating their cell phones or hand set.

*Use of computers*

Due to communication revolution, both urban and rural youth have become computer users. They learn how to operate computer, laptop, desk top or tablet very well. They prefer to study computer and computer application. They are very much successful computer users.

*Use of Internet*

The youth of today are not only computer users, but they are also expert in internet using. They use internet frequently to know informations of various kind they require. All have hand set internet. This has become possible due to communication revolution.

*Use of Internet café*

The youth of today are internet café users. They visit internet café and try to know different types of information.

*Use of dating and chating*

Due to communication revolution, the youth are not only internet café visitors, but they are also engaged in dating and chating.

*Use of facebook*

The youth of today have their facebook account. They post their messages on their face book account. They also share facebook account with friends, relations and others. All these have become possible due to communication revolution.

*Use of twitter*

Due to communication revolution, youth of today have become twitter user. They use twitter for the purpose of communication.

*Use of WhatsApps*

The communication revolution has resulted in making our youth WhatsApp users. They use WhatsApps for communication.

*Use of YouTube*

Communication revolution has also made our youth YouTube users. They use YouTube for the purpose of communication.

*Follower of pop or popular culture*

The youth of today are followers of pop or popular culture. They prefer modern dresses, ornaments, hair styles, songs, music and dance. This has become possible due to communication revolution.

*Follower of Global dresses*

The youth of today are follower of global dresses, ornaments and hair styles which do not discriminate between males and females. This has become possible due to communication revolution.

*Use of entertainments channel at TV or internet*

The youth of today are users of entertainment channels on T.V. screen and internet.

*Attraction towards costly travel*

Due to communication revolution, youth have been attracted towards costly travel. They want to travel on aeroplane or air bus and A.C. I or A.C. II train ticket.

*Accommodation in costly hotels*

The youth of today want to stay in five stars or three star hotels and share tasty luxurious food items.

*Meals of costly restaurant*

The youth of today have been attracted towards costly food items of costly hotels and restaurants due to communication revolution.

*Interest in Global Matches of sports*

Due to communication revolution the youth of today are attracted towards global sports of cricket matches, table tennis matches, badminton matches, *kabaddi*, footballs and athletes.

*Study of e-newspapers*

The youth of today want to study e-news papers to get news of different kinds due to communication revolution.

*Use of e-library*

The youth of today visit e-library to study their subjects. This has become possible due to communication revolution.

*Visit to e-knowledge centre*

The youth of today want to visit e-knowledge centre for the purpose of study. This has become possible due to communication revolution.

*Study through internet*

The youth students of today want to make study and preparation of examination through internet. The internet has become teaching aid for them. They have become dependent on internet for their study. They download reading materials and YouTube lectures from internet for the purpose of study.

*Use of e-books and e-Journals*

The youth students of today visit website to contact e-book and e-Journals for the purpose of study and research. This has become possible due to communication revolution.

*Education in IT and Management Institution*

The youth of today prefer education in IT and management institutions. These institutions have A.C. smart classes, A.C. Libraries, A.C. canteen and high fee structure. This has become possible due to communication revolution.

*Service as IT and Management Professionals*

The youth of today want to do service in IT and management sectors as IT and management professionals. This is also due to communication revolution.

*Preference of foreign travel*

The youth of today as IT and management professionals want to visit foreign countries to enjoy holidays and tour. They have advance planning of travel.

*Service and settlement in foreign country*

The youth of today, want to do service in foreign countries on high packages. They want to earn quickly. They believe in eat drink and be merry. They want to settle in foreign countries.

*Thinking above caste, religion and language*

The youth of today has crossed the boundary of caste religion language and region. For them these boundaries are of no value.

*Intercaste marriage*

The youth of today prefer intercaste marriage and inter-religious marriages. For them caste has no role to play in marriage.

*Rise of new classes*

For youth of today new classes have emerged. They are engineers, doctors, management and IT professionals, business professionals and so on. These classes are above castes, religion, region and language.

*Preference of class marriage*

Due to communication revolution, class marriage has come in to existence. An engineer boy with an engineer girl, a doctor boy with a doctor girl, a management boy with management girls, a professor boy with professor girl, and so on.

*Very late marriage*

The youth of to-day prefer very late marriage. They want to marry after 30 years and below 40 years.

*Live in relationship*

Due to communication revolution, the youth of today want to live in relationship. They do not want to remain as married couple. But they want to live in relationship.

*No interest in procreation of child*

The youth today do not want to produce child. They want to enjoy bodily pleasure, but do not want to reproduce children. This has happened due to communication revolution.

*Procreation by Surrogacy Mother*

The youth of today are interested in procreation through surrogacy. They find out a woman who wants to become surrogacy mother. They adopt the child born by surrogacy.

*Always in search of new jobs*

The youth of today are always interested in search of new jobs. They start searching for new jobs soon after joining the first job. This has become possible due to communication revolution.

***Impact on Woman***

Communication revolution has brought profound impact on woman of today. The impact of communication revolution on woman can be discussed under following sub-headings:

- Online information about woman empowerment
- Online information of International woman day
- Information about National woman day
- Information about National Women Commission
- Information about State Woman Commission
- Information about human rights of women
- Information about Woman Acts and statutes
- Information about Constitutional safeguards
- Information about woman problems
- Information about woman crime
- Information about woman Thana (Mahila thana)
- Information about woman welfare schemes
- Information about woman safety measures
- Information about woman health and family welfare
- Information about woman rehabilitation scheme
- Information about woman educational institutions
- Entrance of woman in I.T. and Management Institutes
- Woman in multinational companies
- Rise of Women IT and Management Professionals
- Rise of Woman entrepreneurs
- Foreign travel by woman
- Love marriage and inter-caste marriage
- Woman cell phone users
- Woman internet users
- Woman computer operators
- Woman migration and settlement in foreign countries

Now, let us discuss these impacts of communication revolution on woman one by one in detail.

*Online information about woman empowerment*

Due to communication revolution, information about woman empowerment is available online. The woman of today visits websites of Ministries and organisations to know about them.

*Online information of International woman day*

Woman of today has online information about the celebration of international woman day.

*Online information about National woman day*

Woman of To day has online information about the celebration of national woman day.

*Information about National woman commission*

Now-a-days, woman of today has online information about the national woman commission and how to approach it for solving problems. They visit website for this purpose about State woman commission. Women visit website of the commission to seek help and solve their problems.

*Information about human rights of woman*

Women of today have online information regarding their human rights. They visit the sites of human rights commission, if they feel that their human rights are being violated.

*Information about women Acts and statutes*

Women of today have online information about woman Acts and statutes. They are taking help of these acts, if and when they require it to get justice and fight against in justice.

*Information about Constitutional safeguards*

Now-a-days, women have information of their Constitutional safeguards. They are visiting websites to know their Constitutional provisions.

*Information about women problems*

The women of today have online information about their problems when they are in journey, office, public place and even alone in homes. They remain alert.

*Information about woman crime*

The woman of today has online information about crime committed against her. She remains alter and takes help of online in case of trouble.

*Information about Mahila thana (Woman Thana)*

Women of today have online information about Mahila thana where they can visit to report crime against them. They also visit Mahila thana website for online FIR.

*Information about women safety measures*

Women of today have online information about their safety at workplace, journey, public place, local transport and even in house. They visit websites to get safety during trouble. They also take help of Mahila helpline and PCR.

*Information about Women welfare schemes*

Woman of today have online information about woman welfare schemes launched by the Government. They visit the site to get benefit and know in detail.

*Information about woman health and family welfare*

Women of today have online information about woman health and family welfare programmes.

*Information about woman rehabilitation scheme*

Women of today have online information about woman rehabilitation schemes. They visit websites for this purpose.

*Informations about woman educational institutions*

Women of today have online information of different educational institutions where they can take admission for study. They visit websites of those institutions to get detail information and to take final decision.

*Entrance of woman in IT and Management Institutes*

Due to communication revolution, woman of today has entered in IT and management institutes for technical and professional education.

*Rise of woman IT and Management professionals*

Due to communication revolution, woman of today have emerged as IT professionals and management professionals.

*Rise of woman entrepreneurs*

Due to communication revolution, women have emerged as entrepreneurs. They have established their own companies, business, trade or start up work.

*Woman in multinational companies*

Due to communication revolution, women have got job opportunities in multinational companies at high packages.

*Foreign travel by women*

Women of today are making foreign trips related to their jobs and business.

*Love marriage and Intercaste, marriage*

Women of today are doing love marriages and intercaste marriages. They also live in relation. Some of them decide to remain unmarried and serve the society.

*Women cell phone users*

Due to communication revolution, women cell phone users have risen up.

*Women internet users*

Due to communication revolution, woman have emerged as internet users.

*Women as computer operator*

Due to communication revolution, the demand of women computer operator has gone up. Women are getting appointment as computer operator in different institutions.

*Women migration and settlement in foreign counties*

Women of today are migrating foreign countries. They are staying there getting citizenship and establishing their settlement in foreign countries.

***Impact on Scheduled Tribes***

The communication revolution has also brought significant impact on Scheduled Tribes. The impact of communication revolution on Scheduled Tribes can be discussed under the following sub-headings:

- Scheduled Tribes as cell phone users
- Scheduled Tribes as computer and internet users
- Scheduled Tribes in IT and management institutes
- Scheduled Tribes as IT and management professionals
- Scheduled Tribes in entrepreneurship, business and trade
- Foreign travel by Scheduled Tribes
- Scheduled Tribes as computer operator
- Scheduled Tribe in multinational companies
- Foreign migration and settlement by Scheduled Tribes
- Rise of professional class
- Inter-caste and inter-religion marriage
- Scheduled Tribes Job in multinational companies
- Information of tribal cultures
- Information of tribal problems
- Information of acts and statutes
- Information of Constitutional provision
- Information of scholarship and welfare programmes
- Information regarding reservation of seats
- Information about S.T. Commission
- Information about Ministry of Tribal Affairs
- Information about S.T. Thana and helpline
- Online FIR facility
- Online marketing facility
- Online ticket reservation
- Online hotel reservation
- Online food supply order

Now, let us discuss about these impacts one by one.

*Scheduled Tribes as cell phone users*

Due to communication revolution, Scheduled Tribes have emerged as cell phone users. In Scheduled Tribes, almost all adult and young members have cell phones for the purpose of communication.

*Scheduled Tribes as Computer and Internet users*

Due to communication revolution, Scheduled Tribes have emerged as computer and Internet users. They are well trained and skilled in use of computer and Internet for the purpose of communication.

*Scheduled Tribes in IT and management institutes*

Due to communication revolution, students of Scheduled Tribes have entered in IT and management institutes for I.T. and management degrees. They are coming out after getting success.

*Scheduled Tribes as IT and management professionals*

Due to communication revolution, the young students of STs are emerging as IT and management professionals. They are getting jobs in management institute and technical institutes.

*Scheduled Tribes Job in Entrepreneurship, business and trade*

Due to communication revolution. Youth STs are entering in entrepreneurship, business and trade.

*Foreign travel by Scheduled Tribes*

Due to communication revolution, members of Scheduled Tribes are making foreign tripes because they have also become multinational company's employee.

*Scheduled tribes as computer operator*

Due to communication revolution, members of Scheduled Tribes have got jobs as computer operators in different institutions.

*Foreign migration and settlement of Scheduled Tribes*

The Scheduled Tribes members who are working in multinational companies, are not only making foreign trips for enjoyment. Rather they are migrating in foreign countries, getting citizenship and establishing their settlement in foreign countries.

*Rise of professional class*

Due to communication revolution professional classes have emerged in Scheduled Tribes. Now, they are divided in to engineer, doctor, lawyer, technical professionals, management professionals, I.A.S., I.P.S. and other professional classes.

*Inter-caste and inter-religion marriage*

To professional tribals, tribe, caste, region, religion and language has no boundary for marriages. They are preferring inter-tribe, tribe-caste, inter-religious marriages, but within same professional class. For example engineer boy with engineer girl, doctor boy with doctor girl, professional boy with professional girl, lawyer boy with lawyer girl, IAS boy with IAS girl, IPS boy with IPS girl and so on.

*Scheduled Tribes Job in multinational companies*

Due to communication revolution, members of STs have got employment in multinational companies on good and high packages.

*Informations of tribal cultures*

The tribals of today have online information of tribal cultures due to communication revolution. They visit websites and know online informations of tribal cultures prevalent in the world.

*Information of tribal problems*

Due to communication revolution, online informations of tribal problems are available. Tribals visit the website to know those informations.

*Information of tribal Acts and statutes*

Communication revolution has provided online informations about tribal Acts and statutes. Interested people visit the sites to know those acts and statues.

*Information of Constitutional provisions*

Communication revolution has made online available constitutional provisions of Scheduled Tribes. The interested candidate visits websites to know in detail.

*Information of scholarship and Welfare Programmes*

Communication revolution has provided informations about tribal scholarship and welfare programmes online. Interested candidates visit the website to known in detail.

*Information regarding reservation of seats*

Communication revolution has provided informations of seat reservation in admission, employment, service and election of MP, MLA and Mukhia for tribals. The tribals visit websites to know about them in detail.

*Information about S.T. Commission*

Information about S.T. commission has been made available online. The interested candidates visit the sites to know about them in detail.

*Information about Ministry of Tribal Affairs*

Information about Ministry of Tribal Affairs has also been made available online. The interested candidates visit the sites for detail information.

*Information about S.T. Thana and helpline*

The communication revolution has made available information about S.T. Thana and helpline online. The tribals visit website to know in detail and solve their problem.

*Online FIR Facility*

The communication revolution has brought facility for online FIR in Thana-police. Tribals visit websites of Thana-police for online FIR.

*Online marketing facility*

Due to communication revolution tribals are also availing online marketing facility. They place online supply order and do payment online. They receive home delivery of goods.

*Online ticket reservation.*

Due to communication revolution, tribals are also availing online plane, train, ship, A.C. buses reservation facility.

*Online reservation in hotels and restaurants*

Due to communication revolution, tribals are also availing online reservation facility in hotels and restaurants.

*Online food supply order from restaurants*

Due to communication revolution, tribals are also availing facility of online food supply order to a restaurant and make online payment to get home delivery.

***Impact on Scheduled Castes***

Communication revolution has brought a number of impacts on life and culture of Scheduled Castes. The impact of communication revolution on SCs can be discussed under following sub-headings:

- SCs as cell phone users
- SCs as computer users
- SCs as internet users
- SCs in IT and Management Institutes
- SCs as IT and Management Professionals
- SCs in entrepreneurship, business and trade
- SCs Jobs in multinational companies

- SCs as computer operators
- Foreign travel by SCs
- Foreign migration and settlement by SCs
- Travel in AC train and car by SCs
- Rise of professional classes in SCs
- Stay of SC in AC hotels
- Inter-caste and inter-religion marriage
- Information about SCs cultures
- Information about SCs problem
- Information about Constitutional safeguards
- Information about Acts and statutes
- Information about scholarship and welfare programmes
- Information about reservation of seats
- Information about S.C. Commission
- Information about S.C. Thana and helpline
- Online FIR facility to SCs
- Online marketing facility to SCs
- Online ticket reservation facility
- Online enrolment in hospitals
- Online meal supply order
- Online cinema tickets or eyelex ticket
- Online entertainment
- Photography through mobiles and communication of selfie

Now, let us discuss about these impacts one by one.

*SCs as cell phone users*

Due to communication revolution, SCs have emerged as cell phone users. Almost all SCs family, all young and adult members have cell phones. Thus, they have become smart phone users.

*SCs as computer users*

Due to communication revolution, SCs have emerged as computer users. They either have own desktop, laptop, hand tablet or they have received training of operating computer in computer training centres. In this way, young SCs members have become computer users.

*SCs as Internet users*

Due to communication revolution, young SCs members have emerged as internet users. With the help of desk top, laptop and hand tablets, they are able to visit websites for their works. Thus, they are expert in using internet. They can download any kind of information from internet websites.

*SCs in IT and Management institutes*

Communication revolution has attracted SC boys and girls to take admission in information technology and management institutes for study and research. They are getting degree in IT and management successfully.

*SCs as IT and Management professionals*

Due to communication revolution, SCs boys and girls have emerged as IT and management professionals.

*SCs in entrepreneurship, business and trade*

Due to communication revolution, SCs boys and girls have intered in entrepreneurship, business and trade enterprises. Some have been attracted towards start up works.

*SCs Jobs in Multinational company*

Due to communication revolution SCs candidates have been able to get jobs in multinational companies as IT engineer or managers on handsome packages.

*SCs as computer operator*

Due to communication revolution SCs candidates have been able to get employment as computer operators in different institutes. This revolution has brought employment opportunities to tribal youth in IT sectors and private institutes.

*Foreign travels by SCs*

Due to communication revolution, SCs candidates have been able to get employment as IT engineers and managers. They make foreign trips by airways for company work.

*Foreign migration and settlement by SCs*

SCs candidates working in multinational companies are migrating to foreign countries, getting citizenship and establishing their settlements there. Thus, communication revolution has made them NRIs.

*Travel by AC train and car*

Due to communication revolution, SCs candidates have started travelling in AC train buses and cars.

*Rise of professional classes in SCs*

Due to communication revolution, SCs candidates have become professional class conscious. Now, they identify themselves as engineer, doctor, professor, lawyer, manager, trader, IT expert company owners and so on.

*Stay of SCs in A.C. hotels*

Due to communication revolution, SCs candidates have started seeking accommodation in costly A.C. hotels for which payment of bills is reimbursed by the company where they work.

*Inter-caste and inter-religion marriage*

Duet to communication revolution, SC candidates have started doing class marriages. For marriage they have crossed ethnic boundaries like caste, tribe, race, language, region and religion. They prefer marriage within classes. For example an engineer boy with an engineer girl, doctor boy with doctor girl, I.I.Tian boy with I.I.Tian girl, manager boy with manager girl, professor boy with professor girl, lawyer boy with layer girl, communication expert boy with communication expert girl.

*Information about SCs cultures*

Due to communication revolution, SCs candidates have become aware of cultures of each other. It is because information about culture of each S.C. is available on websites.

*Information about SCs problems*

Communication revolution has provided information of SCs problems online. Any SC candidate can visit the site and download them.

*Information about Constitutional safeguards*

Communication revolution has made available informations about Constitutional safe guards on websites. SCs candidates visit sites to download them.

*Information about Acts and statutes*

The communication revolution has made available informations related to SC. Acts and statutes online. SCs candidates visit websites to download them for study.

*Information about scholarship and welfare programmes*

Due to communication revolution , it has become possible to make available informations about scholarships and welfare programmes of SCs online. The SCs candidates visit the website to download them.

*Information about reservation of seats*

The communication revolution has made available information about reservation of seats in M.P., MLA, Mukhia elections, educational institution and Central and State Governments services online. SCs candidates visit the sites and download them for use.

*Information about SCs commission*

Due to communication revolution, it has become possible to know online information about SCs commission, its structure and functions. The SCs candidates visit sites to download them.

*Information about SCs Thana and helpline*

The communication revolution has made us available online information about SCs Thana and helpline. The SCs candidates visit the site to download them and lodge complaints.

*Online FIR Facility to SCs*

The communication revolution has made us available online information about FIR facility. Now, FIR can be done online which stands valid legally.

*Online enrolment in hospitals*

Due to communication revolution, SCs patients have become successful in making enrolment in AIIMS and other superspeciality and multispeciality hospitals for treatment.

*Online meal supply order*

Due to communication revolution, SCs members are able to place online order of meal supply in costly hotels or restaurants. The meal is delivered in house and payment is made online.

*Online cinema tickets or eyelex ticket*

Members of SCs have become able to get cinema and eyelex tickets online. They do payment online and reserve seat in cinema hall.

*Online entertainment*

The communication revolution has brought before SCs the facility of online entertainment on cell phones, and T.V. channels.

*Photographs and selfie*

Due to communication revolution it has become possible to take photographs through cell phones and make communication of selfie for S.Cs.

***Impact on OBCs***

The communication revolution has brought a number of changes in life and culture of members belonging to OBCs. The impact of communication revolution on OBCs can be discussed under following sub-headings:

- OBCs as cellphone users
- OBCs as computer users
- OBCs as internet users
- OBCs in IT and management institutes
- OBCs as IT and management professionals
- OBCs in multinational companies
- OBCs in entrepreneurship, business and trade
- Emergence of classes in OBCs
- Inter-caste and inter-religions marriage
- OBCs as computer operator
- Foreign travel by OBCs
- Migration of OBCs as NRIs
- Travel in AC train, bus and car
- Travel by air
- Stay in costly AC hotels
- Meal of costly hotels
- Follower of Pop culture
- Information about OBCs culture
- Information about OBCs problems
- Information about OBC movements
- Information about Constitutional provisions
- Information about OBCs commission
- Information about seat reservation
- Information about scholarship and welfare programmes
- Information about online FIR and helpline
- Information about availability of train tickets
- Information about availability of plane tickets
- Information about availability of rooms in hotels
- Information about availability of food in hotels
- Information about enrolment number in hospitals
- Photography through phones and selfie communication
- Online entertainment

Now, let us discuss about these impacts one by one in detail.

### *OBCs as cell phone users*

Due to communication revolution, OBCs have emerged as cell phone users. Almost all young individuals of OBCs have cell phones by which they make communication. This has made them cell phones users. Each of them has own mobile set.

### *OBCs as computer users*

Due to communication revolution, OBCs have emerged as computer users. They have desktop, laptop, hand tablet through which they make communication.

### *OBCs as Internet users*

The communication revolution has made young individuals of OBCs as internet users. They have installed internet facility in their smart phones, laptops and desktops. They visit websites to download informations. The internet has connected them to entire world.

### *OBCs in IT and Management Institutes*

Due to communication revolution, candidates of OBCs have got opportunity to get admission in information technology institutes and management institutes. This has brought a great impact on life and culture of OBCs.

### *OBCs as IT and management professionals*

Due to communication revolution, IT engineers and management professionals have emerged in OBCs after getting IT and management degree.

### *OBCs in multinational companies*

Due to communication revolution, candidates of OBCs have been able to get jobs in multinational companies after getting IT and management degree from reputed institutes on hand some packages.

### *OBCs in entrepreneurship, business and trade*

Due to communication revolution, candidates of OBCs have entered in to entrepreneurship, business and trade. They have established their own companies after getting IT and management degree. They are also engaged in start up works.

*Emergence of classes in OBCs*

Due to communication revolution, occupational classes have emerged in OBCs. After getting I.T., management and higher education, they have been divided as IT engineers, management professionals, professors, lawyers, company owners, and others. Thus, formation of occupational classes have taken place in OBCs.

*Inter-caste and inter-religion marriage*

The communication revolution has encouraged inter-caste and inter-religion marriage in OBCs. The communication revolution has created international classes among OBCs. International classes prefer inter-caste and inter-religion marriage. They want to select marriage partners even out side their castes and religion. An IT engineer boy wants to marry with an engineer girl, a management professional boy prefers marriage with a management professional girl, a doctor boy with a doctor girl, a lawyer boy with a lawyer girl, an entrepreneur boy with an entrepreneur girl and so on. This form of mate selection has brought class marriage in place of caste marriage.

*OBCs as computer operator*

The communication revolution has opened opportunity of skill development in OBCs candidates. They are receiving training in computer application and computer sciences. After getting training in computer application, they are getting jobs as computer operations in Governmental and Non-Governmental institutions on payment of monthly salary.

*Foreign Travel by OBCs*

The communication revolution has provided jobs to OBCs candidates in multinational companies. They have to make foreign trips related to their company works. For company work they travel foreign countries several times. Besides, they also make trip to foreign countries to enjoy holidays.

*Migration of OBCs as NRIs*

OBCs candidates are migrating to foreign countries related to their jobs and business. They are getting citizenship and establishing their settlement there. They are becoming NRIs.

*Travel in A.C. Train, bus and car*

OBCs candidates as IT engineers, management professionals and NRIs prefer to travel in A.C. train, bus and car.

*Travel by Air*

Due to communication revolution, OBCs candidates have been able to travel by air. They are making travel of foreign countries.

*Stay in costly A.C. hotels*

OBCs candidate as NRIs, IT engineers and management professionals prefer to stay in costly AC hotels, 3 stars hotels or five star hotels.

*Meal of costly and luxurious Hotels*

OBCs NRIs, IT engineers, management professional, professor, doctor, and business man OBCs prefer to take taste of costly and luxurious food items during holidays. They also prefer costly entertainment.

*Follower of Pop culture*

The members of OBCs have become followers of pop or popular culture. They are following global popular dresses, hair styles, songs, music, dance and languages. This has happened due to communication revolution.

*Information of OBCs culture*

Due to communication revolution, it has become possible to know characteristics of OBCs culture online.

*Information about OBCs problems*

Online informations have been provided regarding OBCs problems due to communication revolution.

*Information about OBCs movements*

Due to communication revolution, it has become possible to get information of OBCs movements online.

*Information about Constitutional provisions*

Due to communication revolution online informations about Constitutional provisions of OBCs have been made available on sites. Candidates of OBCs visit sites to know them in detail.

*Information about OBCs Commission*

The communication revolution has given opportunities of OBCs candidates to know about the structure and function of OBC commission online. Desirous candidates visit the websites of commission to know about them and to lodge complaints to get justice.

*Information about Seat reservation*

The communication revolution has provided online information to OBCs candidates regarding reservation of seats in admission election and Central and State Government services.

*Information about scholarship and welfare programmes*

Due to communication revolution, it has become possible for OBCs students and scholars to know online information regarding their scholarship for study and welfare programmes to bring them in main stream of nation.

*Information about Online FIR and helpline*

Due to information revolution, it has become possible for OBCs candidates to lodge FIR in police station against crime, injustice, exploitation and oppression online.

*Information about availability of train tickets*

Due to communication revolution, it has become possible for OBCs to get online information about availability of train tickets. OBCs candidate visits websites to get train ticket reserved and make payment online.

*Information about availability of plane tickets*

Due to communication revolution, it has become possible for candidates of OBCs to get online information about availability of plane ticket. The OBC candidate visits websites to get plane ticket reserved and make payment of fares online.

*Information about availability of rooms in hotels*

Due to communication revolution, it has become possible to get online information about availability of rooms in hotels of different visiting places. The OBC candidates visit website to get room confirmed online in advance and make payment of room rent in advance.

*Information about availability of food in hotels*

Due to communication revolution, it has become possible for OBCs candidates to get online information about availability of food items in hotels. The OBCs candidates visit website of hotels to place order of desired food items. They make online payment and get home delivery.

*Information about enrolment number in hospitals*

Due to communication revolution, it has become possible for members of OBCs to get online information about enrolment and confirmation of number in superspeciality hospitals all over country and even abroad.

*Photography through phones and selfie communication*

Due to communication revolution, it has become possible to take photography of scenes, sceneries and selfie and communicate them to friends and relatives through smart phones with internet facility.

*Online Entertainment*

The communication revolution has provided OBCs opportunities for online entertainments. Entertainment through smart phones and TVs has become possible.

### *Impact on Children*

Communication revolution has brought a number of changes on life and culture of children. The impact of communication revolution on children can be discussed under the following sub-headings:

- Online information of healthy child rearing practices
- Online information of child feeding process
- Online information about children vaccination
- Online information of children health card
- Online information about children diseases
- Online information about first aids
- Online information of child care centre
- Online information of child nursing home
- Online information of Aaya culture
- Online information of children hospitals
- Online information of child specialists
- Online information for enrolment number in hospitals
- Online information of children dresses shops
- Online information of children toys shops
- Online information of children games
- Children games in cell phones
- Children games on T.V.
- Children games on smart phones
- Children games on computer
- Children games on internet
- Children play schools
- Children school with hostels
- Information on children crimes (Juvenile delinquency)
- Information about crime against children
- Information about orphans and orphanage
- Information about destitute children and their schools
- Information about child entertainment channels
- Information about children sanitation
- Information about lactating mother feeding
- Children as cell phone users
- Children as Smart phone users
- Children as computer users

- Children as internet users
- Information about child abuse

Now, let us discuss about these impacts on children due to communication revolution one by one.

*Online Information of healthy child rearing practices*

Communication revolution has brought before us online informations about healthy child rearing practices. Parents visit the sites and avail benefits of them.

*Online Information of child feeding process*

The communication revolution has provided us online information about healthy child feeding process. The parents visit the sites and get acquainted with those processes.

*Online Information about of children vaccination*

The communication revolution has brought before us online information about children vaccination in different ages. The parents visit the site and take advantages of them.

*Online Information about child health card*

Due to communication revolution, Child Health Card is made available online by the hospital. Conscious guardians and parents visit websites to know about them in detail and get further advantages.

*Online information about children diseases*

The communication revolution has given us online information about the diseases from which a child is expected to suffer during his/her childhood. The parents visit websites to know about them in detail. Suggestion for treatment is also provided online.

*Online information about first aid*

The communication revolution has made us available information about first aid in case of Diarrhoea and other child diseases.

*Online information of child care centre*

The communication revolution has provided us online information of child care centre where care of children are taken properly. Parents visit websites to know in detail about those centres. Those parents who do not have sufficient time, visit these centres for keeping children in care of the centre.

*Online information of child nursing homes*

Communication revolution has also provided online us information about child nursing homes where nursing facilities for children are available. The desirous parents visit these sites for putting their children in child nursing homes.

*Online information of Aaya culture*

Communication revolution has provided us online information about Aaya culture. In this culture, parents who do not have time for rearing child, keep an *Aaya* (maid servant). The maid servant keeps every care of child like own parent. The desirous parents visit websites to get an Aaya for their new born child.

*Online information of children hospitals*

The communication revolution has provided us online information about children hospitals where children can be admitted for treatment during emergency.

*Online information of child specialists*

Due to communication revolution, it has become possible to get online information about child specialist doctors of different hospitals or private practicener.

*Online information for enrolment for treatment in hospitals*

The communication revolution has made us online available information about enrolment number for treatment in a hospital or a private practicener in nursing home.

*Online information for children dresses shops*

Communication revolution provides us online information about children dresses shops. The parents visit those shops personally or give online order for home delivery of kids and children wear after online payment.

*Online Information of children toys shops*

Communication revolution has provided us online information of children toy shops. Parents visit those shops personally for shopping toys or they order for supply toys in house after online payment.

*Online Information of children games*

Due to communication revolution, online information of children games are available. The children visit the sites to get information in detail and to make online purchase of those games after online payment.

*Children games in cell phones*

Children games are also available in cell phones. Children play those games with mobiles.

*Children games on T.V.*

Children games are also available on T.V. The children play those games with T.V.

*Children games on smart phones*

Children games are also available on smart phones. Children play those games with smart phones.

*Children games on computer*

Children games are also available in computers. The children use computers to play those games.

*Children games on internet*

Children games are also available on internet. Children visit the sites for playing games.

*Children play schools*

Communication revolution has provided us online information about children play schools where children are admitted for play under the supervision of a teacher. Besides teaching something through plays, the teacher takes every care of children in play schools.

*Children schools with hostels*

Due to communication revolution, it has become possible to know in detail about children schools with hostels. The parents visit sites to know in detail and to send their children in schools with hostel facilities.

*Information on Children Crimes (Juvenile delinquency)*

Online informations about delinquency has been provided to the parents and guardians. The parents or guardians visit the website to know about then in detail.

*Information about crime against children*

Online informations about crime against children has been made available by the Government concerned institution. Helpline is also made available. The parents visit the sites whenever they require.

*Informations about orphans and orphanage*

Online informations about orphans and orphanage has been made available by the Government and institution. People inform police online regardian an orphan or they inform orphanage to take care of children.

*Information about destitute children and their schools*

Online informations regardings destitute children and their schools are available. Parents visit the site to send their destitute children in those schools.

*Information about Child entertainment channels*

Children of today prefer to see entertainment channels on T.V. and internet. They prefer cartoons and other children entertainment channels.

*Information about children sanitation*

Online information about sanitation and good habit has been made available for children. Interested parents visit the site to get detail information.

*Information about lactating mother food*

Online information about lactating mother and their food has been made available. Lactating women or their guardians visit site to know detail information.

*Children as cell phone users*

Due to communication revolution, the children has emerged as cell phone users.

*Children as smart phone users*

Due to communication revolution, children has started using smart phones.

*Children as computer users*

Due to communication revolution, children has become computer users. They use computers without any hesitation.

*Children as internet users*

Due to communication revolution, children has started using internet on computers or smart phones of their parents.

*Information about child abuse*

Online information related to child abuse has been made available to parents by the Government and concerned institutions. The parents visit the site to know about them in detail.

***Impact on Aged***

Communication revolution has brought a lot of changes on life and culture of aged persons of the society. The impact of communication revolution on aged can be discussed under following sub-headings:

- Aged as cell phone users
- Aged as smart phone users
- Aged as computer users
- Aged as internet users
- Entertainment with T.V.
- Aged as e-news reader
- Aged on social media
- Aged on e-mail
- Information about aged problems
- Information about Aged Care Centres
- Information about old age home
- Information about social security
- Information about crime on aged
- Information about welfare schemes for aged

Now, let us discuss about these impacts of communication revolution on aged one by one in detail.

*Aged as cell phone users*

Due to communication revolution aged have become cell phone users. They are having their own cell phone number. With the help of cell phone, they are able to maintain their contacts with friends, relatives and children residing in different parts of country and abroad.

*Aged as smart phone users*

The communication revolution has made aged persons as smart phone users. They have changed their simple mobile phones with the help of smart mobile phone. They take help of smart phones for communication and selfie.

*Aged as computer users*

The communication revolution has made aged persons as computer users. They have computer set in house. They know to use them and make communication with other persons.

*Aged as internet users*

The communication revolution has made aged persons as internet users. They have internet connection in computer or in smart phone and with the help of internet they are able to know a number of informations and to communicate informations to others.

*Entertainment with T.V.*

The communication revolution has provided the aged persons opportunities to enjoy entertainment channels through T.V. and smart phones.

*Aged as e-news readers*

The communication revolution has made a number of aged persons as e-news reader. They read news through their smart phones.

*Aged on social media*

The communication revolution has made aged social media users. They use social media like facebook, twitter, YouTube, whatsapps and other for the purpose of communication to their friends, relatives and others. They also communicate ideas, reactions and other opinions on social media.

*Aged on e-mail*

The aged have also emerged as e-mail users. They have their own e-mail ID with the help of which they make communication with friends, relatives, children, grand children and others.

*Information about aged problems*

The communication revolution has provided online information about problems which aged of today are facing in the society. They visit the websites to know them a rid try to solve those problem. They also become alert of those problems.

*Information about Aged Care Centres*

Due to communication revolution, information about aged care centre is available online. The aged or their relatives visit websites to know about those centres in detail so that in case of urgency they can take help of these centres for their aged persons.

*Information about old age home*

Due to communication revolution, informations about old age homes are available online. The relatives of aged visit the sites to know facilities and expenses so that in case of urgency aged of family can be kept there under care of old age home.

*Information about social security*

Communication revolution has made information of social security available online. The aged visit those sites to know about them.

*Information about crime on aged*

Communication revolution the aged are able to know has made aged persons available crimes committed against them. The aged persons visit sites to know the nature and extent of crime and become alert. They think about their safety.

*Information of welfare schemes for aged*

Due to communication revolution, the aged are able to know online informations about welfare schemes for the aged launched by the Government. The aged or their sons or daughter visit the websites to know about welfare schemes of aged and how benefit can be achieved.

# 12
# Development Communication

Development is a value loaded concept. It is related to such individuals, families, castes, class and areas which are backwards in relation to others. Hence, they are not in the mainstream of nation. In order to bring them in mainstream of nation, the term development has been conceptualised. The concept of development includes development policies, development planning and development programmes. The development programmes are formulated, implemented, monitored, evaluated and followed up. Thus, development process includes a number of steps.

Communication is related to exchange of news or informations of various types. Communication involves communicator or sender, receiver, channel, messages form, code, topic and scene. Language and acts as medium of communication between sender and receiver and *vice versa*.

The term "development communication" is made up of two terms. In fact, it is combination of two terms: development and communication. The meaning of development communication is to understand development from the approaches, methods, techniques and theories of communication. Development and communication are interrelated and interdependent. Communication sends message of development to the people and development provides means to the communication. Thus, communication makes development fruitful and development makes communication fruitful. In this way, development and communication maintain their co-existence.

## Process of Development Communication

Development communication is a both way process. In this process, the sender of one message becomes receiver for another message. In this way development communication functions. This process can be understood in either way of observing the Fig. 12.1 given below.

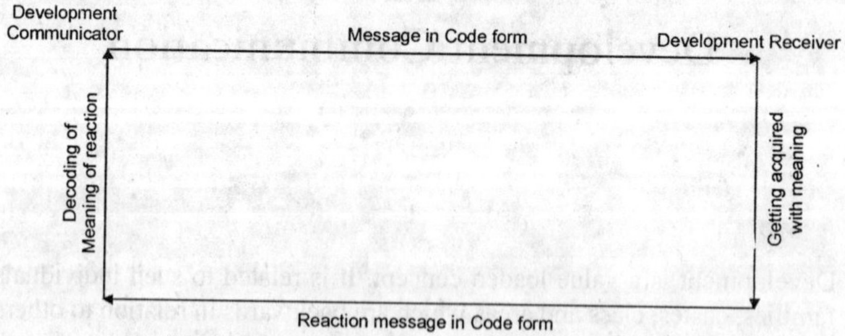


**Fig 12.1:** Development Communication Process

## Elements of Development Communication

The chief elements of development communication are as follows:

- Development communicator
- Development receiver
- Development in message form
- Development channel
- Development code
- Development topic
- Development scene
- Development skill
- Impediments to development communication
- Flow of communication development
- Impact of communication revolution on development communication

Now, let us discuss about these elements of development communication one by one.

### *Development Communicator*

Development communicators are also known as development senders or development messengers. They can be divided in to following three categories:

- Governmental communicator
- Non-Governmental communicator
- International communicator

Now, let us discuss about these development communicators one by one.

***Governmental Communicator***

The following agents and agencies work as Governmental Communicator of development:

- Ward member
- Mukhia
- Panchayat official
- Panchayat mitra
- Village school teacher
- High school teacher
- College professor
- University professor
- Doctor
- Engineer
- Lawyer
- Health workers or Swasthya mitra
- Anganwadi workers
- Block officials
- Thana officials
- District officials
- Technical institutes
- Management Institutes
- Research centres
- Cultural institutes
- Different commissions
- Different Ministries and Ministers
- President
- Prime Minister
- Chief Minister
- M.P.

- MLA
- Mayor
- Municipal corporation
- Municipality
- Mega Municipal Corporation
- District development authority
- Government Radio and T.V. Channel

These are Governmental communicators of development. About them a detail description has been provided under the chapter Agency of Communication (Chapter 9). Hence, detail description of them is not being furnished here.

***Non-Governmental Communicator of Development***

- Family
- Village head
- Village panchayat
- Inter village head
- Inter village panchayat
- Caste panchayat
- Voluntary organisations
- Non-Governmental organisations
- Private schools
- Private colleges
- Private universities
- Private Management Institutes
- Private medical colleges
- Private engineering colleges
- Private nursing Hospitals
- Private law colleges
- Private Law Universities
- Private B.Ed. Colleges
- Private radio and T.V. channels

All above mentioned private agencies or agents work as the communicator of development. Hence, they are known as Non-Governmental communicator of development. They have to follow Government rules and regulations, but they are not Governmental communicators. They have their own autonomy, too. They have also been described under chapter-9.

***International Communicator of Development***

International development communicators are as follows:

- UNICEF
- UNESCO
- Ford Foundation
- Red Cross Society
- CARE
- WHO
- World Bank
- IMF
- UNO
- United Nations Security Council
- World Human Rights Commission
- World Environment Security Council
- World Global Cultural Heritage
- WTO
- World Intellectual Property Rights Council
- Nuclear disarmament
- World Cancer Day
- World AIDS Day
- World Women Day

These world agencies work as international communicator of development. They have also been described under chapter-9.

**Receivers of Development Communication**

The receivers of development communication are public. The receivers of development communication are as follows:

- Children
- Adolescents
- Youth
- Adult
- Aged
- Women
- SCs
- STs
- OBCs

- Patients
- Students
- Village dwellers
- Towns dwellers
- Cities dwellers
- Metropolis dwellers
- Plateau dwellers
- Plain dwellers
- Forest dwellers
- River dwellers
- Mountain dwellers
- Sea shore dwellers
- Island dwellers
- Desert dwellers

These are receivers of development communication.

## Channels of Development Communication

In development communication, verbal and non-verbal channels are used. Thus, channel of development communication maybe divided in to two types:

- Verbal channel
- Non–verbal channel

### *Verbal Channel*

Verbal channel used in development communication may be of following types:

- Oral channel
- Written channel
- Visual channel
- Audio-visual channel

#### *Oral channel*

This is most prevalent form of development communication channel. This channel is used by both illiterate and literate people. People want to hear news of development from development communicator. When communication is made in same dialect, by the communicator, people understand the news easily. They see and hear communicator communicating development related news. This influences the receiver public more than simply writing and reading of news.

Governmental, Non-Governmental and international communicators meet the people first. They communicate development news and try to convince the people for whom development news is meant. The people see the communicator specking and hear their news speech of development. They also make conversation with members of community. Only then they take final decision about accepting or rejecting the development news.

In order to make development communication more effective, morning prayer is organised, procession is held, and slogan shouting is made. This makes development news more effective among the people.

## Written Channel of Development Communication

Besides oral communication, development communicators also use written channel for communicating development news among the people. The written channel includes newspapers, booklets, pamphlets, wall writing, bulletin, slogan writing and others.

This channels influences more literate people who are regarded as elite of the society. The elites of the society make people aware of development news by reading. They communicate written news orally to the people. This also brings great influence on people. Written channel is used to influence development beneficiaries by the communicator. The communicator visits among the people, does wall writing, distributes books, booklets, bulletin and pamphlets, copy of newspapers etc. The people go through those written channels and become convinced regarding development programmers.

### *Visual channel*

The development communicator also uses visual channel of communication to influence development beneficiaries or people. He/She visits among the people, shows different pictures, posters, symbols, impact pictures, on development programmes to make people convinced towards development programmes. In this channel, the different aspects and benefits of development programmes are focused among public through photographic symbols or graphic symbols. For this purpose visual aids are also taken besides distribution of printed photographic symbols.

*Audio-Visual channel*

The development communicator also uses audio-visual channel of communication to influence development beneficiaries and public. The development communicator organises video show, cinema, T.V. show, development serial, video conferencing, seminar, conference and meeting among the people. The people are extracted and influenced by audio-visual channel of development communication.

**Non-verbal Channel of Development Communication**

Besides verbal channel, the development communicator also uses non-verbal channel for communicating development news among the people. While communicating development news, the development communicator uses his\her face, body and body parts as channel of communication. Non-verbal channel of development may be as follows:

- Head channel
- Fore Head channel
- Nose channel
- Ear channel
- Mouth channel
- Cheek channel
- Lip channel
- Teeth channel
- Tongue channel
- Neck channel
- Hand channel
- Finger channel
- Stomach channel
- Waist channel
- Thigh channel

Thus, a communicator uses his face, body and entire body parts as non-verbal channel of development communication. While making verbal communication he\she uses his\her non-verbal channel to bring a balance in communication.

***Message Form***

The development communicator uses following message forms for development communication:

- Words
- Sentence
- Song
- Tales
- Proverbs
- Idioms
- Phrases
- Riddles
- Music
- Dance
- Symbols
- Case study
- Body language
- Sloagan

**Development Code**

The development communicator uses development code for communicating development news. These development codes may be of following types:

- Descriptive code
- Factual code
- Impact code
- Confusion removing code
- Diagnostic code
- Incouraging code
- Humour code
- Religious code
- Welfare code
- Social code
- Cultural code
- Body language code

With the help of above codes, the development communicator attempts to send development messages among the people.

**Topic of Development Communication**

The topic of development communication may be as follows:

- Village
- Women
- Children
- Youth
- Adult
- Aged or Senior citizen
- Scheduled Castes
- Scheduled Tribes
- OBCs
- Education
- Health
- Economy
- Religion
- Politics
- Environment
- Sanitation
- Poverty alleviation
- AIDS
- Cancer
- Leprocy
- Culture
- Art
- Craft
- Towns
- Cities
- Metropolises
- Railways
- Airways
- Transportation
- Communication
- Island
- Desert
- Forest
- Plain
- Plateau
- Flood
- Epidemic

- Starvation
- Festivals
- Fairs
- A number of other areas

**Scene of Development Communication**

The development communicator also presents scenes related to development programmes to influence people such as:

- Family planning
- Benefit of small family
- Impact of education
- Benefit of scientific agriculture
- Benefits of small business
- Benefits of service
- Benefits of modern treatment
- Benefits of Ayush medicines
- Benefits of animal husbandary
- Benefits of dairy
- Benefits of goatery
- Benefits of poultry
- Benefits of piggery
- Benefits of floriculture
- Benefits of vormi composte
- Benefits of chemical fertilizer
- Benefits of weedicides
- Benefits of insecticides
- Benefit of self-help group
- Exploitation of children and child labour
- Women exploitation and oppression
- Aged exploitation and oppression
- Benefit of Social security programmes
- Benefits of women development programmes
- Benefits of children development programmes
- Youth development programmes
- AIDS control programme
- Cancer related programme
- Malaria related programme
- T.B. related programme
- Leprosy related programme

- Safe drinking water programme
- Social development programme
- Cultural development programme
- Political development programme
- Environmental preservation programme
- Danger of pollution

In this way, sources of development related programmes before a communicator may be related to different aspects, areas and segments of society.

**Types of Development Communication**

The communication development may be of following types:

- Interpersonal development communication
- Mass development communication

In development communications, the communicator uses both types of communication interpersonal and mass.

**Inter Personal Communication**

In this type of development communication, the development communicator meets individually and personally to development beneficiaries by moving village to village and door to door. He\she communicates orally about the benefits of development programmes. Besides, oral communication he or she also takes helps of written, visual and audio-visual channels to convince the beneficiaries. In this type of development communication, the personal contact between communicator and the beneficiary is a must. Thus, a number of developmental agencies establish contact with public personally for communicating advantages of development programmes. Interpersonal communication may be between two individuals, an individual and a group, and a group and an individual.

**Mass Communication**

When development communication is made to the masses without meeting them personally, but using highly developed technology of communication from a place by a development communicator, it is known as mass communication.

In this development communication, the development communicator neither meets any one personally, nor visits door to door. He/She rather takes helps of developed information technology to communicate development related messages to the people. These developed means of communication are radio, T.V., computer, internet and print media.

## Communication Flows in Development Communication

In development communication, one finds following types of flows:

- Downwards flow
- Upwards flow
- Diagonal flow
- Horizontal flow

### *Downwards Flow*

In early periods, the flow of development communication was top to bottom; i.e., down wards. Development policies, strategies, programmes, implementation, monitoring, evaluation and follow up actions were taken by the people sitting at top position. Thus, in development communication, the people were not involved. They were only beneficiaries, not policy formulator, implementor, monitor, evaluator and follow actor. As a result, people started treated those imposed development programmes as burden on their head. Thus, downwards flow of communication was not taken as good.

### *Upward Flow of Development Communication*

The upwards flow of development communication came into existence as a reaction against downwards flow of communication. In downwards development communication development related messages follow the path of downwards to upwards. Now, the role of beneficiaries in formulating policies, strategies, programmes, plans and implementing, monitoring, evaluating and follow up actions came in to existence. Thus, when the flow of development communication goes from public to authority, it is called as downwards flow of communication. It is opposite to upwards flow of communication in which flow of communication goes from authority to public.

### *Diagonal Flow of Development Communication*

Diagonal flow of development communication has come in to existence to create coordination between different departments of the Government. The different departments of the Government are education, health, communication, trade, business, and so on. For the purpose of over all development coordination between different departments is a must. The coordination between different departments is maintained through diagonal flow of development communication.

### *Horizontal Flow of Development Communication*

This type of flow of development communication has come in to existence for people organisations and institutions who are placed at same level in hierarchy. When the flow of communication is between people of same level organisations or institution, it is called as horizontal flow of communication.

## Impact of Communication Revolution on Development Communication

The communication revolution has brought a great influence on development communication. Now, it has become very easy to communicate development news to the people. The impact of communication revolution on Development Communication can be discussed under following sub-heading:

- Online information of development policies
- Online information of development strategies
- Online information of development programmes and their implementation
- Online information of monitoring agencies
- Online information of evaluating agencies
- Online information of delivery system
- Online. information of follow up action
- Online information of public reactions
- Online information of corruption
- Online information of action taken
- Online information of budgetary provisions

Now, let us discuss about these impacts on development communication one by one in detail.

### *Online Information of Development Policies*

Due to communication revolution, it has become possible to know information about development policies of the Government online. Interested people visit the sites of different Ministries to know information about development policies of the Government. The people become acquainted with the intimations related to development policies online.

### *Online Information of Development Strategies*

The communication revolution has made people known about development strategies of the Government. The development strategies of Government has been made available to the people online. The interested people visit the websites of the Ministries to know about them in detail. Without strategy, development policies cannot achieve success.

### *Online Information of Development Programmes and their Implementation*

Following policies and strategies, development programmes are formulated and implemented. The information about development programmes formulated and implemented are made available online by the Ministries concerned. The people visit the websites to know about them in detail.

### *Online Information of Monitoring Agencies*

The communication revolution has made people available online informations about monitoring agencies of development communication. The people visit the site of different Ministries to know associated agencies of monitoring of development programmes.

### *Online Information of Evaluating Agencies*

The communication revolution has made us known online about evaluating agencies related to development programmes. The people visit the site to know about them and use them for several development related works. The reports of evaluation committee is also made available online. The interested people visit the site to know the bindings of the evaluation agency.

### *Online Information of Delivery System*

Under development programmes goods are delivered and assets are delivered for distribution among beneficiaries. Online information about delivery system is provided by the Government. The concerned people visit the site to know about delivery of goods and services.

### *Online Information of Follow up Action*

Online information of follow up action is provided by the Government. On the basis of evaluation report follow up action is taken. The follow up action includes continuation or discontinuation of a programme.

### *Online Information of Public Reactions*

Due to communication revolutions, it has become possible to make available the reactions of public towards a development programmes. The reactions of people are taken into consideration by the Government.

### *Online Information of Corruption*

Due to Communication revolution, it has become possible to provide online information of corruption involved in development programmes.

### *Online Information about Action Taken*

Due to communication revolution, it has become possible to provide informations about action taken on corrupt officials.

### *Online Information of Budgetary Provisions*

Due to communication revolution, it has become possible to provide online information about account. The income and expenditure is made available online.

# 13
# Business Communication

Today we are living in an age of globalisations. This age is also known as an age of marketisation. In the age of marketisation, business and trade have emerged as most preferred profession of corporate houses. This age is also known as age of Corporate industrialisation. Although in every age of history of mankind business has played significant role, but in the age of globalisation a number of multinational companies have emerged, which are involved in global business and trades. Multinational companies are owned by corporate houses. They have entered in business of education, health, communication, transportation, tourisms, hospitality, industries, railways and air services. Besides, they entered also in business of commodities of day to day use such as ration, oil, ghee, soap, surf, spicies, footwear, branded clothes, branded jewellery. Multinational companies have made world as a great market complex where day-night marketing, trade and business take place through ATM card, debit card, credit card, e-banking and cashless transaction by sitting on one place. This has become possible with the help of computer and internet, Supply of goods and transfer of money can take place by sitting on internet and computer. Multinational corporate houses claim their goods and services superior than other companies. This has increased competition among cooperate houses and MNCs. In order to prove their products better than others and attract the customers, they organise beauty competition of global, national, regional and state-level. The services of girls who compete and emerged as Winner or beauty queen is used to propagate the products of concerned companies. The corporate houses or MNCs have emerged as Cultural merchant. They establish Cultural Corporation.

Today, we have world level competition among cultural traders. They have great competition among themselves. In order to compete, they spend more and more on communication to attract their customers. The communication revolution has brought a great change on business, trade and market. In order to compete in global market more and more emphasis is being paid on business communication.

## Meaning of Business Communication

The meaning of business communication is to understand, describe, explain and know business from the point of view of approach, technique, method and theory of communication. Its chiefs purpose is to communicate business among more and more customers so that more and more profit can be earned.

## Process of Business Communication

The business communication is a both way process. This process includes a message sender and a message receiver. But message sender at one time becomes message receiver at other time. In this way reciprocal exchange of messages goes on, Besides sender and receiver, the messages are sent in code form. The sender communicates messages to receiver in code form. The receiver decodes the messages received. He/she expresses his\her reaction messages in code form after decoding them. Now, the reaction of receiver goes to sender in code form. The sender decodes the reaction and tries to understand the message conveyed as reactions expressed by receivers. The process of business communication can be understood in better by the diagram given below:

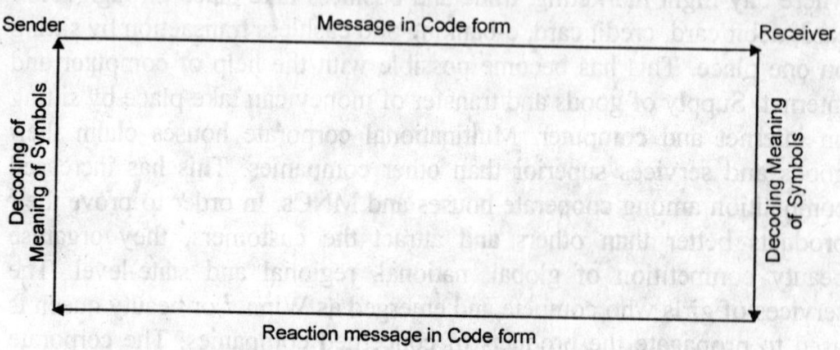


**Fig. 13:** Process of Burinen Communication

From the above diagram, it is quite dear that it is a communication of business news between sender and receiver and *vice versa.*

**Elements of Business Communication**

The chief elements of business communication are as follows:

- Business news sender
- Business news receiver
- Business news in message form
- Channel of business communication
- Code of business communication
- Topic of business communication
- Scene of business communication
- Types of business communication
- Flows of business communication
- Impact of Communication revolution on business communication.

Now, let us discuss about these essential elements of communication one by one.

***Business News Sender***

The business news Senders are managers of different multinational companies, corporate houses and business enterprises. They send different types of messages to their customers. Thus, all producers—Small or big—are business news sender.

***Business News Receiver***

The business news receivers are public who for the businessman or trader, are consumers. Because they consume goods produced by traders.

***Business News Message Forms***

The business communication sends messages to the consumers in different forms such as words, sentence, proverbs, Idioms, phrases, riddles, songs, poetry, tales, photographs and others. Through these forms of message, the business communicator approaches to the customer. They propogate their brand names again and again.

***Channels of Business Communication***

The business communicator uses following types of channels to propogate their products among customers and attract them to buy their products:

- Verbal Channel
- Non-verbal Channel

*Verbal Channel*

The verbal channel of business communication may be devided in to following types:

- Oral
- Written
- Visual
- Audio-Visual

*Oral Channel*

This is most important channel of business communication. In order to sell their products more and more, the business communicator meets with people, have conversation, tells about the benefit of his products and convinces the people to buy more and more his product. For this purpose, the business communicator employs sell boys or sell girls who visit door to door along with some free samples of the product.

*Written Channel*

The business communicator also uses written channel to propagate his/her products among people or customers. He/she makes advertisement in newspapers, news bulletin, news and Journals. He/she also publish booklets and books on his/her products. He/she also distributes pamphlets along with newspapers and in markets and fairs to attract more and more people to buy his\her products.

*Visual Channel*

The business communicator also uses visual channel of communication to attract more and more people for buying his\her product. He/she prints the names of great hero, heroin, beauty queen, athletes, academician, musicians, singer, writer on his\her products to attract the people. Seeing great people propagating and using the product, people are attracted to buy them. For this purpose, the business communicators print the name and figures on pamphlets and products packets to attract the people.

*Audio-Visual Channel*

The business communicator also takes help of audio-visual channel of communication. For this purpose, each business company has brand ambassador who appears on audio-visual media to advertise the products of companies. For example Baba Ramdev, Amitabh Bachchan, Hemamalini, Sachin Tendulker and so on. The brand ambassador appears frequently on radio, T.V. and other audio-visual media to attract and convince people to buy products.

***Non-verbal Channel***

The business communicator also uses non-verbal channel to advertise their products among the people. The brand ambassadors of different companies make a balance between their verbal and non-verbal behaviour. While speaking, their body, face and body parts also take parts in communication. The body language of brand ambassadors attract more to the people for buying products of company.

## Method of Communication in a Business Organisation

There are two methods of communication in a business organisation. They are as follows:

- Internal communication
- External communication

***Internal Communication***

When people of a business organisation make communication with each other on a business issue, this kind of communication is known as internal communication. This type of communication enhances team spirit and team feeling among members of a business organisation. This is also very helpful in achieving common goal of business organisation.

The internal communication may be informal or formal. This types of communication may take place between two individuals, an individual and a group, a group and an individual or people of one department with an another department of the same organisation.

When communication of workers with organisation chief takes place without any formal order, this communication is known as informal communication. The organisation chief meets with workers individually in informal ways to incourage them and take them in to confidence. The workers become pleased to see the big boss in their chamber talking and discussing informally like family members.

But when the chief or big boss of a business company meets with his\her workers following a formal order, this type of communication is known as formal communication. In this type of communication, date, time and agenda of meeting is dully pre-fixed. The discussions of the meeting is recorded.

From above discussion, it is clear that the business chief communicates with his\her business workers formally and informally both.

In internal communication, generally oral channel of communication is followed. The business organisation chief and workers sit together, discuss problems and try to solve them. This happens generally in case of informal communication.

The formal communication in an organisation takes place with the help of written order of the chief. The workers of the organisation are informed through a written notice in which date, time and agenda of the meeting are mentioned. Following notice, chief and workers sit together for a meeting. The proceeding of meeting is recorded on a register or through voice recording device. Works are performed as per written decision taken in the meeting. Written channel is used for formal communication.

In internal communication visual channel is also taken in to account. In meeting of chief and workers, slides, internet without multimedia and pager are used. These are visual channels of communication.

In internal communication, audio-visual channel is also used. For example use of video-conferencing, internet with multimedia and audio-visual aids.

Besides above mentioned verbal channels of communication, non-verbal channels of communication are also used. The business chief and workers communicate also through their face, body and body language.

### External Communication

When business chief or boss or workers of an organisation makes communication with chief boss or worker of an another organisation, it is known as external communication. These people may be customer, dealer, distributor, media, persons, Government official, common people, lawyer, doctor, professor, engineers, traders, and other authorities, letter, notice, invitation, price list, sale order, purchase order, customer report, service call centre, bulletin, advertisement, tender, record and so on are methods and techniques of external communication.

Now-a-days, business corporate houses take care of customer care, customer report and customer suggestion to sell their products more and more. They invite suggestions of customer so that they could make improvement in the quality of the products. They try their best to fulfil desires of customers. Thus, they spend a huge amount on external communication. It is because without the support of customers they cannot sell their products in a better way.

The external communication is generally made in formal way. This communication is generally based on records. But corporate houses are attempting to make external communication informal.

In external communication all channels—oral, written, visual and audio-visual are used for business communication.

The non-verbal communication channel like face, body and body parts movements are also used for the purpose of business communication.

The business communicator maintains a balance between verbal and non-verbal behaviour. The body language of brand ambassadors attracts and brings more influence upon the customers.

### Code of Business Communication

In business communication, business code occupies significant place. All business communicators use their code to differentiate its product from others. They have their own seal, amblem, brand ambassador and formula. The code of one corporate house is different from the other corporate house. They have their own brand names, seal, amblems and brand ambassadors.

### Topic of Business Communication

The entire business communication revolves round some topics. The topic of business communication are as follows :

- To improve quality of product
- To improve sell
- To bring Organisation in profit
- To compensate business loss
- To appoint and utilise brand ambassador
- To attract more and more customers
- To bring coordination in different organisations
- To market products effectively
- To use media effectively for advertisement
- To provide attractive look to packets
- To solve problems of organisation

### *Scene of Business Communication*

In business communication, scenes dealing with business occupies significant place. The business communicator uses attractive scenes to attract customers. They display model boys, model girls, brand ambassador, attractive scenes, effective scenary influencing pictures, diagrams and sketches in their business communication. Thus, business scene and symbols occupy significant place in business communication.

### *Types of Business Communication*

The business communication may be of two types:

- Interpersonal business communication
- Mass business communication.

#### *Inter personal business communication*

It takes place individually and personally. The communicator meets with customers personally.

#### *Mass business communication*

It takes place between communicator and people with developed media. Such as news papers, radio, T.V., internet and so on.

## *Flows of Communication in Business Organisation*

In business organisation, flows of communication follow following paths:

- Down wards flow
- Upwards flow
- Diagonal flow
- Horizontal flow

### *Down wards flow*

In all traditional business organisation, the flow of communication was down wards. All important decisions were taken by persons sitting at the top. The decision of top boss was communicated to workers. The decision of top boss was communicated to workers by different officials under whom the workers used to work. Thus, the flow of communication in a multilayered business organisation used to occur. A number of weaknesses appeared in such type of flow of communication. They are as follows:

- This type of communication flow created dictatorship nature and environment in a business Organisation.
- The messages communicated by chief boss were broken and communicated in own ways by different officials at different level. As a result business communication loss took place.
- This type of communication flow was also more time consuming.
- In the action process of communication flow, unnecessary delay was bound to occur.

In order to over come these associated difficulties with business communication, another types of business communication flow was developed.

### *Upwards Flow*

The upwards flow of business communication came in to existence after knowing the weaknesses of downwards communication. This flow provided due regards to workers in business communication. Now, workers were involved in business communication. The workers of an organisation began to integrate themselves with organisation. As a result a healthy coordination developed between bosses and workers. Today upwards flow has become important for any kind of organisation.

### *Diagonal Flow*

In an organisation, several departments are integated. Each department performs its own function. But all departments are integrated to whole organisation. The diagonal flow is found among several departments of the same organisation.

### *Horizontal Flow*

Horizontal flow is found between officials or workers of same status. The communication between officials or between workers is an example of horizontal flow.

## Impact of Communication Revolution on Business Communication

The communication revolution has brought a great influence on business communication. The impact of communication revolution on business communication can be discussed under the following heading:

- Online information of products of different companies
- Online information of different market centres
- Online information of traders, merchants and companies
- Online information about quality assurance
- Online marketing facility
- Online payment facility
- Online delivery facility
- Online information of customer care centre
- Online meeting with customers
- Online in formation of customer reaction
- Online information of discount to customers
- Online information of special offer to customers
- Online information of stock available
- Information about manufacturing defects
- Information about return of price

Now, let us discuss about these impacts one by one in detail.

***Online Information of Products of Different Companies***

The communication revolution has provided us online information about products of different companies such a surf, soap, fan, watch, jewellery, rice, oil, cloth, medicine, freeze, radio, T.V., camera, computer, internet and so on. The customers have alternative choice to select a product of a company among several choices.

***Online Information of different Markets***

The communication revolution has made us aware of different kinds of markets in the world. The people visit the website to search a market of their requirement. They make order and payment online and get delivery very in home.

***Online Information of Traders, Merchants and Companies***

Due to communication revolution, online information related to different brands, traders, markets and companies is available before us. The interested customers visit the sites to get detail information about brands, traders, merchants and companies. They select brand and products of their choice. They place online orders, make online payment and get delivery in their houses. The communication revolution has made it possible.

***Online Information of Quality Assurance***

Due to communication revolution, online information of quality assurance by different brands and companies are available to customers. The customers visit websites to know about them. They know about assurances provided by companies on quality products. In case of quality dissatisfection the company assures the return of price with postal expenses.

***Online Marketing Facility***

The communication revolution has provided us online marketing facility in the country and abroad. The customers can visit the website and place supply order in any market of the world.

***Online Payment Facility***

The communication revolution has provided us online information about payment facility. The customers can make online payment for products they have purchased from any markets in the world.

***Online Home Delivery Facility***

Due to communication revolution home delivery facility of products is available online. The company assures the customer to supply products in home after receiving payment online.

***Online Information of Customer Care Centre***

Due to communication revolution, online information of customer care centres are available on company sites. The customers visit the sites to know customer care centres and their number. They make any kind of complaints on customer care centres.

***Online Meeting with Customers***

Due to communication revolution, it has become possible to organise a meeting of company boss with customers. The company boss appears online before customers, have discussion with them and assures them about quality product and make change as per their suggestions.

***Online Information of Customer Reaction***

Due to communication revolution, it has become possible to get reactions of customers online and make change as per reaction.

***Online Information of Discount to Customers***

Due to communication revolution, it has become possible to know about the discounts announced by the companies for the customers.

***Online Information of Special offer to Customers***

Due to communication revolution, it has become for the customer to know online about special discount offer to be provide to customer by companies within fixed days.

***Online Information of Stock Available***

Due to communication revolution, it has become possible for the whole-sellers and part-sellers to know about the stock available.

***Information about Manufacturing Defects***

Due to communication revolution, it has become possible for wholesellers or part-sellers to inform company about manufacturing defects.

***Information about Return of Price***

Due to communication revolution, it has become possible to know about return of price in case of manufacturing defects online to the customers.

# 14

# Approaches to Study of Communication

It is fitness of the thing to present here approaches by which study of communication can be made by researchers. The study of communication can be made by three approaches. They are as follows:

- Anthropological approach
- Sociological approach
- Ecological approach

Now, lets us discuss about these approaches one by one.

**Anthropological Approach**

In order to study communication from the point of view of Anthropology, it is essential to focus our attention on physical and cultural features of man. It is because man is the only communicating animals in this world who uses different symbols to communication his ideas, experience and messages for his fellows. According to bio-cultural evolutionists, man is master of animal kingdom. He occupies top most position in animal kingdom. He is only cultural animal of animal kingdom. Hominidae was minimum condition for the evolution of culture. For being superior animal of animals kingdom some such changes occured in physique of man due to which he became master of animal kingdom and creator of culture. These changes were as follows:

- Bipedal walk
- Erect posture

- Freely opposable thumb
- Sterioscopic and chromatic vision
- Developed brain
- Creation of symbols

Due to above changed physical features in man, some such powers developed in him, which made him master of animal kingdom. These powers were—

- Tool Making power
- Speaking power
- Expression power

***Tool Making Power***

Due to erect poster and bipedal walk, hands of man became free and freely opposable thumbs were developed. Now, feet were able to walk and hands were able to perform works. Due to opposable thumbs, it become possible to take out bulbs, to break flowers, fruits and leaves, to collect seeds, and to fashion stone pieces in to tool. Due to developed brain, he began to provide desired shapes to tools of hunting and gathering. The tools making power made man victorious of nature.

***Speaking Power***

Due to erect posture and bipedal walk, larynx slipped down to digestive canal and head became straight on neck. The larynx became first resonator where the air of digestive canal gets struck and get a shape of sound. Mouth cavity became the second resonator. In mouth cavity, the air of digestive canal get struck with teeth, lip, tongue and palate. They became speech organs. The nasal cavity developed as third resonator. Due to development of speech organs, man became a speaking animals. Along with speech, he also develops his body language. The verbal language and non-verbal language or body language became the speaking power of man.

***Expression Power***

With the development of verbal and non-verbal languages man developed expression power. Now, he began to express his ideas, emotions, feelings, desire, needs, pleasure, sorrow, victory, defeat, acceptance, refusal, benefit, loss, knowledge, science and a number of events taking place in world around him. Due to development of expression power man became a communicative animal. Gradually, he developed communication skill. Thus, he became a rational, logical and communicative animals.

**Cultural Feature of Communication**

Man is a cultural animal. Culture itself is a social heritage because culture is acquired in society through socialisation process, which transforms an infant in to child, a child in to adolescent, an adolescent in to young, a young in to adult and an adult in to old. Like culture, communication is also acquired in society. Thus, like culture communication is also a social heritage. The cultural features of communication can be studied under following heading:

- Kinship terminology in communication
- Terms of address in communication
- Terms of reference in communication
- Ethnic terminologies in communication
- Cultural terminology in communication
- Songs and Geet in communication
- Folk tales and myth in communication
- Poetry in communication
- Ballads in communication
- Proverbs in communication
- Riddles in communication
- Funs in communication
- Action jokes in communication
- Inter-ethnic communication
- Religious communication
- Political communication
- Economic communication
- Health communication
- Play, Games and Sports communication
- Migration communication
- Cultural media and agents of communication

Now, lets us discuss about them one by one.

### Kinships Terminology in Communication

The cultural has provided to a community kinship terminologies by which a person communicates with his/her consanguineal and affinal relatives or kins. Each individual kin is termed by an independent term. Thus, for each kin, there is a terminology. This is known as descriptive terminology. Besides, descriptive terminology, classificatory kinship terms are also used in a culture. In cultural communication, the same terms is used for a class of relatives. For example—uncle, aunt, cousin, *samadhi* and *samadhin.* These classificatory terminologies are frequently used in cultural communication of a community. This is very significant cultural feature of communication.

### Terms of Address in Communication

Terms of address are important cultural features of communication. In cultural communication, terms of address are used at the time of addressing community members for example, respected, dear, ladies and gentlemen, *Mukhiya ji*, *Purohit ji*, uncleji, aunti ji, *Bhaiya ji*, *Didiji*, *Baba* and so on. Thus, terms of address are cultural features of communication.

### Terms of Reference in Communication

Terms of reference are also very important cultural feature of communication. In day to day communications specific communication terms of reference comes in to existences. The terms of reference may be related to a person, place, animal, God, Goddesses, marriages, holy books, earthquake, flood, epidemic, aged, children, woman, priest, *Jajaman* and so on. The terms of reference depends upon the context in which communication is going on and the context in which terms are used. For example, *Papaji, Mukhiaji, Guruji, Mamaji, Bhaiyaji, Chachaji* etc.

### Ethnic Terminology in Communication

The use of ethnic terminology is a cultural feature of communication. The members of village community use ethnic term in their day to day communication. They use the term *Brahmin*, *Rajput*, *Yadav*, *Koeri*, *Kurmi*, *Barahi*, *Lohar*, *Halwai* and so on. Those terms are also used as terms of reference for a person who belongs to a particular ethnic group. For example, *Panditji, babusaheb, yadavji, Barahi mistri, Lohar mistri, halwai bhai* and so on. The persons are addressed by his\her caste or ethnic identity.

### *Cultural Taboos in Communication*

Communication taboo is one of significant cultural features of a community. In community, some members have to follow avoidance rule in communication. Generally, it is followed in case of avoidance relatives. The avoidance relatives communicate with each other following avoidance rule. They communicate indirectly because they cannot appear face to face. They take help of an another kin for the purpose of communication. A child becomes medium of communication between avoidance relatives. *Sas-damad, sasur-damad, sas-putoh, sasur-putoh, Bhawoh-Bhainsur, Jyeshtha Sali*—younger sisters husband are avoiding relatives. They do not communicate directly.

Again sex based taboos are also found in culture of a community. All males of a community cannot make communication with all females of the same community. Females have limited scope of communication. They have to follow taboo in communication with members of other families and castes. Women are also tabooed to talk with stranger males and even females. These taboos are followed in traditional society.

### *Songs and Geet in Communication*

The use of songs and geet is very interesting feature of communication culture. On the occasion marriage and birth communication between different relatives takes place through songs and geet. Joke songs and Geet are also sung on these occasion.

### *Folktales and Myth in Communication*

The use of folktales and myth is a cultural feature of communication. The members of folk and peasant society quote folktales and myths in their day to day communication. Thus, cultural communication takes place through folktales and myths.

### *Poetry in Communication*

In folk and traditional society, there are a number of folk poets who make communication with members of the community. They create poetries and communicate their members. This is also very significant cultural feature of communication.

### *Ballades in Communication*

Ballades are cultural feature of communication. Ballades are sung to communicate characters and roles of great cultural hero or heroin. Some caste members earn by making communication of great hero or heroin by singing ballades.

### *Proverbs in Communication*

Proverbs are cultural feature of a community. Members of community use proverbs frequently in their day to day communication. The use of proverbs make communication interesting.

### *Riddles in Communication*

Riddles are cultural feature of a community. The members of a community use frequently riddles in their daily communication. The use of riddles make communication very interesting among community members.

### *Funs in Communication*

Funs and jokes are cultural features of a community. But they play significant role in daily communication among members of a community. The members of a community make fun and cul jokes incourse of communication.

### *Action Jokes in Communication*

Action jokes are very interesting cultural features of a community, The members also make communication through action jokes like throwing mud, colour, turmeric paste, and paint on the body of a person. These action jokes make communication very interesting.

### *Inter-ethnic Communication*

In a multi caste or tribe village inter-ethnic communication takes place following cultural rules of communication. They members of different castes use terms of address according to social hierarchy.

### *Religious Communication*

Religion is very significant feature of a communication. The religion involves sacred centres, sacred specialists, sacred performance, ancestor worship, animal worship, tree worship, bird worship, snake worship, spirit worship, festivals and fairs of a community. Religious communication takes place on these occasions. The priest mediates the communication between Gods and Goddesses and other spirits. They are communicated through *mantra*, *bhajan*, *kirtan*, offerings, worships and sacrifice.

### *Political Communication*

Political institutions are cultural features of a community. They are family head, council of elders, village head, village Panchayat, inter village Panchayat, inter village head, caste Panchayat and others. These institutions performs function in maintaining law and order in community. Political communications are made through these cultural institutions of community. They play significant role in communication of political culture.

### *Economic Communication*

Economic communication is also a cultural features of a community. Economic institution are part and parcel of cultural institutions. Economic institutions like production, consumption, trade, market, reciprocity, hospitality, gift, and loan are governed by culture of a community. Different economic institutions play significant role in communication.

### *Health Communication*

Health communication is an integral part of culture of a community. There are cultural practices related to health in every community. Different aspects of health are communicated through cultural practices.

### *Play, Games and Sports Communication*

The communication of play, games, and sports is interesting cultural feature of a community. The play of children, games of young and sports of adult are communicated by their experts and players. Thus, play games and sports are related to anthropological approach to study communication.

### *Migration Communication*

Migration is a cultural feature of a community. The members of community migrate at a suitable places for service, works, business, pilgrimage, health check up, fairs and so on. The benefits of migration is communicated by conversations among community members. Disadvantages associated with migration are also communicated by conversation.

### *Cultural Media and Agents of Communication*

The anthropological approach to the study of communication also includes study of cultural media and cultural agents of communication. Every community has its own cultural media and agents which deal with cultural communication. The study of songs, myths, tales, music, drama, dance, cultural traders and agents occupy significant place in anthropology of communication.

## Sociological Approaches to the Study of Communication

In order to approach communication from the point of view of sociology, the following types of sociological study of communication can be made:

- Communication between different age groups of society
- Communication between sex groups of society
- Caste and communication in society
- Religion and communication in society
- Occupation and communication in society
- *Purohit-Jajman* communication
- Communication in folk society
- Communication in peasant society
- Communication in town society
- Communication in city society
- Communication in metropolis society
- Communication in global society
- Communicational problems of society
- Communication skill in society
- Development communication in society

- Business communication in society
- Health communication in society
- Educational communication in society
- Religious communication in society
- Political communication in society
- Communication agent in society
- Communication media in society

Now, lets us discuss about them one by one.

### *Communication between Different Age Groups of Society*

Different age groups of a speech community are participant of communication. The members of same age group have friendly communication. For example children, adolescent, youth, adult and aged. These are different age groups of the society. They have intra age group and inter age group communication. Members of different age groups do not have friendly communication till adolescent periods. But as soon as they become 16 years of age, they are treated as friends even by adult members of the community. The aged persons wait to have more and more communication with children whom they like very much. Grand children are loved more than own childrens. Similarily, grand child wants to communicate more and more with grand parents than their own parents. These are social features of communication between age groups.

### *Communication between Sex Groups of Society*

Male and female are sex groups of the society. Both are participants of communication in a society or speech community. But for both sexes different verbal languages are used. For example, he is singing and she is dancing. Communication between different sex groups reveals gender based language, i.e. separate language for male and female of the society. Again females of the community have to follow a number of taboos. Females cannot speak with strangers, males having avoidance relations and males with different caste groups. They cannot represent his family and husband on any occasion of social importance. These are sociological features of sex based communication.

### *Caste and Communication in Society*

Caste is a social endogamous group whose members follow taboos related to food, water, marriage and occupation. In caste system different castes occupy hierarchical position fixed by the society. The members of same caste and members of different castes communicate with each other following rules of society. The members of same caste communicate by observing avoidance rule and following age and sex distinction.

The members of different castes communicate following hierarchical position. They use terms of address and terms of reference following their position in caste hierarchy.

Females of high castes are tabooed to have communication with males of other castes and even females of other castes. Females of low and middle hierarchical status castes can communicate with high caste males using hierarchical terms of address.

Children of high caste do not want to play and communication with children of lower castes.

Thus, communication according to caste is a sociological feature.

### Religion and Communication in Society

In a society, members of different religions reside together. They speak the same language. Thus, they are members of same speech community. Being members of same speech community, they are participants of the communication.

In multireligious community, the members have to communicate with members of same religion as well as with other religion. Thus, intra religious and inter religious communication is a sociological feature. Adult males of different religious groups communicate frequently in day to day life. But children and women do not have frequent communication, though they are of same village community.

### Occupation and Communication in Society

In society, each individual and family are bound by an occupation. The occupation may be traditional and modern. Hunting-gathering, shifting cultivation, pastoral, settled agriculture, artisan and labour are traditional occupation. But service, business, trade, start up works are modern occupation. In society intra occupational and inter occupational communication is a sociological features. The members of same occupation talk frequently about process, technology, produce, product, market, profit and loss in their day to day life. The members of different occupational community make communication about different aspects of their occupation. Thus, as a member of speech community intra occupational and inter occupational communication is a feature of society. In occupational communication only adult members take part.

### *Purohit-Jajman Communication*

In society *purohit* and *Jajman* are bound together by *Jajmani* system. The village priest is known as *purohit* in this system. The functional castes are termed as *pawania*. The *purohit* and *pawania* call agriculturists as *Jajman*. Communication among *purohit*, *jajman* and *pawania* is a sociological feature of society. The relation among *purohit*, *pawania* and *Jajman* is mainted through communication to perform work at different occasions for which they are paid in cash, kind and both.

### *Communication in Folk Society*

The folk society is simple society. Their means and agents of communication are very simple. They have face to face relation and do not require any formality for communication. For the members of folk society, scope of communication is 24 hours. They can meet with each other anytime and have communication informally on urgency.

Besides informal communication, the members of folk society have formal communication on the occasion of birth, marriages, death, Panchayat meeting, organisation of festivals and so on. The family head, village head, village priest, inter village head, inter village priest act as traditional agents and media of communication in folk society. School teacher, *Mukhiya*, *Panchayat mitra*, *Gram mitra*, B.D.O., C.O., aganwadi, health sub-centres, health centre, community health centre, saddar hospital, referral hospital, MLA, M.P., Ministries, Chief Minister, Prime Minister all are modern agent and media of communication in folk society. International and Non-Governmental agents are also functioning in peasant society.

Now, members of folk society are users of cell phones, mobile phones, smart phones, internet, computer, facebook, YouTube, Google, Twitter. Thus, communication revolution has brought a great change in life and culture of both society. Now, they have also become member of global village society. They use oral, written visual and audio-visual channel of communication. They also use body language in communication. The study of verbal and non-verbal symbols provides significant clues for communication in folk society.

### *Communication in Peasant Society*

Peasant society is a society whose members subsist on agriculture and allied works. Peasants living in an area and speaking same language are participants of communication. They follow intra family, inter family, intra caste, inter caste, and inter village communication. They also have peasant organisation in which they have formal communication. But in day to day life they have informal communication. In birth, marriage and death rituals, they follow formal communication. There are verbal and non-verbal channels of communication. The verbal channels may be oral, written, visual and audio-visual. The non-verbal channel includes their body part.

In peasant society there are a number of traditional agents of communication such as family head, village head, priest, functional castes, artisian castes, middleman, medicine man, artists, dancers, musicians, poets, singers and so on. School teachers, *mukhiya*, Panchayat officials, block officials, district official, health sub centre, health centre, community health centre, referral hospital, sadar hospital, medical college, post office staff, MLA, M.P., Ministers, Chief Minister, Prime Minister are modern agents of communication for peasant society. Besides, Redcross, CARE, UNICEF, Ford foundation, WHO, and World Bank are international agents of communication functioning among peasant society. A number of N.G.Os. are also working as agents of communication in peasant society.

The members of peasant society are also now members of global village society. They now to communicate with cell phones, mobiles, smart phones, computer, internet, face book, twitter, YouTube, WhatsApp. They use oral media, print media, press media, electronic media, and satellite media for various purposes. Communication revolution has brought drastic change in life and culture of peasant society.

### *Communication in Town Society*

Towns have more concentration of population than villages. They have road, water and electricity connectivity. They are controlled by municipality. The town dwellers live as members of a community. In towns, we have intra family and inter family communication. The communication takes place through a conmen dialect or a linguafranca, which varies from region to region. In towns, members of different castes and religion reside together. Therefore, they follow generally formal method of communication. They visit in the house of each other by a formal information and invitation. But some families living nearby also follow informal method of communication.

The town dwellers use oral, written, visual and audio-visual channels of communication. They also use non-verbal channel through their body language.

The town dwellers use oral, print, press, electronic and satellite media of communications. They have modern agents of communication.

### *Communication in City Society*

Cities have more concentration of population than towns. It covers more geographical areas. The controlling administrative agency in city society is municipal corporation. Cities are well connected through roads, water and electricity. In cities members of different castes, religious groups and occupational groups reside together as a community members. In cities one finds intra family, inter family, intra caste, inter caste, intra religion, inter religion and intra regional and inter regional communication. In family communication takes place through mother tongue. But in community or in market communication takes place through linguafranca. But in education Government approved languages are used for communication.

Among city dwellers multilingualism is very common. Digglosia is also very common in city dwellers. The city dwellers utilise services of modern agents of communication. They use verbal and non-verbal channels for communication. In verbal channels, they use oral, written, visual and audio-visual channels. But in non-verbal channel, they use body language. The verbal and non-verbal codes are used by senders and decoded by receivers.

The city dwellers use oral, press, print, electronic and satellite media of communication. They are users of mobiles, cell phones, smart phones, computer, internet and social media like twitter, facebook, YouTube and WhatsApp. There are a number of cafe in cities for this purchase. Marketing is being done online. Traders, producers and customers all are utilizing internet and online services. The communication revolution has influenced the life and culture of city society to a great extent.

### *Communication in Metropolis Society*

Metropolises are those cities whose population is more than 15 lakhs. The metropolises dwellers have well connection of road, water, electricity, railways, and airways. They are great centres of service, trade, business, health, hospitality and communication centres. In metropolises, there are caste and region based organisations. There are also language based organisations. In family, communication takes place through mother tongue. But in organisations and markets, communication takes place through linguafranca. But in schools and Government communications occurs through language. The administration of metropolises lies in control of Mega Municipal Corporation or Maha Nagar Nigam.

The metropolise generally follow informal method of communication in their family and neighbourhood. Sometimes, they also follow informal method of communication with their fellow workers with whom they meet daily, work together and have familial relation. But generally in work organisation they follow formal method of communication specially with high big boss.

The metropolise dwellers generally have Governmental, Non-Governmental and International agents of communication. They are very much dependent on media for communication. They use press media, print media, electronic media, satellite media and social media for communication. They are well acquainted with communication system of mobiles, cell phones, smart phones, computer, internet and social media such as face book, twitter, YouTube, WhatsApp, and so on.

The communication revolution has greatly influenced social life and culture of metropolises. The incidence of cyber crimes, computer and internet related crimes have also come in to existence. Enemy countries are also using these means to distabilise the Government of a country and cause damage of life and property of enemy countries.

The metropolise dwellers use verbal channels like oral, written, visual and audio-visual. They also use non-verbal channel like body language at the time of communication. In fact, they support their oral communication with body language which makes communication more effective.

### *Communication in Global Society*

Now-a-days, we are living in an age of communications revolution. The communication revolution has made us member of a global society. The members of this society are integrated through computer, cell phones, mobiles, smart phones, internet and social media like facebook, twitter, YouTube, WhatsApp and so on. They maintain social relation and social interaction through well developed information technology. The global society has global producer, global consumers and global markets. They do marketing of desired products online and make payment online. They receive products in home.

Members of global society use generally space media and social media. They rely too much on print, satellite and social media. They are governed by WTO and intellectual property rights. This society has given a new definition of distance and time. Now talking and marketing to a distant place is possible in few seconds. Now, the world is in the hand of members of global society.

The communication revolution has influenced life, culture, society, economy, polity, health and communication of global society to a great extent. The members of global society has crossed the limit of ethnic boundaries. They have developed a secular thought which is above caste, creed, sex, colour, language, region and religion. The members of the society believe in eat, drink and be merry.

### *Communicational Problems of Society*

The study of communication can also be approached through problem of society. There are a number of factors which influence the communicational system of the society. They are flood, earth quakes, storms, lightening and other natural calamities. These natural calamities paralyse the communication system of the society. It takes much time to restore them.

Again communicational problems of society is also related to its types such as folk, peasant, urban, metropolis and global. Each types of society has its own problems related to communication.

### *Communication Skill in Society*

The study of communication can also be approached through the study of communication skill. The communication skill of different societies are different. The communication skill of folk, peasant, urban, metropolis and global societies are different. Again in each society the communication skill of different sex groups and age groups are different. This difference in communication skill provides significant clues for pattern of communication prevalent between societies.

### *Development Communication in Society*

The study of communication can be approached through development communication in a society. The development communication in a society attempts to know development from approaches, methods and techniques of communication. Each society attempts to know communication of development through intra personal, inter personal and mass communication methods. It also follows formal and informal methods of communication. The agents of development communication may be traditional, modern, Governmental, Non-Governmental and International. The media of development communication may be folk media, mass media, press media, print media, electronic media, satellite media and social media like facebook, twitter, YouTube and WhatsApp. The channels used for communication in a society may be verbals like oral, written, visual and audio-visual and non-verbal like body language. The participants of development communication are members of society who may be men, women, children adult and aged.

### *Business Communication in Society*

The study of business communication in a society can also be approached from the point of view of approaches, methods and techniques of communication. These attempts are made to study business communication from the point of view of communication. Here, the business pattern of a society is understood by using intra personal, inter personal, informal, formal and mass communication method. Attempts are made to know the media of business communication. The media employed in business communication may be folk media, mass media, print media, electronic media, satellite media and social media sites like facebook, twitter, YouTube, WhatsApp and so on.

The channels used for business communication may be verbal as well as non-verbal. The verbal channels are oral, written, visual and audio-visual. The non-verbal channels are body languages. Body language supplements the oral communication. They create a balance between verbal and non-verbal behaviours associated with communication. The agents of business communication may be Governmental, Non-Governmental, private or international. The message senders of business communication are business personnels, firms and companies. The receivers of business news are customers and consumers. The customers and consumers are attracted by different effective techniques of communication. They are given quality assurance, discount assurance and special offer assurance.

### *Health Communication in Society*

The study of communication can also be made from the point of view of health. Health communication means understanding health from the approaches, methods and techniques of communication. There are a number of health communication agents in society. They are traditional, modern Governmental, Non-Governmental and international who propagate about different aspects of health among the people. The health communicators take help of verbal and non-verbal channels of communication. The verbal channel indues oral, written, visual and audio-visual channels. The non-visual channel includes body languages. The health communicators use folk media, mass media, press media, print media, electronic media, satellite media and social media in order to propagate health development and communicate the concept of good health.

The communication revolution has promoted the practice of health tourism. The online ticket reservation, number allotment in hospitals, accommodation, reservation and online order of food have made health tourism very easy.

### *Educational Communication in Society*

Education communication is an attempt to understand education from the point of view of approaches, methods and techniques of communication. The senders of education are agents or communicators of education. They may be traditional or modern, Governmental or non-Governmental, formal or informal. The receivers of education are public or people.

The communicators use verbal and non-verbal channel of communication to propagate educational development. The non-verbal channel includes body languages. The verbal channel includes oral, written, visual and audio-visual behaviours. The communicators maintain a balance between verbal and non-verbal behaviours. While communicating different aspects of education.

The communicators use folk media, mass media, press media, print-media, electronic media, satellite media and social media to propagate educational programmes and associated benefits to the people.

The communication revolution has brought the concept of e-learning, e-knowledge centre, e-library, e-book, e-journals, e-teachers, professors and experts.

### *Religious Communication in Society*

The study of communication in a society can be approached from the point of view of religion. Each society has a religion. The members of society are followers of religion. There are a number of religious agents or communicators who acts as message sender of a religion. These agents may be traditional or modern, formal or informal. The followers are receivers of a religion. The communicators use formal or informal method to send religious messages. They use verbal and non-verbal channels of religious communication. The verbal channel includes oral, written, visual and audio-visual channels. The non-verbal channels include body languages. The communicators attempt to make a balance between verbal and non-verbal behaviours. The communicators use folk media, mass media, press media, print media, electronic media, satellite media, and social media like facebook, twitter, YouTube, WhatsApp and so on.

The communication revolution has brought a great impact on religious communication in society. Now, pilgrimage of different places of religious importance has become very easy and comfortable.

### *Political Communication in Society*

The communication in a society may be approached from the point of view of political organisations and political institutions for smooth functioning of a society. There are political institutions, which bring control in the society. Political institutions may be traditional or modern, formal or informal. But they act as agents or communicators of political communication in society. The political agents or communicators are message senders. The people are message receivers. The political communicators use verbal and non-verbal channels. The verbal channels are oral, written, visual and audio-visual. The non-verbal channels are body languages. The political communicators use folk media, mass media, press media, print media, electronic media, satellite media and social media for political communication.

The communication revolution has brought a great impact on political communication.

### *Communication Agents in Society*

The study of communication in a society can also be approached from the point of view of communication agents. There are a number of communication agents in a society. They may be traditional, or modern, formal or informal and Governmental or Non-Governmental. These agents play significant role in different types of communication.

### *Communication Media in Society*

There are a number of media in a society which propagate different types of news, views and events occurring in and around the society. They are folk media, mass media, press media, print media, electronic media, satellite media and social media such as facebook, twitter, YouTube, and WhatsApp. These media play significant role in communication in a society.

## Ecological Approach to the Study of Communication

The study of communication can be made from the point of view of ecology. Ecology is a science which deals with interaction between environment and organism. But this term is also used for habitat or human settlement. As environment of world is not same every where, therefore human settlements are also not same everywhere. Thus, in each type of ecology, a special type of communication system has come in to existence. We can make study of communication from the point of view of ecology in following ways:

- Communication in forest ecology
- Communication in Mountain plateau ecology
- Communication in plain ecology
- Communication in desert ecology
- Communication in coastal ecology
- Communication in Island ecology
- Communication in glacial ecology

Now, let us discuss about communication in these ecology one by one.

### *Communication in Forest Ecology*

The study of communication can be made from the point of view of ecology found in forest. In forest areas, we find human settlements. The forest dwellers make their living by forest produce and forest resources. The forest dwellers have their own communication system. They have their own agents and media of communication. They use verbal and non-verbal channels of communication. Forest dwellers are now also users of mobiles, cell phones, smart phones, computer, internet and social media. The communication in forest ecology can be discussed under following headings:

- Demographic communication in forest ecology
- Health communication in forest ecology
- Education communication in forest ecology
- Water resources and conservation in forest ecology
- Economic communication in forest ecology
- Business and trade communication in forest ecology
- Religious communication in forest ecology
- Political communication in forest ecology
- Cultural communication in forest ecology
- Development communication in forest ecology
- Entertainment communication in forest ecology
- Communication agents and media in forest ecology
- Floral-faunal communication in forest ecology

Now, let us discuss about these aspects of communication in forest ecology.

### *Demographic Communication in Forest Ecology*

In forest ecology forest villages are found. They are different from revenue villages. Forest village dwellers do not have ownership of land. The ownership of land lies in the hand of forest department. The forest department allots land for house and cultivation in forest areas on lease. The forest villages also have their own demographic features. The demographic features of forest dwellers and forest villages can be studied from the point of view of communication. The age groups, sex groups, sex ratio, marital status, occupational status, marital distance, educational status, religious status, political status of forest villages and migration can be studied from the point of view of communication. The languages spoken in forest villages can be explored. Their cultural grammar, lingua-franca, and body languages can be studied. The different types of channels used by forest dwellers such as oral, written, visual and audio-visual and non-verbal such as body languages can provide significant clues regarding demographic feature of communication. The communication agents of forest villages can be explored. They may be traditional, modern, Governmental, Non-Governmental, and international.

The media of communication of forest dwellers can be explored.

They may be folk media, mass media, press media, print media, electronic media, satellite media and social media.

The impact of communication revolution in forest ecology can also be explored. Mobile users, cell phone users, smart phone users, internet users, computer users and social media users can be explored and analysed in context of forest ecology.

### *Health Communication in Forest Ecology*

The health communication study can be approached through forest ecology. Forest ecology also provides significant information regarding health communication. The birth, rate, death rate, infantmortality, mother mortality, diseases, family planning, modern health centres, hospitals, nursing houses, medicine shops, alternative medicine, sanitation, health education, health programmes in forest ecology can be explored and communicated to Government institutions, media persons for information and health policy.

The health agents or communicators, health related verbal and non-verbal channels, health media—folk, mass, press, print, electronic, satellite and social of forest ecology can also be explored. The impact of communication revolution in forest ecology and communicational barriers of forest ecology can also be studied. In this way, the study of forest ecology will provide significant informations regarding health communication.

### *Education Communication in Forest Ecology*

The study of forest ecology provides us very valuable informations regarding education communication. It can reveal us news about schools, colleges, universities, medical colleges, law colleges, technical institutes, management institutions enrolment, non-attendance, dropouts, literates, illiterates, matriculates, intermediates, graduates, post-graduates, technical and management degree holders, teachers, professors, scholarships and a number of educational programmes of forest ecology. It can also highlight educational channels, agents, communicators and media of education communication in a forest ecology. The impact of communication revolution on education and educational problems of forest ecology can also be explored.

### *Water Resources and Conservation in Forest Ecology*

The study of water resources and their conservation in forest ecology can also be made from point of view of communication. Water resources of forest ecology such as streams, ponds, water falls, rivers, wells, tube-wells, artisn wells, their utility and conservation can be explored from the point of view of communication. They can be photographed and brought to media for the purpose of communication.

### *Economic Communication in Forest Ecology*

The economic institutions of forest ecology such as production, consumption, distribution, exchange, market, trade, reciprocity, hospitality, gift, loan, credit and saving, can be explored from the point of view of communication. The economic communicators, channels and media of forest ecology can also be explored and described. The impact of communication revolution in forest ecology and communicational problems of a economy in forest ecology can also be studied.

### *Business and Trade Communication in Forest Ecology*

The important business centres, shops, malls, markets, business enterprises and traders of forest ecology can be explored from the point of view of communication. They can be highlighted on media. Business and trade media, channels and communicators of forest ecology can also be explored and highlighted. Impact of communication revolution on business and trade of forest ecology also provides significant news from the point of view of communication. Communication barriers of business and trade can also be explored and highlighted.

### *Religious Communication in Forest Ecology*

Religious communication in forest is very interesting areas of research. Each forest ecology has its followers of religions, religious centres, religious performances, religious festivals, religious fairs. These religious aspects of forest ecology can be explored and highlighted in media. The religious agents, channels and media can also be explored and highlighted. The religious problems can also be studied, published and highlighted.

### *Political Communication in Forest Ecology*

Each forest ecology has traditional political institutions and modern political institutions. Each political institution has its own officials and functionaries. They perform significant function in smooth functioning of the society. These institutions can be explored and highlighted in media. Again each forest ecology has followers of different parties, caste and tribe leaders, caste/tribe elites. They can be explored and reported to media. Political awareness and participation of forest ecology can also be explored and highlighted. Impact of communication revolution on political communication and barriers of political communication can also be studied and highlighted through media.

### *Cultural Communication in Forest Ecology*

In forest ecology a number of ethnic groups reside. Each ethnic group exists as cultural unit. Thus, each ethnic group has its own culture of family, marriage and kinship. They have own story, legends, ballades, folktales, drama, dance, music, songs and play, games and sports. These cultural aspects of forest ecology can be explored and highlighted on media for the purpose of communication.

### *Development Communication in Forest Ecology*

Each forest ecology has its own problem of development such as health, education, social, economic, political, religious and communicational. Keeping these aspects in mind our Government has formulated policies related to development of forest ecology. The policies, plans, programmes, their implementation, beneficiaries, monitoring, evaluation, follow up actions and problem of development in forest ecology can be explored and communicated to people and the Government through different types of media. Development communicators, channels and media in forest ecology can be studied and highlighted.

### *Entertainment Communication in Forest Ecology*

The traditional entertainments and modern entertainment prevalent in forest ecology can be explored and highlighted. The different plays of children, different games of adolescents, different sports of adults can be studied, recorded and reported to the media for communication to Government and other people. The entertainment communicator, channels and media prevalent in forest ecology can be studied and reported. The problem of entertainment communication can also be explored and highlighted.

### *Communication Media and Agents in Forest Ecology*

The communication media of forest ecology such as folk, mass, press, print, satellite and social can be explored and highlighted to understand communicators ecologically. The communicational agents or communicators, traditional, Governmental, Non-Governmental and international—can also be studied and highlighted.

### *Floral-Faunal Communication in Forest Ecology*

Forest ecology is marked by a number of floral and faunal species. Attempts should be made to record floral and faunal species in forest ecology for the purpose of communication.

## Communication in Mountain-Plateau Ecology

The plateau and mountaineous areas have different ecology. People inhabiting hilly areas have different cultures. Different floral and faunal species are found in plateau areas. The policies, plans, programmers of hill ecology are different. Ethnic and demographic compositions are different. Economic, educational and health problems are quite different. Communication agents, channels, media and problems are quite different. In this way, hilly areas provide significant clues to be studied communicationally.

The communication in mountain and hill ecology can be approached under following sub-headings:

- Demographic Communication in plateau ecology.
- Health Communication in plateau ecology.
- Educational Communication in plateau ecology.
- Economic Communication in plateau ecology.
- Religious Communication in plateau ecology.
- Political Communication in plateau ecology.
- Business and trade communication in plateau ecology.
- Water resource communication in plateau ecology.
- Cultural Communication in plateau ecology.
- Development Communication in plateau ecology.

- Transport communication in Plateau Ecology
- Administrative communication in plateau ecology.
- Entertainment Communication in plateau ecology.
- Communication agents and media in plateau ecology.
- Floral-Faunal communication in plateau ecology.

Now, lets us discuss about these aspects of communication in plateau ecology one by one.

### *Demographic Communication in Plateau Ecology*

Demographic communication of plateau can be approached ecologically. Each plateau ecology has its own demographic features. The chief demographic features are population, ethnic groups, age group, sex groups, sex-ratio, marital status, occupational status, religious group, birth rate, death rate and migration. These demographic features of plateau ecology can be explored and highlighted in media to attract attention of policy-makers.

### *Health Communication in Plateau Ecology*

The health of people living in hilly areas needs to be explored from the point of view of communication. Birth rate, death rate, infant mortality, mother mortality, safe delivery, vaccination of children, diseases like diarrhoea, Chicken pox, T.B., Malaria, leprosy, AIDS, cancer, drinking water facility, sanitation facility, housing facility, health promotion schemes, health practitioners, hospitals, medical colleges, alternative medicines and a number of health related factors in a plateau and hill ecology should be explored and communicated to health policy makers, programme makers and programme implementers. Medical media and communicators also need to be explored in plateau area. Impact of communication revolution on health of plateau ecology should also be explored.

### *Educational Communication in Plateau Ecology*

Education among people of plateau area needs to be explored from the point of view of communication. Schools, colleges, universities, technical institutes, management institutes, medical colleges, law colleges, education colleges, engineering colleges, teachers, professors, professional institutes, syllabus, hostels, enrolment, attendance, dropouts, reservation policies, medium of teaching and libraries in plateau areas can be explored and communicated to policy makers and programme formulators. Educational media can also be explored.

### *Economic Communication in Plateau Ecology*

The economic institutions prevalent in plateau areas also need to be communicated to policy makers and plan formulators. The economic institutions like production, consumption, distribution, exchange, trade, market, labour, loan, credit, hospitality, gift, and reciprocity in plateau areas can be explored and highlighted in media. The economic communicators, economic media and economic channels of plateau area can be studied and reported. The impact of communication revolution on economic institutions of plateau areas needs to be studied and highlighted.

### *Religious Communication in Plateau Area*

Sacred centres, sacred performances, sacred specialists, festivals, fairs, pilgrimage, tourism, channels, media, communication agents and religious problems of plateau area can be explored from the point of view of communication. The impact of communication revolution on religious communication can also be discussed and highlighted.

### *Political Communication in Plateau Ecology*

The political systems, traditional and modern, of plateau ecology can be studied with a view to understand them from the point of view of communication. Functions of traditional political institutions and modern political institutions can also be studied and highlighted. Existence of political parties, political awareness and political participation can also be explored and communicated. Political leaders, elites, agents, media and channels should be explored and highlighted. Impact of communication revolution on politics and political systems of plateau area can also be explored and highlighted.

### *Business and Trade Communication in Plateau Ecology*

The business and trade agency of communication in plateau areas need to be explored and communicated. The plateau ecology also provides opportunities to business man and traders, who do business and trading in plateau areas. The businessman, traders, their trade and business, business transport, business agent, business channels, business media, and business problems of plateau area can be studied and highlighted in media. The impact of communication revolution on trade and business of plateau ecology can also be explored and communicated.

### *Water Resource Communication in Plateau Ecology*

Water resources of plateau ecology such as rivers, ponds, streams, water falls, artisan wells, wells, hand pumps can be explored from the point of view of communication.

### *Cultural Communication in Plateau Ecology*

Cultural institutions like marriage, family and kinship of plateau areas can be explored and communicated. Cultural agents, cultural media, cultural channels and cultural problems of plateau area can be studied and explored. Performing cultural arts like music, song, and dance can be explored and highlighted.

### *Development Communication in Plateau Area*

The development plans, programmes, implementation, beneficiaries, monitoring, evaluation, follow up actions of plateau area can be explored and communicated. Development agents—traditional and modern, media, channels and problems can also be explored and highlighted. The impact of communication revolution can also be discussed.

### *Transport Communication in Plateau Ecology*

The surface ways, water ways, railways and airways of plateau areas should be explored and communicated. Different transport agencies, media, channels and problems of transport communication can be explored and highlighted.

### *Administrative Communication in Plateau Ecology*

The administrative machinaries of towns, cities and villages should be explored and highlighted. Administrative agents, cannels, media, should also be highlighted. Impact of communication revolution can also be explored and highlighted.

### *Entertainment Communication in Plateau Ecology*

The plays of children, games of adolescents, sports of young and adults should be explored and communicated. Entertainment agents, channels, media and problems of plateau ecology can also be explored and highlighted.

### *Communication Agents and Media in Plateau Ecology*

The communication agents—traditional and modern and media, folk, mass, press, print, electronic, satellite and social—should be explored and highlighted.

### *Floral-Faunal Communication in Plateau Ecology*

The flora and fauna of plateau ecology should be explored and highlighted.

## Communication in Plain Ecology

The plain ecology can be explored from the point of view of communication. Demographic, ethnic, social, economic, political, religious, health, education, entertainment and administrative features of plain ecology can be studied, reported and highlighted to understand them from the point of view of communication.

Communication in plain ecology can be discussed under following sub-headings:

- Demographic communication in plain ecology
- Health communication in plain ecology
- Educational communication in plain ecology
- Development communication in plain ecology
- Religious communication in plain ecology
- Political communication in plain ecology
- Economic communication in plain ecology
- Business and trade communication in plain ecology
- Cultural communication in plain ecology
- Administrative communication in plain ecology
- Entertainment communication in plain ecology
- Communication agents and media in plain ecology
- Floral-faunal communication in plain ecology

Now, lets us discuss about these communications in plain ecology one by one.

### *Demographic Communication in Plain Ecology*

The demographic features of plain ecology such as population, age groups, sex groups, sex ratio, ethnic groups, marital status, occupational status, religious status, migration and immigration in plain area should be explored and studied from the point of view of communication.

### *Health Communication in Plain Ecology*

The health statistics or indicators of plain ecology such as birth, death, infant mortality, child mortality, mother mortality, disease, treatment, medicine, medical institutions, shops, family welfare, health promotion scheme should be explored and communicated. Health agents, health channels and health media should also be explored and analysed to highlight the features. Impact of communication revolution on health can also be discussed.

### *Educational Communication in Plain Ecology*

The educational aspects such as school, college, universities, research institutes, technical institutes, management institutes, medical college, law college, engineering college, skill development institutes, Ayurvedic, Homoeopathy, Unani, Yoga and Siddha colleges, teachers, professors, resource persons, hostels, books, witting materials and so on of plain ecology can be recorded and highlighted for policies, plans and programmes. Reservation of seats in admission and employment should also be recorded and reported to Government and people. Fellowships for study and research also needs attention for communication. The educational agents—traditional and modern media—folk, mass, press, print, electronic, satellite and social and channel verbal and non-verbal—should also be studied to highlight educational communication. The impact of communication revolution on education communication should also be recorded and highlighted to the people and Government.

### *Development Communication in Plain Ecology*

The areas, agencies, channels, media, policies, plans, programmes, beneficiaries, monitoring and evaluation of development should be explored and highlighted for the policy maker and the people.

***Religious Communication in Plain Ecology***

The plain ecology has followers of a number of religions. It has several sacred and pilgrimage centres and specialists. The plain ecology has a number of festivals and fairs. The religious groups, sacred centres, pilgrimage centres, sacred specialists, sacred performance, worship and sacrifice, festivals, fairs, religious agents, media, channels, impact of communication revolution on tourism should be recorded and highlighted systematically from the point of view of communication.

***Political Communication in Plain Ecology***

The plain ecology has its own traditional and modern political institutions. They have their own elites, leaders and path showers. They have political awareness and participation. They have their own agents, media and channels. Thus, political institutions, elites, leaders, path showers, agents, media, channels, problems and impact of communication revolution in plain should be recorded and highlighted.

***Economic Communication in Plain Ecology***

The pain ecology has its own economic institutions. The economic institutions of plain ecology should be explored from the point of view of communication. The process of production, consumption, distribution, exchange, trade, market, loan, credit, reciprocity, hospitality, gift and presentation, should be explored and highlighted. The economic agents, traditional and modern, media—folk, mass, press, print, electronic, satellite and social—channels—oral, written, visual and audio-visual and non-verbal body languages should be recorded and reported. The impact of communication revolution on economic communication should also be explored and highlighted in media.

***Business and Trade Communication in Plain Ecology***

The study of business and trade communication in plain ecology provides significant information regarding adoption of trade in a special type of ecology. The plain ecology has its own producers, consumers, businessman and traders. They can be recorded and reported from the point of view of communication. The agents, channels and media associated with business communication can be studied and reported. The impact of communication revolution on business and trade of plain areas can also be explored with view to provide informations to policy makers and others.

### *Cultural Communication in Plain Ecology*

Plain ecology has its own ethnic groups and their cultures. Each ethnic group has its own culture. The cultural features like family, marriage and kinship of each ethnic groups can be studied from the point of view of communication. The cultural youth organisation, dancing floor, wall paintings, abode of Gods and Goddesses, graveyards or *Ashmashan*, can also be explored and highlighted. Dance, music, songs, drama, folk proverbs, idioms, phrases, riddles should also be explored and highlighted. The cultural communication agents, channels, media and problems of cultural communication should also be explored and highlighted. The impact of communication revolution on cultural communication should also be recorded and highlighted.

### *Administrative Communication in Plain Ecology*

The administrative machinary and institutions of rural and urban areas of plain ecology should also be explored from the point of view of communication. The administrative agents, media, channels and problems of communication should be studied and highlighted in media. The impact of communication revolution on administration of plain ecology should also be recorded and highlighted.

### *Entertainment Communication in Plain Ecology*

Plays of children, games of adolescents and sports of adults of a plain ecology should be explored from the point of view of communication. Again parks, cinema halls, restaurants should also be explored and highlighted. Entertainment agents, channels media and problem of media communication should also be explored and highlighted. The impact of communication revolution on entertainment industries should also be explored and highlighted.

### *Agents and Media of Communication in Plain Ecology*

Attempt should be made to explore and highlight all types of agents and media of communication working in plain ecology.

***Floral-faunal Communication of Plain Ecology***

Attempts should be made to record flora and fauna of plain ecology from the point of view of communication. The local terminology of each flora and fauna should be recorded and highlighted. The cultural relation of flora-fauna should also be explored and highlighted. Floral-faunal medicines should also be recorded for communication.

**Communication in Desert Ecology**

The desert ecology has its own demographic, social, cultural, political, religious, educational, health, business, trade, entertainment, administrative, communicational and transportational communication features. Therefore, these features of desert ecology should be studied from the point view of communication. We can discuss communication in desert ecology under following headings:

- Demographic communication in desert ecology
- Social communication in desert ecology
- Cultural communication in desert ecology
- Economic communication in desert ecology
- Political communication in desert ecology
- Religious communication in desert ecology
- Educational communication in desert ecology
- Transportational and tourism communication in desert ecology
- Health communication in desert ecology
- Entertainment communication in desert ecology
- Business and trade communication in desert ecology
- Development communication in desert ecology
- Communication agents and media in desert ecology
- Floral-faunal communication in desert ecology

Now, lets us discuss about these types of communication one by one.

***Demographic Communication in Desert Ecology***

The desert ecology has its own demographic features such as ethnic groups, age groups, sex groups, sex ratio, marital status, occupational status, educational status, religious status, and migrational status. These demographic features of desert ecology can be explored, reported and highlighted from the point of view of communication.

### *Social Communication in Desert Ecology*

Each desert ecology has its own ethnic composition. Each caste/tribe exists as a social unit. Intra caste and inter caste relation should be explored. Besides different types of social organisations such as marriage, family and kinship should also be explored and highlighted from the point of view of communication. The problems of women, children, adolescent, youth and aged should be explored and highlighted. Social welfare schemes of desert ecology should also be highlighted. Social customs and practices should also be explored and communicated to media. The channels, media, agents and problems of social communication should be highlighted and explored. The impact of communication revolution on social communication should also be recorded and highlighted.

### *Cultural Communication in Desert Ecology*

The desert ecology has its own cultural features. The ethnic groups of desert ecology have their own cultural customs of marriage family and kinship. They have their own house types, household furnitures, household utensils, dress, and ornament. They have their own culture of maintaining relation and expressing disagreement. They have own language, folk tales, songs, ballads, proverbs, and jokes. They have own musical instruments and players. They have own drama and dance. These cultural features of ethnic groups living in desert ecology should be explored and highlighted. Cultural agents, cultural media, cultural channels, and cultural communication problems should be explored and highlighted. The impact of communication revolution on cultural communication should also be explored and communicated.

### *Economic Communication in Desert Ecology*

Each desert ecology has its own system of production, consumption, distribution, trade, market, loan, credit, reciprocity, hospitality, gift and exchange. These economic institutions of desert ecology should be explored, reported and communicated. Economic agents, media and channels should also be explored. problems of economic communication should be explored. Impact of communication revolution on economic communication should also be discussed.

### *Political Communication in Desert Ecology*

Each desert ecology has its own traditional and modern political institutions, elites, leaders, functionaries, workers and supporters. Each desert ecology has own political participation and awareness. Each desert ecology has its own political problems. These political institutions and organisations should be explored and highlighted. The political agents, media, channels and problems of political communication should also be explored and highlighted. The impact of communication revolution on political institutions should also be studied.

### *Religious Communication in Desert Ecology*

The desert ecology has followers of a number of religious groups. The different religious groups, their sacred centres, sacred specialists, sacred performances, festivals, fairs, pilgrimage and so on should be explored and communicated. The religious media, agents, channels and problems should also be explored and highlighted. The impact of communication revolution on religious group should also be explored and highlighted.

### *Educational Communication in Desert Ecology*

Literacy, literacy rates, schools, colleges, universities, research institutes, medical colleges, engineering colleges, management institutes, hostels, teachers, professors, books, journals and libraries of desert ecology should be explored and highlighted. The educational agents, media, channels and problems should also be explored and highlighted.

### *Transportational Communication in Desert Ecology*

The transportation system of desert ecology such as animal transport, surface transport, road ways, water ways and water transport, railways, and airways should be explored and highlighted.

### *Health Communication in Desert Ecology*

The health institutions like Anganwadi Kendras, health sub-centres, health centres, community health centres, hospitals, sardar hospitals, medical colleges and hospitals, private hospitals, private medical colleges and hospitals, plural medical systems, doctors, *vaidya*, medicine man, categorisation of diseases, folk medicine and folk way of treating diseases of desert ecology should be explored and reported. The problem associated with health communication should also be explored. The health agents, media, channels and impact of communication revolution on health should be explored and highlighted.

### *Entertainment Communication in Desert Ecology*

The means of entertainments of desert ecology such as plays of children, games of adults, sports of young, games of adults and aged, singing, dancing, story telling, joke making, parks, zoo, hotels, restaurants, cinema halls, and so on should be explored and highlighted.

### *Business and Trade Communication in Desert Ecology*

Desert ecology has its own business and trade perspective. The business man and traders attempt to purchase the things produced by the people and to supply those things to the people which they do not produce. Thus, producers, consumers, traders and business-man of desert ecology should be recorded and preserved. Business and trade agents, media, channels and problems should be explored and communicated.

### *Devlopment Communication in Desert Ecology*

The development programmes, welfare programmes, areas of development, policies of development, implementation of programmes, beneficiaries, monitoring, evaluation and follow up of programmes, development problems, development agents, development media, development agents and channels should be explored and highlighted. Impact of communication on development should be recorded and highlighted.

### *Media and Agents of Communication in Desert Ecology*

Different types of Communication agents and media of desert ecology should be explored and communicated.

### *Floral-faunal Communication in Desert Ecology*

The names of all flora and fauna available in desert ecology should be explored and their relationship with culture of desert ecology should be highlighted. Their medicinal values should also be highlighted.

**Communication in Coastal Ecology**

Coastal ecology has its own cultural, social, religious, political, economic, business and trade, educational, health and communication features. Hence, these characteristics of coastal ecology should be explored, preserved and highlighted. We can discuss the communication in coastal ecology under following sub-headings:

- Demographic communication in coastal ecology
- Social communication in coastal, ecology
- Cultural communication in coastal ecology
- Political communication in coastal ecology
- Religious communication in coastal ecology
- Economic communication in coastal ecology
- Business and trade communication in coastal ecology
- Health communication in coastal ecology
- Educational communication in coastal ecology
- Transportational communication in coastal ecology
- Development communication in coastal ecology
- Entertainment communication in coastal ecology
- Agents and media in coastal ecology
- Floral-Faunal communication in ecology

Now, lets us discuss about these communications one by one in detail.

***Demographic Communication in Coastal Ecology***

The coastal ecology has its own demographic characteristics such as ethnic group, age group, sex group, sex ratio, fertility, mortality, educational status, marital status, religious status and migration. These demographic features of coastal ecology should be recorded and highlighted. The demographic problems should also be explored. Impact of communication revolution on demographic features of coastal areas should also be reported.

### *Social Communication in Coastal Ecology*

The coastal ecology has a number of ethnic groups. Each group has its own social norms and values. They maintain intra family, inter family, inter caste and inter religion relation by reciprocal exchange of visits, invitation, gift and presentation. These social features should be explored and highlighted.

### *Cultural Communication in Coastal Ecology*

The ethnic groups living in coastal ecology has its own cultural features. They follow cultural traditions of marriage, family and kinship. They have their own material culture and performing art culture. They sing song, tell stories, play musical instruments and sing *bhajan* and *kirtan*. They have their own cultural agents, cultural media and channels. They also face problems in their cultural communication. These cultural features of coastal ecology should be recorded and highlighted.

### *Political Communication in Coastal Ecology*

The ethnic groups living in a coastal ecology have their own traditional and political functionaries who look after customary laws and bring control in the society. They have their traditional leaders and elites. Besides, they have also modern political functionaries who look after modern law and development. They have political awareness and political participation. They have political agents, media and channels. They face problems related to political communication. The communication revolution has brought a change on political communication. These features of political communication in coastal ecology should be explored and communicated.

### *Religious Communication in Coastal Ecology*

The people of coastal ecology has its own religious features such as followers of religions, sacred centres, sacred specialists, sacred performances, fairs, festivals, worship, sacrifice and others. These religious features need to be explored and highlighted. Religious media, agents and channels should also be explored. Religious tourism, hospitality and accommodation facility should be studied and highlighted. Impact of communication revolution should also be studied.

### *Economic Communication in Coastal Ecology*

The economic institutions of coastal areas such as production, consumption, distribution, exchange, trade, market, loan, credit, reciprocity, hospitality, gift and exchange system should be explored and highlighted. The economic communication problem should also be studied. The economic agents, media and channels should be explored and communicated. The impact of communication revolution should be studied.

### *Business and Trade Communication*

The producers, consumers, traders and business man of coastal ecology should be explored. The agents, media and channels of business communication should be studied. The problems of business and trade communication should be explored and highlighted. Impact of communication revolution on trade and business of coastal ecology should be studied and highlighted.

### *Health Communication in Coastal Ecology*

The institutions and practices related to health such as Anganwadi Kendra, sub health centres, health centres, community health centres, referral hospitals, sadar hospitals, medical colleges and hospitals, plural medical system, folk medicine, herbal medicines, *Jhar phuk* method, medicine shops, health tourism, family welfare, family planning, infant mortality, mother mortality, vaccination, health promotion scheme and sanitation situations should be explored and highlighted. The health agents, media, channels and problems should also be studied. The impact of communication revolution on health should be explored.

### *Educational Communication in Coastal Ecology*

The educational institutions such as schools, colleges, universities, medical colleges, engineering colleges, law colleges, B.Ed. colleges, teachers, students, literacy rate, enrolment, non-attendance, dropouts, scholarships, hostels, books, libraries, play-grounds, sanitation should be explored and highlighted. Educational agents, media and channels should be studied and highlighted. Impact of communication revolution should also be discussed.

### *Transportational Communication in Coastal Ecology*

The transport systems such as animal transport, watersways, roadways, airways, and railways should be explored and highlighted. The problems of transportation should be highlighted. The transport media, agents and channels should be explored and highlighted. Impact of communication revolution should be discussed.

### *Development Communication in Coastal Ecology*

Development aspects such as policies, strategies, plans, implementation, monitoring, evaluating and follow up actions in coastal ecology should be explored, reported and communicated. Impact of communication revolution on development issues should also be explored and highlighted.

### *Entertainment Communication in Coastal Ecology*

Plays of children, games of adolescents and sports of young, recreation of aged, zoo, parks, garden, restaurants, cinema halls and other entertainment institutions should be explored and highlighted. The agents, media and channels of entertainment should be discussed.

### *Agents and Media of Communication in Coastal Ecology*

All types of agents and media of communication working in coastal areas should be explored and highlighted.

### *Floral-Faunal Communication in Coastal Ecology*

All species of flora and fauna of coastal areas should be explored and highlight. Their relation with coastal culture should also be explored and highlighted.

## Communication in Island Ecology

Islands are land part of sea. They are surrounded by sea. Island has its own communication. The social, cultural, demographic, political, religious, economic, health and educational communications of island ecology are different. Therefore, we can present communication in island ecology under following sub-headings:

- Demographic communication in Island ecology
- Social communication in Island ecology
- Cultural communication in Island ecology
- Political communication in Island ecology
- Religious communication in Island ecology
- Economic communication in Island ecology
- Business and trade communication in Island ecology.
- Educational communication in Island ecology
- Development communication in Island ecology
- Health Communication in Island Ecology
- Entertainment communication in Island ecology
- Agents and media communication in Island ecology
- Floral and Faunal communication in Island ecology
- Transport Communication in Island Ecology

Now, lets us discuss about these types of communications in Island ecology one by one.

***Demographic Communication***

The Island ecology has its own demographic features such as age groups, sex groups, occupational status, educational status, marital status, sex ratio, fertility and migration. These demographic features of island ecology should be explored and highlighted for policy makers, programme formulators, implementors, evaluators and follow up officials. The demographic agents, media, channels and problems should be explored and highlighted. Impact of communication revolution on demographic communication should also be explored and communicated.

***Social Communication in Island Ecology***

The ethnic groups, inter and intra family, inter and intra clan, inter and intra caste, inter and intra tribe, caste interactions and inter relations should be explored and highlighted. Social pathological problem should also be explored and highlighted. Agents, media, channels and problems of social communication should also be explored and highlighted. Impact of communication revolution on children, adolescents, young, adult and aged should also be explored and highlighted.

### *Cultural Communication in Island Ecology*

Cultural institutions of family, marriage, kinship, youth organisation, dancing floor, graveyards, house types, household furnitures, assets, dress, ornaments, ways of seeking blessings from elders, ways of providing blessings to youngers in island ecology should be explored and highlighted. Agents, media, channels and problem of cultural communication should be explored and highlighted. Impact of communication revolution on cultural communication should also be studied.

### *Political Communication in Island Ecology*

The traditional and modern political institutions of island ecology should be recorded and highlighted. Elites, leaders, political parties, political awareness and political participation should be explored and highlighted. Agents, media, channels and problems of political communications should be explored and highlighted. Impact of communication revolution on political institutions should also be explored and highlighted.

### *Religious Communication in Island Ecology*

The religious institutions and religious groups, sacred centres, sacred specialists, sacred performances, festivals, fairs, dances, *Bhajan-kirtan*, *Ramleela*, *Krishnaleela*, donation, pilgrimage, accommodation and other should be explored and highlighted. Agents, media, channels and problems of religious communication should be explored for communication. Impact of communication revolution on political institutions should also be recorded and highlighted.

### *Economic Communication in Island Ecology*

The communication related to economic institutions and organisations should be recorded and reported. Impact of communication revolution on economic institutions should also be explored and highlighted. The economic problems should also be communicated.

### *Business and Trade Communication in Island Ecology*

Producers, consumers, businessman, traders, industries, trades and markets should be explored and highlighted. Agents, media, channels and problems of trade and business should be explored and highlighted. Impact of communication revolution on business and trade should be explored and communicated.

### *Educational Communication in Island Ecology*

Traditional and modern educational institutions such as youth organisation, schools, colleges, universities, medical colleges, engineering colleges, management institutes, technical institutes, research institutes, law colleges, teachers, students, books, library, playing grounds, sanitation, media, agents, channels, problems and impact of communication revolution on educational institutions of island ecology should be explored and highlighted.

### *Development Communication in Island Ecology*

Development policies, strategies, plans, programmes, implementation, monitoring, evaluation, following actions, media, channels, and problems of development communication should be explored and highlighted.

### *Health Communication in Island Ecology*

Health institutions such as *anganwadi kendra*, primary health sub centres, primary health centres, subsidiary health centres, community health centres, referral hospitals, sadar hospitals, medical colleges and hospitals, doctors, nurses, para-medical staff, medical stores, plural medical systems, medical agents, media, channels, problems and impact of communication revolution should be explored and highlighted.

### *Entertainment Communication in Island Ecology*

Plays of children, games of adolescents and young, sports of adult, entertainment means of aged, traditional drama, dance, music, should be explored and highlighted. Agents, media, channels, problems and impact of communication revolution should also be explored and highlighted.

### *Agents and Media Communication in Island Ecology*

All types of agents and media of communication in Island ecology should be explored and highlighted.

*Floral-faunal Communication in Island Ecology*

Floral-faunal species of island ecology should be explored and highlighted and their relationship to cultural ecology should be highlighted.

*Transport Communication in Island Ecology*

The transport systems of island ecology such as head load, animal transport, roadways, waterways, railways and airways should be explored and highlighted.

## Communication in Glacial Ecology

The glacial ecology has its own demographic, social, cultural, economic, political, religious, health, educational, developmental, recreational, transportational and Floral-faunal characteristics. Each of these features are significant from the point of view of communication. The communication in glacial ecology can be discussed under following sub headings:

- Demographic communication in glacial ecology
- Social communication in glacial ecology
- Cultural communication in glacial ecology
- Political communication in glacial ecology
- Religious communication in glacial ecology
- Economic communication in glacial ecology
- Business and trade communication in glacial ecology
- Transportational communication in glacial ecology
- Health communication in glacial ecology
- Educational communication in glacial ecology
- Developmental communication in glacial ecology
- Entertainment communication in glacial ecology
- Agents and media of communication in glacial ecology
- Floral-faunal communication in glacial ecology

Now, lets us discuss about these communications in glacial ecology one by one.

### *Demographic Communication in Glacial Ecology*

The glacial ecology has its own population showing age group, ethnic group, sex group, educational status, marital status, migration, religion, sex ratio, fertility and mortality. These demographic characteristics of glacial ecology should be explored and highlighted from the point of view of communication.

### *Social Communication in Glacial Ecology*

Intra family, inter family, intra lineage, inter lineage, intra clan, inter clan, intra caste, inter caste, intra tribe and inter tribe, intra village and inter-village relationships should be explored and highlighted.

The status of women, children and aged should also be explored. Agents, media, channels, problems and impact of communication revolution should also be explored and highlighted.

### *Cultural Communication in Glacial Ecology*

Cultural institutions such as marriage, family, kinship, youth organisation, dancing floor, grave, art, drawing, printing, folklores, agents, media, channels, problems and impact of communication revolution should also be explored and highlighted for the purpose of communication.

### *Political Communication in Glacial Ecology*

Traditional and modern political institutions, elites leaders, political parties, political awareness, political participation, agents, media, channels, problems and impact of communication revolution should be explored and highlighted for communication.

### *Religious Communication in Glacial Ecology*

Followers of religions, sacred centres sacred specialists, sacred performances, worship, *puja-path*, sacrifice, life cycle rituals, festivals, fairs, pilgrimage centres, religious tourism, agents, media, channels, problems and impact of communication revolution on religions, religious performances and religious organisations should also be explored and highlighted for the purpose of communication.

***Economic Communication in Glacial Ecology***

The economic institutions like production, consumption, distribution, exchange, trade, market, loan, credit, dairy, fishery, goatery, poultry, duckary, small trade, business, enter-prises, labour and service should be explored and highlighted for the purpose of communication. Agents, media, channels, problems and impact of communication revolution should also be explored and communicated.

***Business and Trade Communication in Glacial Ecology***

Producers, consumers, traders, businessman, trading centres, markets, transportation, problems, media, agents and channels of business and trade communication should be explored and highlighted for communication.

***Transportational Communication in Glacial Ecology***

The transport system of glacial ecology such as head load, shoulder load, animal transport, surface transport, waterways, railways and airways, agents, media and channels of transport communication should be explored and highlighted. Problems of transport should also be explored. Impact of communication revolution should also be explored and highlighted.

***Health Communication in Glacial Ecology***

The health institutions of glacial ecology such as anganwadi kendra, health sub centres, subsidiary health centres, community health centres, health centres, referral hospitals, sadar hospitals, medical colleges and hospitals, superspeciality hospitals, multi speciality hospitals, traditional health healers, plular medical systems, medical stores, medical shops, private practitioner should be explored, recorded and communicated. Agents, media, channels, problems and impact of communication revolution should also be explored.

***Educational Communication in Glacial Ecology***

Educational institutions of glacial ecology should also be explored for the purpose of communication. For examples schools, colleges, universities, technical institutes, management institutes, medical colleges, engineering colleges, law colleges, B.Ed. colleges, teachers, students, hostels, books, book stores, playground and sanitation in educational institution. The agents, media, channels, problems, and impact of communication revolution should also be explored and communicated.

### *Developmental Communication in Glacial Ecology*

Development areas, policies, planning, strategies, formulation of programmes, beneficiaries, monitoring of programmes, evaluation of programmes and follow up actions, agents, media, channels, problems and impact of communication revolution should be explored and communicated.

### *Entertainment Communication in Glacial Ecology*

Plays of children, games of adolescents, sports of young and adult and recreation means of aged, dance, drama, songs of glacial ecology should be explored and communicated. The agents, media channels, problems and impact of communication revolution should be explored and highlighted.

### *Agents and Media of Communication in Glacial Ecology*

Media and agents of communication in glacial ecology should also be explored and communicated. Problems of communication, agents and media should also be explored and communicated. Impact of communication revolution on media and agents should be explored and highlighted.

### *Floral-Faunal Communication in Glacial Ecology*

Floral and Faunal species of glacial ecology should be explored. Their cultural relation with ethnic groups and values in society should be explored and communicated.

# 15
# Ethnography of Human Communication

Ethnography is a science, which deals with systematic recording of culture of a community. The science which deals with systematic recording of communication culture of a speech community is known as ethnography of communication.

The speech community is a community whose members participate in communication through a common language, dialect or linguafranca.

The idea of ethnography of communication in anthropology was introduced by a scholar named Dell Hymes. Dell Hymes had published an article entitled, "The Ethnography of Speaking" in 1962. In this article, he attempted to review several weak intellectual areas where anthropologists can contribute. The speech was one of them. According to Hymes, ethnography of communication was a neglected area of research in anthropology. The ethnography of communication can be termed as ethnography of speaking. This attempt can fill up the gap between what is described in grammars of a linguistic study and what is described in an ethnographic study. Traditionally, a linguist attempted to study structural differences between languages and their historical developments and an ethnographer studied nature and function of culture. The mutual interest of linguist and ethnographer has been recognised inseparability of language and culture. Every community has a language by which its members fulfil variety of culture specific goals.

For smooth functioning of community, the members must have not only linguistic competency, but also communicative competency. The linguistic competency is also associated with grammatical knowledge of mother tongue, which is a acquired before adulthood. The communicative competency deals with knowledge about what is appropriate to say or not to say in a specific cultural context. In this way, the ethnography of communication is concerned with situations and uses of speaking as an activity in its own cultural context. Ethnography of communication is concerned with those aspects of human behaviour by which culture meets communication. It provides interdisciplinary understanding of human expressive behaviour.

The fieldwork method is soul of ethnography of communication. For fieldwork, an ethnographer of communication focuses on speech community as its unit of study. The ethnographer of communication attempts to understand the way by which communication is patterned and organised as system of communicative events within a speech community and the ways by which they interact with all other systems of culture.

It is also fitness of the thing to deal here the meaning of speech community. It certainly does not coincide with a society or a culture. It is because in a society or in a culture language is never spoken uniformally by all members. The spoken language varies to a great extent in the same society differentiating men from women, young from old, poor from rich, and so on. Even within a small geographical space of a village or a town, spoken languages varies considerably, depending upon many social and linguistic criteria. Therefore, all those who share specific rules for speaking and interpreting speech and alteast one speech variety belong to a speech community.

In order to understand different units of communicative behaviour or speech behaviour, ethnographic description and analysis can be made by three conceptual terms, which are as follows:

- Speech situation,
- Speech event, and
- Speech act.

**Speech Situation**

The speech situation is context in which speaking takes place. For example, family dinner, marriage feast, birth day party, death rituals, festival celebration, village Panchayat meeting, fair, pilgrimage, hunting expedition bathing ghat, playground, graveyard, seminar, symposium, conference and a large number of such situations in which speaking takes place in a society every day. Each speech situation is different from others with regards to type of participants and objectives behind it. This implicitly determines the nature of communicative behaviour. The behaviour is characteristically different from situation to situation. For example, the speech behaviour during a community feast would not be same as during hunting expedition or a fishing expedition. The speech behaviour during birth ceremony is not same as during death ceremony. The speech behaviour during victory is not same as during defeat. Again, the speech behaviour during success is not same as during failure. In this ways, we can say that speaking varies from one circumstances to another circumstances.

## Speech Act

The speech act is the minimal unit of speech for anthropological analysis. The speech act is expressed by greeting, compliment, approval, disapproval, question, apology, and so on. The speech act of speakers may be an individual or a group. The latter may be found in religious congregations, school prayer meetings and like. The speech act varies in size from a single word like thanks/excellent to a long sentence or a story.

## Speech Event

When a number of speech acts are arranged in a recognised sequence and are governed by the social rule of a given society, they constitute speech events. For example, intensive interview, dialogue, conversation, with another persons, enquiry over phone and so on.

The boundary between successive speech events may be drawn by change in composition of participants, an intermittent silence, a deliberate remarks to change the topic of conversation to a new one etc.

However, under some special circumstances, a speech act becomes a speech event. For example shouting of the term fire in cinema hall or public place. Similarly, shouting shame in a public meeting.

It is very important to mention here that a speaker is expected to produce such speech acts, which are suitable for speech events of specific situations. It is just as speakers of a language are expected to speak grammatically correct and meaningful sentences. If the speaker does not fulfil this condition, his speech is considered as out of context or he may be considered as silly or abnormal in extreme cases.

## Components of Ethnography of Communication

There are seven components of ethnography of communication, which need to be analysed by an ethnographer. They are as follows:

- Sender (addresser)
- Receiver (addressee)
- Message form
- Channel
- Code
- Topic
- Setting

Now, let us discuss about these components of ethnography of communication one by one.

***Sender (addresser)***

In speech events, it is senders who sends messages to receivers. In other words, we can say that communication takes place between speaker and hearers or receivers. The speaker speaks through speech events and the hearer listen to them. Here participants of communication are speakers and hearers. In this way, communication takes place between human speakers and hearers. But in a number of cultural circumstances, the communication takes place between human and non-humans. For example between a person and spirits, between human individuals and animals, plants, birds, insects. The non-humans also appear as communicator during dreams, rituals, festivals, and other occasions. Thus, in humans communication, the senders are human and non-human both. Humans and non-humans are participants of communication.

***Receiver (addressee)***

As referred above, the participants of human communication are senders and receivers or speakers and hearers both. Again, as senders or speakers of human communication are both human and non-human, in the same way receivers of human communication are also humans and non-humans both. Besides human individuals, they may be God, Goddess, spirit, animals, bird, insects, snakes, lizard, tree, plant and others.

***Message Form***

In ethnography of communication message form occupies significant place. The message form may be of various types such as a word, a sentence, a stanza, a paragraph, story, ballad, song, proverbs, riddles, jokes and so on. But participants of communication—sender and receiver—should know the meaning of messages conveyed in different forms.

### *Channels*

In the study of ethnography of communication, the exploration and description of channels of communication is also of great value. In the communication the sender uses verbal and non-verbal channels. The verbal channels are oral, written, visual and audio-visual. But besides, these verbal channels, non-verbal channels are also used such as body gestures, facial expressions, and movements of body parts in cultural context and cultural variations.

### *Code*

The code caries hidden meaning through which communication takes place. The hidden meaning of code is shared commonly by both sender and receivers, i.e., participants of communication. Varieties of codes are used in communication by a speaker. The may be related to different cultural situations and contexts. The code may be categorised—social, cultural, religious, political, economic, health, educational, victory, defeat, approval, disapproval, joy, sorrow, war, peace, flood, storm, natural calamity, epidemic, friendship, enmity. The drum code, flag code, clapping code, flower code, sword code, whistling code, broom code, blood code, are some of codes, which are used very often by speakers and hearers.

### *Topic*

In the study of ethnography of communication the topic of communication occupies significant place. It is because entire speech events revolve round the topic of communication. Message forms, channels, and codes are used by the speakers, according to the topic of communication.

### *Setting*

The setting is related to scene and situation in which participants of communication are expected to follow and use. Thus, besides participants, setting and situations are also important. The setting and situation have cultural variation. For example, joking between joking relatives are easily acceptable under normal situations, but it is not accepted in death situation or a misfortune in a family. Action jokes are acceptable during marriage rituals, but not in death ritual. Practical jokes are acceptable on 1st April, but not on other day.

**Method of Studying Ethnography of Communication**

The method used in study of ethnography of communication is primarily intensive field-works method. The fieldwork may be carried out in other culture or in own cultures. Participant observation technique is used. The observation is used to observe the speech events or to objectify the speech events. and provide scientific description. Participation is used to understand speech events from the point of view of native. Finally, a balance is attempted between observation and participation. The interview of participants of communication is organised, modes of thought and behaviours of speech community is explored and recorded. They are compared to other cultural group to understand the phenomenon from the point of view of cultural relativism. This methodology minimises the perceptual and analytic bias of researcher.

**Importance of Ethnography of Communication**

The study of ethnography of communication is significant from the following points of view:

- It enhances understanding of cultural system of language.
- It correlates language to social organisations.
- It shares knowledge and behaviour which are transitted from generation to generation.
- It contributes to the study of cultural to cultural maintenance.
- It provides important cludes to culture history.
- It initiates more and more cross-cultural comparisons of uses.

# 16
# Structure of Human Communication

The scope of communicational anthropology is incomplete without description of human communication. Hence, it is quite suitable to discuss here the structure of human communication. For the purpose of study, the structure of human communication can be broadly divided into two categories:

- Non-verbal structure of communication
- Verbal-structure of communication

### Non-verbal Structure of Communication

Besides verbal communication, significance of gestures, facial expressions, postures and tone of voice has been recognised since classical period. The Greek and Roman scholars had codified these components of oratory. In Indian context, the art of non-verbal expressions had attracted the attention of scholars between 4th and 1st century B.C. They were codified in Bharata's *Natyashastra*. Bharata's *Natyashastra* has left for us a number of dance poses called *mudras*. *Mudras* express human emotions in subtle way without using the spoken language. This is also true for many classical dance forms prevalent all over the world. In dance forms gestures become the medium of expressing emotions.

During 19th century non-verbal communication was established as an area of linguistic research. It had achieved scientific status with the publication of conversational necessities. Following scientific approaches, experiments and rigorous documentation were initiated following using charts, graphs, formulae, sketches, to record hand gestures and facial movements in oratory and dance routines. In fact, non-verbal communication is an integral part of our communicative behaviour. For example whistling, hissing, murmuring, clapping, figure gesturing, eye-gesturing, face gesturing, mouth gesturing, teeth gesturing, bowing, sitting with crossed leg, sitting folding one leg and so on. These and a number of non-verbal communications indicate anger, happiness, frustrations, greeting command, love, hatred and other feeling. These could also be expressed by spoken languages.

From the above account it is quite clear that non-verbal expressions are very significant communicative behaviour. Their study provides significant clue of human communication. There are a number of modes of non-verbal human communication, which either substitute or supplement the spoken languages in normal network of human communication.

The various modes of non-verbal human communication are as follows:

- Para linguistics
- Kinesics
- Proxemics
- Chronemics
- American sign language

Now, let us discuss about these modes of non-verbal communication one by one.

**Paralinguistics**

Paralinguistics is science which deals with vocal patterns and emotional expressions in the same way as facial expressions and emotions have innate relationships. All extra speech sounds such as hissing, shushing, whistling, imitation sounds, speech modifications like quality of voice, (sepulchral, whiny, giggling), very high pitch, hesitation and rate of talking form the integral part of para language. A number of researches in para languages in primates including man were conducted in 1950s, but it was Charles Darwin who attempted to deal with relationship between non-semantic aspects of speech and expression of emotions in man and animals. His observation was that animal can also express-emotions in specific situations such as courtship, conflict and others.

Since the time of Darwin, many advances have been made to study para linguistics with the help of sophisticated machine. These studies have followed two different direction. Voice as an indicator of personality and voice as an indicator of states of human mind. But both areas depend upon voice as a conveyer of emotions.

## Kinesics

The science which deals with articulation of body is termed as kinesics. This kind of study in non-verbal communication was introduced in 1950s to study movements resulting from muscular and skeletal shift in the process of communication. This includes all actions such as physical, physiological, automatic reflexes, postures, facial expressions, gestures, and other kind of body movements. It was a scholar Bird Whistell who first became interested in body movements while undertaking anthropological field work in 1946 among Kutenai Indians of Western Canada. He began to propose models for organisation of kinesics behaviour. He considered verbal and non-verbal aspects together. He favoured contextual approach in place of proponents of clinical approach to the study of kinesics.

## Proxemics

The science which deals with space as channel of non-verbal behaviour is known as proxemics. The space cannot be seen in the same way as facial expression, body movement or a tone of voice. But it is a vital part of every social encounter. Like Kinesics, the study of proxemics is also linked to anthropology. Edward Hall in his book, *The Hidden Dimension* (1966) initiated the systematic investigation in to cultural space. He had defined proxemics as the study of man's perception and use of space. According to him, it is a much closer to complex activities and their derivatives known to ethnologists as territoriality. He had dealt with four types of social distances such as intimate, personal, social and public which seems to be present in every culture. He had made a study of use of space in five cultures, namely Germany, England, France, Japan and Arab and tied them to national character. In case of German door is taken very seriously. It is because door preserves the integrity of the room and provide protective boundary between people. The concept of centre is an organising principles for the Japanese. His concept of space should not be confused with the concept of personal space. The concept of personal space is psychological and deals chiefly with individual meaning of crowding, territoriality, architectural design and not so such with intercultural variation. Under proxemic study non-verbal behaviour associated with centre, periphery, corner, door, direction, distance, window, courtyard, boundary, kitchen garden, cowshed, bathroom, latrine, worship room, veraudah, balcony, dancing floor, graveyard, cremation ground, grazing ground, school, hospital, community hall, Panchayat bhawan, seat of village and inter village head and so on are taken into consideration.

## Chronemics

The science which deals with non-verbal behaviours associated with time as channel of communication is known as chronemics. It is also common in cultural behaviour. When people meet together on several occasions they use time in communication through their non-verbal behaviour. Social-cultural meaning of time appears in day to day encounter through non-verbal behaviour such as early morning, morning, midday, evening, night, months, years, seasons, occurance of earthquakes, flood, epidemic, birth, death, marriage and so on.

## American Sign Language (ASL)

We have discussed earlier that one of remarkable differences between man and other non-human animal is that man is uniquely endowed with speech faculty. That is why he can express different shades of meaning with the help of language. But deaf children cannot speak. But they also make communication among themselves. They acquire and create language through their non-verbal behaviour to express themselves as efficiently as normal children. This shows clearly that human language can not only be expressed through creating sounds. The hand and body movements of deaf carry definite meaning. The deaf speakers are capable of creating new sentences in their own gestural way. The deaf children learn sign language, if it is used around them. Deaf children, who grow up in American homes, acquire American sign language (ASL). It has been estimated that ASL is the third most commonly used non-English language in United States.

ASL was developed from French Sign Language (FSL), French sign language was developed in a Paris school in 18th century. It was brought in USA by one of teachers of Paris school named Laurent Clercoin the beginning of 19th century. The teacher was brought to USA by Thomas Gallaudet. He taught not only the deaf children, but also trained other teachers in USA. As a result ASL was evolved. ALS is different, from

British Sign Language (BSL). ASL is based on four key aspects of visual information. They are classified as shape, orientation, location and movements of hands and palms. The shape of hands may be flat hand, fist hand, cupped hand etc. to convey different messages. Orientation of hand may be palm up, palm down, palm towards signer and so on. The location of hand may be at chin, waist and movement of hand will be upword or downward. In addition to these, a number of non-mannal components are involved in ASL such as head movement, eye movement, facial expressions, gestures, raising eye brows, narrowing eye brows, widening eyes, expression with finger spelling and so on. Different countries have evolved different sign languages according to their linguistic requirement. These sign languages are used by millions of deaf people to express themselves easily and efficiently. Even news bulletin are being broad cast for the hearing impaired viewers of T.V. with the help of sign language.

## Verbal Communication

Verbal communication is communication through sound language or verbal language. The members of same speech community make verbal communication among themselves quite easily because they know the same language. But when a member of one speech community meets with members of another speech community he/she is not in a position to communicate. It is because he/she does not know the language of another speech community. We hear a parrot calling our names or uttering names of Gods and Goddesses. But parrot does not understand what it pays. Similarly, when we hear two speakers speaking in unfamiliar language, we do not understand the meanings. When we hear a speaker speaking in high pitch, we understand that he/she is angry or annoyed. These examples reveal clearly that language is a two way process.

So far as speech is concerned, it is involved in associating sounds with meaning and meaning with sounds. This is quite different from writing. In writing meaning is associated with signs or a visual symbol. Therefore, the structure of verbal communication, requires a clear-cut understanding about followings:

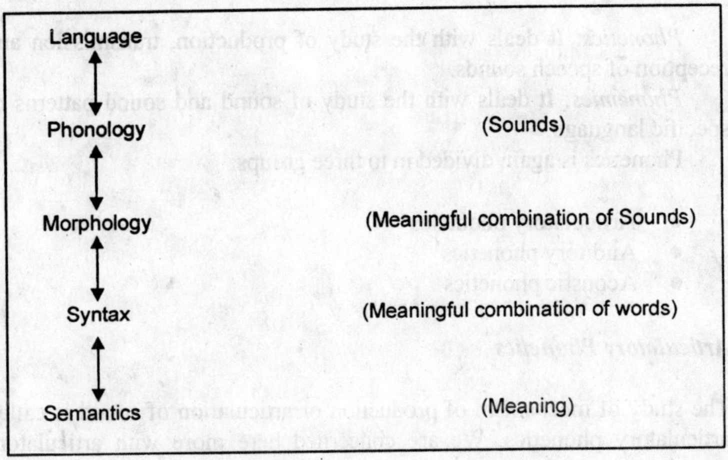


**Fig. 16.1:** Structure of verbal Communication

From the above figure it is quite clear that in order to know verbal communication, we need to know how sounds are produced, how sounds are combined meaningfully to form words, how words are combined meaningfully to form sentences, how meaning is attached to words and sentences. Thus, phonology, morphology, syntax and sementics constitute the basics of verbal communication. Each one of them are full flagged sciences.

Now, let us discuss about them in detail one by one.

## Language

Language is a means of communication. In language, sounds are produced knowingly following rules of phonology, morphology syntax and semantics.

## Phonology

Phonology is a science which deals with study of all sounds produced by speech organs. Phonology is divided in to two groups:

- Phonetics
- Phonemics

*Phonetics*: It deals with the study of production, transmission and reception of speech sounds.

*Phonemics*: It deals with the study of sound and sound patterns of specific language.

Phonetics is again divided in to three groups:

- Articulatory phonetics
- Auditory phonetics
- Acoustic phonetics

***Articulatory Phonetics***

The study of mechanism of production or articulation of sound is called articulatory phonetics. We are concerned here more with articulatory ponetics.

***Auditory Phonetics***

The study of perception of speech sound *via* ear is known as auditory phonetics.

***Acoustic Phonetics***

The study of physical properties of sound is called acoustic phonetics.

**Speech Organs**

In verbal communication, speech organs play significance. In communication, the air of food canal is pushed out and sometimes pushed in. The air of food canal is pushed out through larynx, pharynx and vocal cords. The larynx pharynx act as 1st resonator when air of food canal assumes sound form. Mouth cavity functions as 2nd resonator and nasal cavity functions as 3rd resonators. Thus, the air of food canal can assume sound shapes through these resonators. Sounds could not be produced without air. Most of sounds are produced by pushing air out of digestive canal through lungs, oral or nasal cavity. Hence, these sounds are known as pulmonic sound. Since the movement of diaphragm pushes out the air, these are called agressive. The mechanism through which we produce English speech sounds is commonly known as pulmonary aggressive air stream mechanism. Many other languages have inagressive sounds produced by sucking in the air, instead of pushing out air. The main organs of speech are jaws, lips, teeth, teeth ridge, known as alveloar ride, tongue, hard palate (roof of oral cavity), soft plate (known as velum), uvula, pharynx, larynx, and vocal cords. The tongue is so important in production of sound that it has been divided in to four areas: tip, blade, front and back—which help in production of different speech sounds.

We produce many interesting types of sounds such as voiceless, voiced, oral and nasal. The mechanism of different sounds production reveals that when air moves from lungs, it moves up through trachea known as wind pipe and then through opening between vocal cords or glottis. When vocal cords are open, air stream passes smoothly in to supra glottal cavities to produce voiceless sounds. For example sounds like |P|, |T|, |K|, |S|. These are voiceless sounds. But when vocal cords are together, the air stream has to push open the glottis. This causes a vibration due to which voiced sounds are produced. For example |b|, |d|, |t|. When we close our ear opening with finger or put hand on throat, we clearly feel velocities in glottis in uttering voiced sounds. Pin, bin, tin, seal, zeal are distinct set of voiced and voiceless sounds in English.

Like voiced and voiceless sounds, we can also distinguish between oral and nasal sounds. Take example of |m|, |n|, and |o|, |ng|. When we produced these sounds, the air not only escapes through oral cavity, but a part of it also escapes through nasal cavity and nostrils. This happens due to Uvula at the end of soft palate (Velum). When we produce an oral sound, the uvula is raised to touch the back of throat by blocking the nasal passage. This causes the air to pass through oral cavity. Hence oral sounds are produced. But when we produce a nasal sound, the velum is lowered giving way part of air to pass through nasal cavity. Hence nasal sound is produced. These phonetic features enable us to classify the speech sound of English in to four classes—voiceless, voiced, oral and nasal.

Depending upon manners of articulation and places of articulation, voiceless, voiced, oral and nasal sounds may further be analysed as follows:

**Stops**

Stops are those sounds which are produced when the air flows completely block off in oral cavity. Stops may be of following types:

- Voiceless bilabial stop
- Voiced bilabial stops

- Voiceless alveolar stop
- Voiced alveolar stop
- Voiceless velar stop
- Voiced velar stop
- Glottal stop

Now, let us discuss about these stops one by one:

***Voiceless bilabial stop***

These sounds are produced when the air flow is blocked off by complete closure of both lips. For example, the sound |P| in word pin.

***Voiced bilabial stop***

When the articulation is same as voiceless bilabial stop, but the sound is voiced, it is termed as bilabial stop. For example, the sound |b| in word bin.

***Voiceless alveolar stop***

These sounds are produced when the tongue touches the alveolar ridge behind the upper teeth. For example, the sound |t| in the word tin.

***Voiced alveolar stop***

When the articulation is same as above, but the sound is voiced, it is termed as voiced alvelar stop.

***Voiceless Velar Stop***

When the tongue is raised and touches the ridge soft polat or velum at the time of articulation, it is termed as voiceless velar stop. For example, the sound |k| in the word kind.

***Voiced Velar Stop***

When the articulation is exactly same as above, but the sound is voiced, it is known as voiced velar stop. For example—sound |g| in the word gag.

### *Glottal stop*

When air is stopped completely at glottis due to closure of vocal cords in articulation, it is termed as glottal stop.

### Fricatives

Fricatives are sounds produced when air stream is not completely stopped as in case of stops, but is not allowed to flow freely from the mouth. This happens due to a narrow passage created in oral cavity for air to passout. Some function is created due to narrowness of passage. The friction can be observed by putting the hand or a small piece of paper before the mouth. The fricatives may be of following types:

- Voiceless labiodental fricative
- Voiced labiodental fricative
- Voiceless interdental fricative
- Voiced interdental fricative
- Voiceless alveolar fricative
- Voiced alveolar fricative
- Voiceless alveopalatal fricative
- Voiced alveopalatal fricative
- Glottal fricatives

Now, let us discuss about these fricatives one by one.

#### *Voiceless labiodental fricative*

These sounds are produced with the help of lower lip and upper teeth. For example, the sound |b| in word bin.

#### *Voiced labiodental fricative*

These sounds are produced in the sounds manner as voiceless labiodental fricative, but here sounds are voiced. For example, the sound |v| in word vine.

#### *Voiceless interdental fricative*

These sounds are produced by the air between the tip of tongue and upper teeth. For example, the sound |th| or |θ| in the word thin or theeta.

***Voiced interdental fricative***

This is voiced variant of the above sound. For example, the sound |d| in words then, this and that.

***Voicedless alveolar fricative***

These sounds are produced when the air stream passes through the narrow opening between tip of tongue and alveolar ridge. For example, the sound |s| in word sit.

***Voiced alveolar fricative***

This is the voiced variant of the above sound. For example, the sown |z| in zebra.

***Voiceless alveopalatal fricative***

The sounds are created when the air passes through tip of tongue and the roof of mouth. For example, the sound |s| in the word ship.

***Voiced alveopalatal fricative***

This is voiced variant of above sound. For example, the sound |s| in measure or decision.

***Glottal fricative***

These sounds are produced by partial abstraction of air flow by the vocal cords or glottis. For example, the sound |h| in words how or here.

**Affricates**

When same sounds are produced initially by the abstraction of air flow as in case of stops and slow release gairs in case of fricatives, they are termed as affricates. Affricates in English consonants are as follows:

- Voiceless alveopalatal affricate
- Voiced alveopalatal affricate

Now, let us discuss about these affricates one by one is detail.

***Voiceless alveolarpalatal affricate***

These sounds are produced when the tip of tongue touches alveolar ride or just behind it. For example, the sound |č| in word church.

***Voiced alveo palatal affricate***

When the above sound is voiced, it is called as voiced alveopalatal affricate. For example,—the sound |č| in the word church.

**SIBLIANTS**

When fricatives |s|, |z|, |š|, |ž| and affricates |č| and |ǰ| are together, they are termed as SIBLIANTS as they produced a typical hissing noises.

**Liquids**

Liquids are those sounds which are produced with some obstacles to the air flow in mouth, but are not sufficient or strong enough to cause friction. The air in these cases flows easily and smoothly. The liquid may be of following types:

- Lateral alveolar liquid
- Non-lateral alveolar liquid

Now, let us discuss about these liquids one by one.

***Lateral alveolar liquid***

These sounds are produced when tongue blade is raised and the tip touches the alveolar ridge. The sides of tongue are lowered to allow the air to flow out. For example, the sound |f| in word life.

***Non-lateral alveolar liquid***

These sounds are produced with tongue blade raised to touch alveolar ridge, and many speakers curl the apex of tongue back in to a retroflix position. Most often due to retraction of tongue root, this sound causes throat constriction. For example, the sound |r| in word right.

## Glides

Glides are referred to as some vowels because of their vowels like articulation. In pronunciation of these sounds the air passes smoothly.

The glides may be of following types:

- Palatal glide
- Labiovelar glide

Now, let us discuss about these glides one by one.

### *Palatal glide*

These sounds are produced when the body of tongue is arched in high front position towards the hard palate and the air flow is quite smooth. For example, the sound |y| in the word yes.

### *Labiovelar glide*

These sounds are produced by raising the back of tongue towards the velum and rounding of lips. For example, the sound |w| in words like which and which and witch.

## Vowels

The production of vowel sounds takes place with the help of position of tongue, opening between lips and position of jaws.

The vowels in English are of following types:

- Short high front vowel
- Short mid front vowel
- Short low front vowel
- Short high back vowel
- Short mid back vowel
- Short low back vowel
- Short central low vowel

Now, let us discuss about these short or lax vowels one by one.

***Short high front vowel***

These vowel sounds are produced when the position of tongue is high and frontal in the mouth. For example, the sound |i| in word bit.

***Short mid front vowel***

These vowel sounds are produced when the position of tongue is frontal, but slightly. For example, the sound |e| in words get and mes.

***Short low front vowel***

These vowel sounds are produced when the tongue is in forward position, but the blade of the tongue is almost on the floor of the mouth. For example, sound |ae| in the word bat.

***Short high back vowel***

These vowel sounds are produced when back of tongue moves up work towards velum. For example, the sound |U| in word put or foot (fut).

The lips get rounded in the production of these sounds.

***Short mid back vowel***

These sounds are produced when the tongue movement is associated with minor lip rounding. For example, the sound $\partial$ in the word caught.

***Short low back vowel***

These sounds are produced when the position of the tongue is low and retracted. For example, the sound |a| in words hot (hat), pot (pat).

***Short central low Vowels***

These sounds are produced when the tongue balade touches the floor of mouth. For example, word |U| in luck and bus.

### *Reduced Vowels*

The reduced vowels are of following types:

- Reduced high central vowel
- Reduced mid central vowel.

Now, let us discuss about these vowel sounds one by one.

### *Reduced high central vowel*

These vowel sounds are produced as an unstressed syllable in the word. This is represented by the symbol |i|. This is commonly referred to as barred |i|. For example, sound |i| in the word chicken.

### *Reduced mid central vowel*

These vowel sounds are also produced unstressed as in case of reduced high central vowels, but by the symbol |$\partial$| which is in the form of upside down and reversed |e|. For example, the last vowel of the word sofa.

### *Long Vowels*

The long vowels differ from the short vowels not only because they are longer, but also because they sound higher then short vowels. Long English vowels have two parts; an initial louder vowel followed by a less loud vowel. Because of these two parts long vowels are also known as diphthongs: The diphthongs are of following types:

- Long high front vowel
- Long mid front vowel
- Long low front vowel
- Long high back rounded vowel
- Long mid back rounded vowel
- Long low back vowel

Now, let us discuss about these long vowels one by one.

### *Long high front vowel*

This is represented by the symbol |iy| in word bead or |biyd|. Its two parts

***Free Morphemes***

The morphemes which stand by themselves as single words without any attachment are termed as free morphemes. The free morpheme are many. For example, boy, man, girl, woman, dog, tree, bird, animal, and, but, when, how, because, on, near, above and son on. Free morphemes can further the divided in to two types:

- Lexical morphemes
- Functional morphemes

*Lexical morphemes*

Lexical morphemes are those morphemes, which are found as ordinary nouns, adjectives and verbs. For example, man, boy, girl, black, red, go, study, write, read and many others.

*Functional morphemes*

The functional word used in language in the form of pronouns, conjunctions, prepositions, articles, pronouns and so on are termed as functional morphemes. For example, and, but, when and others.

***Bound Morphemes***

Bound morphemes do not stand alone like free morphemes. They are typically attached to another morphemes. That is why they are termed as bound morphemes. For example, prefix and suffix which we use in language are example of bound morphemes. When they are alone, they are meaningless, but when they are bound to a morpheme as prefix or suffix, they become meaningful. For example, player and evolutionist. In these words—er and –ist are bound morphemes. They are meaningless when they are alone. But when they are attached to free morpheme play and evolution, they because meaningful.

Bound morphemes are of two types:

- Derivational morpheme
- Inflectional morpheme

*Derivational morpheme*

Derivational morphemes are those morphemes which make either a new word or a word of different grammatical category from the stem. For example, morpheme –ness in the word kindness. Here the morepheme—ness changes the adjective form in to noun form. Similarly, the morpheme—ment in entainment. Here verb form is changed in to a noun form. Prefixes like re, pre, ex, dis, co, un and others also belong to this category.

*Inflectional morphemes*

Inflectional morphemes are those morphemes which do not produce new words or a word of different meaning, but certainly indicate change in the grammatical function of he stem. For examples, played, going, boys etc. The morphemes –ed, –ing and –s are inflectional bound morphemes.

With the help of these classifications we can attempt a morphological description of a sentence. For example—

| The | Girl | —'s | Kind | Ness |
|---|---|---|---|---|
| (Functional) | (Lexical) | (Inflectional) | (Lexical) | (derivational) |
| impress | –ed | the | Teach | er |
| (Lexical) | (Inflectional) | (Functional) | (Lexical) | (derivational) |

**Morphs and Allomorphs**

Just like allophones of particular phone, there are allomorphs of a particular morpheme. Like phonemes, morthemes also have a number of variants. These variants are known as allomorphs of concerned morpheme. In other words, when a morpheme has alternative phonetic forms, these forms are allomorphs of that morpheme.

Let us take example of plural morphemes. Predictably, –s, –z and –Iz are allomorphs of regular plural morpheme. While –s occurs after most voiceless phonemes as in case of cats, giraffes, –Z occurs after most of voiced phonemes such as dogs, bees, lambs, etc. |Z usually occurs as sibilants (hussing and hissing sound) as in words horses, dishes etc.

Now, question arises how to understand the plural forms like sheep, geese, oxen, men etc. This problem has been resolved by recognizing that zero-morph is also an allomorph of plural. This takes care of the word sheep by saying that plural form of sheep is sheep. Other forms are said to have individual morphotrical realization rules like ox + plural. The same rule is also applicable to some forms of past like go + past tense.

**Syntax**

When an attempt is made to study the structure and ordering of components within a sentence, we are trying to study what is technically known as syntax of a given language. In fact, the word syntax comes originally from Greek word, the meaning of which is arrangement. Therefore, literally meaning of syntax is analysis of arrangement of words within sentence.

We know very well that merely putting a few unrelated words in row does not make a meaningful and grammatically correct sentence. There are certain very define and stringent underlying rules which are needed to follow for arranging words in meaningful and grammatically correct form.

Most of languages have devised their own methods to show the relationship of one word with another in a sentence. But there are some common devices, too, which are followed in all languages. One of these is word order or proper arrangement of words in a sentence. For example, let us consider the following sentences:

A cockroach frightened Mrs. Nidhi

Mrs. Nidhi frightened a cockroach

The words in both sentences are identical in form and number. Despite this, both sentences convey different meaning. It is because arrangements of words in both sentences are different. The subject of one sentence becomes object of another sentence. That is why, both sentences convey different meaning.

Another commonly used device in many languages is use of function words like of, by, and others. These are basically empty words which do not indicate syntactic relationships and do not refer to identifiable objects, qualities and actions. This will become clear from the example given below:

Mr. Bhim was terrified by a tiger.

He was a very brave hero of *Mahabharata*

The appropriate use of function words and proper arrangement of words in a sentence is broadly called as grammar of a language.

It is internal linguistic knowledge which lies at the sub-conscious level of thought. The children master in these grammatical aspect of a language by the age of 5 years. This helps them to express themselves unambiguously.

In traditional grammar, structure of expression is analysed with the help of commonly used parts of speech. We are already familiar with articles, nouns, pronouns, adjectives, verbs, adverbs, prepositions and conjunctions. Let us recapitulate them with the help or following sentences:

| The | naughty | boy | threw | the | stone | at |
|---|---|---|---|---|---|---|
| (article) | (adjective) | (noun) | (verb) | (article) | (noun) | (Pre-position) |
| the | angry | tiger | and | they | cheered | loudly |
| (article) | (adjective) | noun | (conjunction) | (pronoun) | (verb) | (adverb) |

In addition to the parts of speech, traditional grammar also uses a number of other categories for analysis. The other categories are number, gender, person, tense and voice. In English languages number may be singular or plural. Person may be 1st, 2nd and 3rd, gender may be masculine, femine and neutral, tense may be present, past and future, and voice may by active or passive.

The above classification of English language does not hold true for other language. For example, Sanskrit language has three numbers—*Ekvachan*, *dvivachan* and *bahu vachan*. Many languages do not recognize neutral gender. The local classification varies greatly from culture to culture.

The analysis of traditional grammar can be approached from two directions:

- Prescriptive approach
- Descriptive approach

**Prescriptive Approach**

In 18th century England, some rules were set out for proper use of English language. This was known as prescriptive approach. Grammarians insisted that an infinitive must not be split, or the sentence must not end with preposition. But in common usage we find the teacher correcting sentences as:

I shall (not will) go there.
Baby is taller than I (not me)

The prescriptive approach helps one to understand the linguistic etiquette or proper use of a language. This is also known as social expectation.

**Descriptive Approach**

This approach is different from prescriptive approach. It is because this approach does not take any model of grammar of a language for the analysis of any other language. For example, Latin grammar may be useful guide for the analysis of Italian or Spanish languages, but cannot be useful guide for analysis of American Indian languages. At the end of 19th century a number of native American languages were discovered. Their structures were different. They did not follow any one Grammatical rule. A need was felt to describe their regular structure. This approach was known as descriptive approach to the study of language.

Sentences are not simply random words put together, rather they follow sentence patterns. An analysis which seek to show how the constituents of sentences fit together to form large constituents is commonly known as immediate constituent analysis.

Let us see the arrangement of constituents in the following sentence:

The police caught the thief in the market.

There are eight words in the above sentence. They can be divided in to three phrase line constituents such as below:

The police—Noun phrase (NP)

Caught the thief—Verb phrase (VP)

In the market —Preposition phrase (PP)

Again Noun phrase (NP) can be divided in to following constituents

The Police

The Article

Police Noun

The Verb Phrase (VP) can be divided in to following constituents:

Caught the thief

Caught—Verb

The—Article

Thief—Noun

The preposition phrase is divided in to following constituents:

In the market

In—Preposition

The—Article

Market—Noun

The constituent analysis can also be presented with the help of following tree diagram.

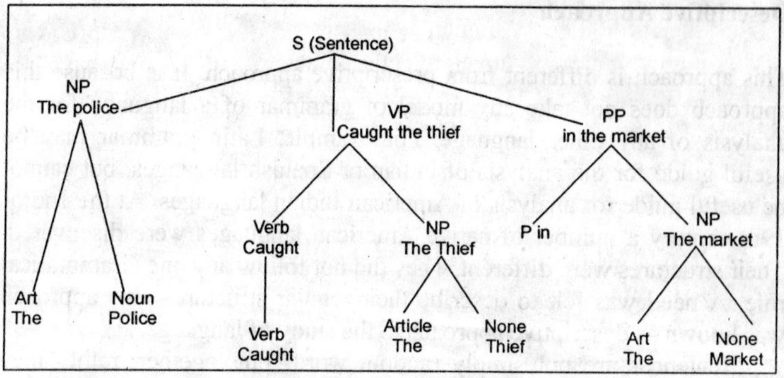


**Fig. 16.2:** Tree Diagram

## Transformational Generative Analysis (T.G. Analysis)

The traditional approaches treat syntax as study of structure of sentences, the contemporary approaches take sentence as the basic unit of analysis. This is known as transformational generative analysis. This analysis was deviced by Noam Chamasky, a reknowned linguistic anthropologists. He brought a revolution in linguistics during 1950s. This revolution had a strong impact on linguistics for a considerably long time thereafter. This approach emphasizes upon describing the languages interms of rules of production of sentences. Although a number of sentences can be formed in any language, but the rules for such production which native speakers follow are surprisingly limited. These rules are found to be similar in type from language to language. Thus, they indicate underlying similarity between languages.

Chomsky grammar is based upon several important assumptions. They are as follows:

- Productivity or creativity
- Speaker's Competence
- Speaker's Performance
- Structure Grammar

Now, let us discuss about these assumptions one by one.

### Productivity or Creativity

Productivity or creativity is very important property of human language.

This means ability of human beings to produce and comprehend an indefinite number of novel utterances, which might they have never uttered before.

**Speaker's Competence**

Every speaker works out for himself or herself a set of rules quite unconsciously. This constitutes a part of his/her linguistic ability. Chomsky asserts that these internalised sets of rules are speaker's competence. The linguist should discover these speaker's competence.

**Speaker's Performance**

According to Chomsky, rules are of greater interest than actual utterances that speaker make during normal conversation. This is speaker's performance. Since competence lies in the human mind, Chomsky aptly suggests that linguistics is an importance branch of cognitive psychology.

**Structure Grammar**

If we assume that speaker has internalised some basic rules of Grammar of the language, every time he/she makes a new sentence. He/she expands the basic rules to accommodate the later. These basic rules come under the phrase structure grammar. Such a grammar contains a series of rewrite rules which show progressive expansion.

The structure grammar can be understood by the sentence given below.

The cat may eat the fish.

The structure rules followed in this sentence are as follows:

S→NP + VP

NP→DET (determiner) + N

VP→VB (verb) + NP

VB→AUX ( auxiliary verb) + V (main verb)

The→DET

Cat, fish→N

May→AUX

Eat→V

On a tree diagram the rules appear as follows:

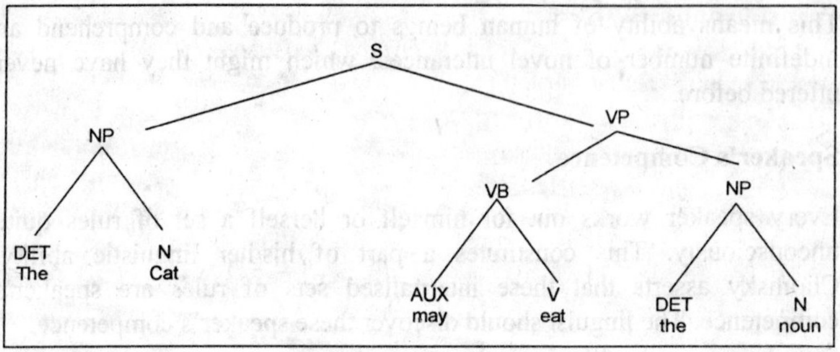


**Fig. 16.3:** Tree Diagram of P-S rules

Although the basic preliminary rules are applied to the most simple sentences, which are able to generate an infinite number of sentences. Thus, when sentences become complex, additional rules are devised in the following manner to comprehend them:

NP→DET +ADJ (adjective) + N
NP→PRO (pronoun)
VP→V+NP+PP
PP→P+NP

The long sentence can be analysed very easily with the help of phrase structure grammar rule. It is because all of them follow the simple rules of syntax. But sometimes, sentences appear within sentences. In these cases grammarians have to follow recursive rules. Recursive rules can be understood with the help of following example:

He thought, he would fight till last.

In the above sentence one sentence is embedded or inserted in to main sentence. It is creating a condition of recursion. Recursion is possible in another condition, when sentences are conjoined or fused using conjunctions such as like, and, but etc. For example—Ram played football but Shyam went fishing. This sentence presents a recursive condition because two sentences have been fused with conjunction, but to make a single sentence. Thus, we can say that recursion is the possibility of repeatedly using the same construction so that there is no fixed limit to the length of sentences. The length of sentence does not matter. It follows some very limited phrase structure, rules, which underlie the complex construction of the sentences.

**Transformational Rules**

Besides, these phrase structure rules which are basically generative in nature, there are a series of rules of transformation that help to derive negative, exclamatory, interrogative and complex sentences from simple declarative sentences. Here an example of reflexive transformation as representative of transformational rule is being provided. In English language we have a number of reflexive pronouns such as myself, yourself, himself, herself, yourselves, ourselves, and themselves. Their distribution is very special in sentence. They cannot function as a subject NP like other pronouns. The sentence herself cursed Geeta (Geeta cursed herself) is ungrammatical. It a reflexive pronoun appears in a sentence, it must have an antecedent else where in the same sentence. In the sentence Geeta cursed herself, the antecedent of herself is Geeta. Which also appears in the same sentence to refer to reflexive pronoun. Further, the reflexive pronoun must to the NP with same person, number and gender as the antecedent. For example if the above example is rewritten as Geeta cursed himself or Ram cursed herself is grammatically wrong. Invariably, we find that if there are two identical noun phrases referring to same individual in a sentence, the second one is substituted by reflexive pronoun, but same as person, number and gender of the first. The above example can be represented by following tree:

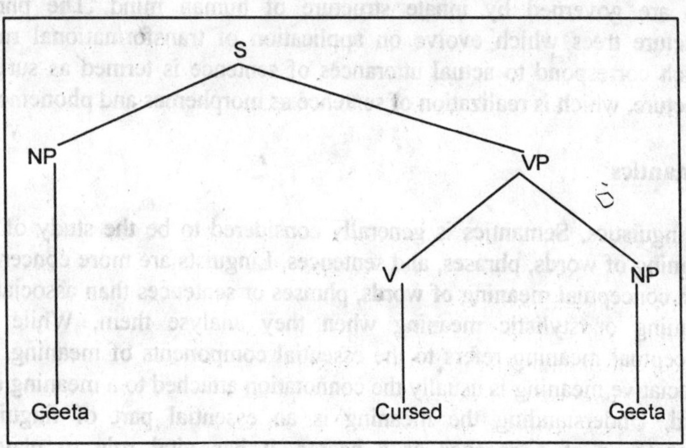


**Fig. 16.4:** Reflexive transformation

The reflexive rule transforms the above phrases structure trees.

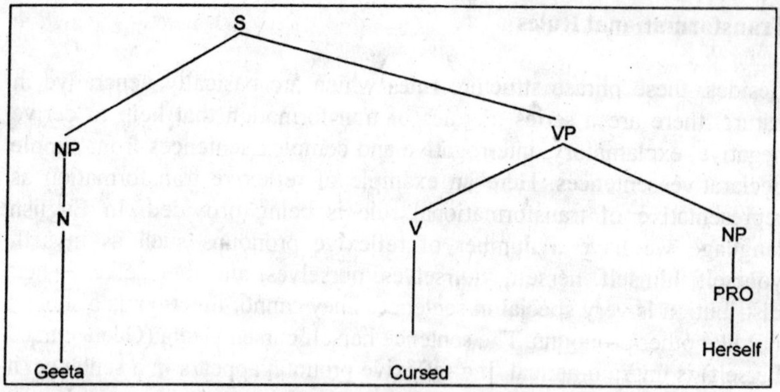


**Fig. 16.5:** Tree diagram of transformation

The reflexive transformation rule states that if there are two occurences of identical second noun phrases within a sentence, replace the record with reflexive pronoun that matches the first in person, number and gender. The phrase structure tree that results from these analytical exercise of syntax has been termed as deep structure by Chomsky. The deep structure is abstract form of a sentence. At this level differences between languages appear to be minimum of non-existent. It is because the relationship between components are mostly conceptual and are governed by innate structure of human mind. The phrase structure trees which evolve on application of transformational rules, which correspond to actual utterances of sentence is termed as surface structure, which is realization of sentence as morphemes and phonemes.

## Semantics

In linguistics, Semantics is generally considered to be the study of the meaning of words, phrases, and sentences. Linguists are more concerned with conceptual meaning of words, phrases or sentences than associative meaning or stylistic meaning when they analyse them. While the conceptual meaning refers to the essential components of meaning, the associative meaning is usually the connotation attached to a meaning of a word. Understanding the meaning is an essential part of linguistic competence of a speaker or a hearer. It has vital role to play in communication. Meaning may be of two different types: Linguistic meaning and speaker's meaning. Linguistic meaning is conceptual and speaker's meaning is associative. While the linguistic meaning is conceptual and deals with conventional translation of the meaning of a word, the speaker's meaning is associative of the context in which speaker speaks.

Let us consider the following examples to understand the difference between them:

What a beautiful nose you have !
What a beautiful nose you have !

Both sentences are same but their meaning may be different. One meaning may be admiring expression of other nose, the other meaning may be satirical or teasing criticising the other nose. Thus, speaker's meaning would be just literal or non-literal depending on the contexts. Non-literal uses of language may include sarcasm or irony or could be used metaphorically, as often being done by poets and writers.

Linguistic meaning may be of different types. Meanings may vary across dialects and between individual speakers. This implies that the same words may be used differently by people speaking different dialects of same languages; and sometimes meaning of same words varies from person to person. Therefore, there may be dialectical and ideolectical differences in meaning which make the field of semantic most challenging for linguist. It is more so for the anthropologists who mostly studies unwritten languages.

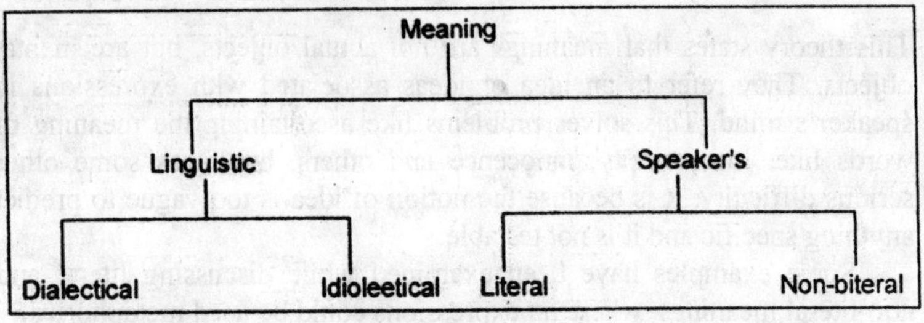


**Fig. 16.8:** Types of Meaning

**Theories of Meaning**

Now, question arises what is meaning? What kind of entity it is? How is it to be understood. Answers of these questions reveal different conception of meaning. Different conceptions of meaning have led to different theories of meaning.

The different theories of meaning are as follows:

- Referential theory of meaning
- Mentalist theory of meaning
- Use theory of meaning
- Lexical relation theory of meaning

### *Referential Theory*

According to this theory, meaning of each expression is actual object it refers to. For example, if names of persons, places, definite objects or descriptive noun phrases are expressed, these convey definite meanings, that is referent of each expression. For example, if speaker says, Ram, Sita, Hanuman, Ravana, the hearer does not have problem in understanding the reference with respect to each of these expressions. But there are certain inherent problems in this conceptualisation. For example, like love, hello, empty etc. have meanings without reference to actual objects. Similarly, this theory has also been questioned when it states; if two expressions have the same referent, the meaning of both of them is same. For example, morning star, evening star and venue express the same meaning, but they do not mean the samething. Thus, this theory is not an absolutely satisfactory theory of meaning.

### *Mentalist Theory of Meaning*

This theory states that meanings are not actual objects, but are mental objects. They refer to an idea or ideas associated with expressions in speaker's mind. This solves problems like ascertaining the meaning of words like, love, empty, innocence and others, but faces some other serious difficulty. It is because the notion of idea is too vague to predict anything specific and it is not testable.

Some examples have been examined while discussing literal and non-literal meanings, where an expressions could be used metaphorically or satirically. From its external appearance or in its written form, it is difficult to subject these ideas or concepts or feeding to any kind of test to find out their exact referents. Thus, mentalist theory of meaning is also not satisfactory.

### *Use Theory of Meaning*

This theory states that meaning of an expression is determined by its use in a particular language community. In a given language community, the speaker's meaning of an expression is more or less standardised. That is why hearers do not have much difficulty in understanding the meaning. Due to a shared process of language acquisition and sharing of a normative pattern of behaviour, the meaning does not become obscure for the hearers. In this theory, conception of use must be made precise, so that there should not be any confusion about the relationship between meaning and use.

### *Lexican Relations*

Meanings are not only associated with words that contain them, but are also in mutual relationship between words. Thus, meaning could be derived either conceptually or relationally. In the semantic description of language, linguists also analyse the relationship between words, which is commonly known as lexicon relations.

Now, let us discuss some of these lexical relations, which are very commonly understood and used.

### Synonyms

Two or more forms are said to be Synonyms, when they have very closely related meanings, which are very often, but not necessarily always, used as each other's substitute in sentences.

Examples are apathetic/passive/indifferent, or pedigree/ancestry/descent, and so on. It is important to mention here that there are no perfect synonyms or words with exact meanings. It is because contextual use of words are basically different.

### *Antonyms*

Words which are opposite in meaning are often termed as antonyms. The common examples of antonymous pairs are male/female, young/old, man/woman, boy/girl, hot/cold and so on. Antonyms are divided in to two sets:—

- Gradable antonyms
- Non-gradable antonyms

### *Gradable Antonyms*

These are used in comparative constructions and negative of one of pairs does not mean the other. For example, the man is not old. This does not necessarily mean that man is young. Here is young/old are antonyms.

***Non-gradable Antonyms***

They are known as complementary pairs. They are not used in comparative constructions. The negative of one of pairs necessarily implies the other. For example, he is not dead certainly implies that he is alive. Similarly, male/female, true/false, married/single etc. are non-gradable antonyms.

**Hyponymy**

When two or more words are in hierarchical relationship, and the meaning of one is included in the meaning of the other, the words are said to be hyponymus to each other. For example, rose flowers, cow/animal, cabbage/vegetable and so on. In these examples, rose is a flower, cow is an animal and cabbage is vegetable, the meaning of flower, animal and vegetable is included in meaning of rose, cow and cabbage, respectively. Moreover, component of each of these pairs are placed hierarchically among each other. In this hierarchical relationship, if more than one word come under the same super ordinate term, the former are co-hyponymus to each other such as rose/lily/chrysanthemum (all being flowers), cow, goat, sheep (all being animal), and cabbage/potato/carrot (all being vegetables).

**Hymophony, Homonymy and Polysemy**

When two or more different written forms have the same pronunciation, they are termed as homophones. For example, flour/floor, to/two, meat/meet, sit/sheat, hit/heat, here/hear, beer/bear and so on.

The words having same written and spoken form, but different meaning are termed as homonyms. For example, bank/bank (one referring bank of a river and another an institution, pupil/pupil (one student and another an organ in eye), mole/mole (one a mark on skin and another an animal) and so on.

Identical words with related multiple meanings due to extension of one meaning to another is termed as polysemons. These words occur in pair. Here meanings are related to each other, though they are used in different context. For example, head/head (head of body and head of institution. Similarly, run/run are polysemous words.

**letonymy**

Vhen two or more words indicate a very close connection with each ther like a container-contents relationship or whole parts relationship or representative symbol relationship, they are termed as metanymous erms. For example, bottle/wine, house/verandah, Governor/Rajbhawan.

# Bibliography


Atchinson, Jean (1983): *Linguistics* (Second edition), Sevenoaks, Kent: Hold and Stonghton.

Akmajian, A., *et al.* (1984): *Linguistics: An Introduction to Language ar Communication* (Second edition), Cambridge: The MIT Press.

Ardener, E. (ed.) (1971): *Social Anthropology and Language,* London: Tavistok.

Bauman, Richard and Joel Sherzer (eds.) (1989): *Explorations in Ethnograp of Speaking* (Second edition), London: Cambridge University Press.

Berlin, Brent (1976): "The Concept of Rank in Ethnobiological Classificatio Some Evidence from Aguaruna Folkbotany," *American Anthropolists.*

Berlin, Brent and Paul, Kay (1969): *Basic Colour Terms: Their Universali and Evolution*, Berkley: University of California Press.

Bloomfield, Leonard (1933): *Language*, New York: Holt.

Blount Ben G. (1974): *Language, Culture and Society*, Cambridge, Mass Winthrop.

Boas, Franz (1911): *Introduction in the Handbook of American India Language*, Bureau of American Ethnology, Bulletin-40, Washington Government Printing Office.

Boas, Franz (1939): *A Report on Committee on Research in American Nativ Languages 1927-1937*, American Council of Learned Societies Bulleti No. 29.

Boas, Franz (1940): *Race, Language and Culture*, New York: Free Press.

Carrol, J.B. (1963): *The Study of Language*, Cambridge: Harvard University Press.

Casson, R.W. (ed.) (1981): *Language, Culture and Cognitive: Anthropologica Perspectives*, New York: MacMillan.

Chatterjee, S.K. (1963): *Language and Literatures of India,* Calcutta: Bengal Publishers.

Chomsky, Noam (1956): *Syntactic Structures*, The Hague: Mouton.

Chomsky, Noam (1972): *Language and Mind* (enlarged edition), New York: Harcourt Brace Jovanovich.

Conklin, Harold C. (1955): "Hanonoo colour Categories", *South Western Journal of Anthropology*, 11: 339-344.

Conklin, Harold (1959) : "Linguistic Play in Cultural Context", *Language*, 35 631-636.

rick, M. (1976): *Explorations in Language and Meaning: Towards a Semantic Anthropology*, London : Malaby Press.

Crystal, David (1991): *A Dictionary of Linguistics and Phonetics* (third addition), Cambridge: Cambridge University Press.

D'Andrade, Roy (1995): *The Development of Cognitive Anthropology*, Cambridge: Cambridge University Press.

Darwin, Charles (1872): *Expression of Emotions in Man and Animal*, London: University of Chicago Press.

Dougherly, J.W.D. (ed.) (1985): *Directions in Cognitive Anthropology*, Urbana and Chicago: University of Illinois Press.

Errington, J.J. (1988): *Structure and Style in Javanese: A Semiotic View of Linguistic Etiquette*, Philadelphia: University of Pennsylvania Press.

Evince-Pritchard, E.E. (1940): *The Nuer*, Oxford: Oxford University Press.

Fasold, R.W. (1984): *Introduction to Social Linguistics* (Vol. 1), New York: Blackwell.

Fergusen, C.A. (1959): 'Diglossia', *Word*, 15: 325-340.

Fischir, J.L. (1958): "Social Influences in Choice of the Linguistic Variant". *Word,* 14: 47-57.

Fisherman, J. (ed.) (1968): *Readings in Sociology of Language*, The Hauge: Mouton.

Frake, C.O. (1961): "The Diagnosis of disease among the Subanam of Mindanao", *American Anthropologist*, 63: 113-132.

Frake, C.O. (1964): "How to Ask for a Drink in Sabanam", *American Anthropologist*, 66(6): 127-132.

Fromkin, Victoria and Robert Rodman (1978): *An Introduction to Language* (Second edition), New York: Holt, Rineheart and Winston.

Gardner, R.A. and B.T. Gardner (1969): "Teaching Sign language to Chimpanzee", *Science*, 165: 664-672.

Giglioli, P.P. (ed.) (1972): *Language and Social Context: Selected Readings*, Baltimore: Penguine Books.

Gleason, H.A. Jr. (1961): *An Introduction to Descriptive Linguistics* (revised edition), New York: Holt, Rineheart and Winston.

Goodenough, W.H. (1957): *Cultural Anthropology and Linguistics, Monography*, Washington: Georgetown University Press.

Greenkery, Joseph (1968): *Anthropological Linguistics*, New York: Random House.

Gudchinsky, S.C. (1986): "The ABCs of Lexico statistics", *Word*, 12: 175-210.

Gumperz, J.J. (1964): "Linguistic and Social Interaction in to two Communities." *American Anthropologist*, 66(6) 137-153.

Gumperz, J.J. and Dett Hymes (eds.) (1972): *Directions in Socio-Linguistics*, New York: Holt, Rineheart and Winston.

Hall, E.T. (1966): *The Hidden Dimension*, New York: Doubleday.

Hall, E.T. (1968): Proxemics, *Current Anthropology*—IX: 83-108.

Hamad, *et al.*, (eds.) (1976) : Origin and Evolution of Language and Speech, New York: *Annals of the New York Academy of Science*, Vol. 280.

Harris, Marvin (1938) : *Rise of Anthropological Theory*, London : Rutledge an Kegan Paul.

Hickerson, N.P. (1980): *Linguistics Anthropology*, New York : Holt, Rinehear and Winston.

Hocket, C.F. (1973): *Man's Place in Nature*, New York: MacMillion.

Hocket, C.F. (1958): *A Course in Modern Linguistics*, New York: Holt, Rineheart and Winston.

Hymes, Dell (ed.) (1964): *Language in Culture and Society*, New York: Harper and Row.

Hymes, Dell (1974): *Reinventing Anthropology*, New York: Vintage Books.

Jacobson, R. and Morris Halle (1956): *Fundamentals of Language*, The Huage: Mouton.

Jolly, Alison, (1972): *The Evolution of Primate Behaviour*, New York: Methuen.

Key, M.R. (1977): *Non-verbal Communication: Research Guide and Bibliography*. Metuchen, N.J. : Scarecrow Press.

Khubchandani, L.M. (1983): *Plural Languages, Plural Cultures: Communication, Identity and Socio-Political Change in Contemporary India*, Honolulu: University of Hawai Press.

Kinkaid, M.D., *et al.* (ed.) (1975): *Linguistics and Anthropology*, Lisse de Ridder Press.

Labov, William (1972): *Socio-linguistic Patterns*, Philadelphia: University of Pennsylvania Press.

Leach, E.R. (1974): *Levi-strauss* (revised edition), London: Fontanal Collins.

Lehmann, W.P. (1983): *Language: An Introduction*. New York: Random House.

Linneberg, E. H. (1967): *Biological Foundation of Language*, New York: Wiley..

Levi-Strauss, Claude, C. (1963): *Structural Anthropology*, Harmonds Worth: Penguine Books.

Levi –Strauss, Claude, C. (1966): *The Savage Mind*, Chicago: The University of Chicago Press.

Lieberman, Philip (1984): *On the Origin of Language*, New York: MacMillan.

Lieberman, Philip (1984): *The Biology and Evolution of Language*, Cambridge: Harvard University Press.

Lyons, John (1978): *Noam Chamsky* (revised edition), New York: Penguin Books.

Malinowski, Brownis Law Kaspar (1922): *Argonauts of Western Pacific*, London: Routledge Kegan Paul.

Malinowski, Brownislaw Kaspar (1926): *Myth in Primitive Psychology*, New York: Narton.

Majumdar, S.N. (1970): *Markism and Language Problem in India*. New Delhi: Peoples Publishing House.

Misra, K.K. (2000): *A Textbook of Anthropological Linguistics*, New Delhi: Concept Publishing Company.

Ogden, C.K. and I.A. Richards (eds.) 1923: *The Meaning of Meaning*, New York: Harcourt.

Pandey, Gaya (2015): *Sampreshanatmak Manavshastra,* New Delhi: Concept Publishing Company.

Parkery, Frank (1986): *Linguistics for Non-Linguistics*. Boston: Little Brown.

Philips, Susan U., *et al.* (eds.) (1987): *Language Sex and Gender in Comparative Perspectives*, Cambridge: Cambridge University Press.

Phitepsen, Gerry and Donal Carbough (1986): "A Bibliography of Field Work in Ethnography of Communication", *Language in Society*, 15: 387-397.

Pine, Kenneth L. (1967): *Language in Relation to a United Theory of Structure of Human Behaviour* (Second Revised edition). The Hauge: Mutton.

Pride, J.B. and Jannet Holmes (eds.) (1972): *Socio-linguistics: Selected Readings*, New York: Penguin Books.

Robins, R.H. (1967): *A Short History of Linguistics*, London: Longmans, Green & Co. Ltd.

Solzmann Zdenek (1993): *Language, Culture, Society: An Introduction to Linguistics Anthropology*.

Sapir, Edward (1921): *Language: An Introduction to the Study of Speech*, New York: Hercourt Brace.

Saville, Troike, Murried (1989): *The Ethnography of Communication: An Introduction* (Second Edition) Oxford: Blackwell.

Sebock, T.A. (ed.) (1977): *How Animals Communicate*, Blomington: Indiana University Press.

Simpson, Jimy (1969): *A First Course in Linguistics*, Edinburgh: The University Press.

Stoss, Brian (1976): *The Origin and Evolution of Language*, Dubuque, Iowa: W.C. Brown.

Swadesh, Morris (1971): *Origin and Diversification of Language*, Chicago: Aldine.

Tedlock, Dennis (1983): *The Spoken Word and the Work of Interpretation*, Philadelphia: University of Pelsynnvania.

Thorne Barrie, *et al.* (eds.) (1983): *Language, Gender and Society*, Rowley, M.A.: Newbury House.

Todd, Loreto (1993): *An Introduction to Linguistics* (5th impression), Harlow, ESSEX: Longman York Press.

Trager, George L. (1972): *Language and Languages*, San Francisco: Chandler.

Tyler, S.A. (ed.) (1969): *Cognitive Anthropology*, New York: Hatt, Rineheart and Winston, Inc.

Wardhaugh, Ronald (1986): *An Introduction to Socio-linguistics*, New York: Blackwell.

Waterman, J.T. (1970): *Perspectives in Linguistics*, Chicago: Chicago University Press.

Whorf, Benjamin L. (1956): *Language, Thought and Reality: The Selected Writings Bejamin Lee Whorf*, Cambridge, Mass: The MIT Press.

Yule, George (1996): *The Study of Language* (Second edition) Cambridge: Cambridge University Press.

# Index